The Muses of Truth and Transformation

Drawing on the author's own experiences as a psychiatrist-psychotherapist, this fascinating new book gathers and analyzes folktales from around the world about adults struggling with conflicts and trying to determine truth. These narratives illustrate how storytelling is crucial to the process of reconciliation.

The stories included within this book feature both familiar and forgotten ones: e.g., "The Fisherman and the Djinn" from Arabia; "Why the Platypus Is Special" from Australia; the Native American, "How Nanapush Brought the Peace Pipe to the People," and the ancient Greek tale of "Baucis and Philemon." The anthology retells the tales and discusses them in terms of psychological and spiritual development – the role of individuation and wisdom in reconciling disputes. The tales reveal astonishing cross-cultural similarities about how to do so, and directly apply to many modern dilemmas. Particularly important is a new paradigm of truth and transformation illustrated by long overlooked tales of the Greek Muses.

The Muses of Truth and Transformation draws on Chinen's research in adult cognitive, emotional, and spiritual development. The new perspective will appeal to Jungian analysts, psychotherapists, as well as students of psychology, mythology, and epistemology.

Allan B. Chinen, MD is a Clinical Professor of Psychiatry (voluntary), University of California, San Francisco, School of Medicine and a Distinguished Life Fellow of the American Psychiatric Association. He is the author of *In the Ever After*, *Once Upon a Midlife*, *Waking the World*, and *Beyond the Hero*, as well as a co-editor of *The Textbook of Transpersonal Psychiatry and Psychology*.

To Roy - who makes it all possible

The Muses of Truth and Transformation

A Jungian Perspective on Timeless Tales

Allan B. Chinen

Routledge
Taylor & Francis Group

LONDON AND NEW YORK

Designed cover image: Getty Images

First published 2025
by Routledge
4 Park Square, Milton Park, Abingdon, Oxon OX14 4RN

and by Routledge
605 Third Avenue, New York, NY 10158

Routledge is an imprint of the Taylor & Francis Group, an informa business

British Library Cataloguing-in-Publication Data
A catalogue record for this book is available from the British Library

Library of Congress Cataloging-in-Publication Data
Names: Chinen, Allan B., 1952– author.
Title: The muses of truth and transformation : a Jungian
    perspective on timeless tales / Allan B. Chinen.
Description: Abingdon, Oxon ; New York, NY : Routledge, 2025. |
    Includes bibliographical references and index. |
Identifiers: LCCN 2024029616 (print) | LCCN 2024029617 (ebook) |
    ISBN 9781032748122 (hardback) | ISBN 9781032748115 (paperback) |
    ISBN 9781003471028 (ebook)
Subjects: LCSH: Folklore—Psychological aspects. | Tales—Psychological
    aspects. | Psychoanalysis and folklore. | Reconciliation. | Conduct of life.
Classification: LCC GR42 .C55 2025 (print) | LCC GR42 (ebook) |
    DDC 398.201/9—dc23/eng/20240902
LC record available at https://lccn.loc.gov/2024029616
LC ebook record available at https://lccn.loc.gov/2024029617

ISBN: 978-1-032-74812-2 (hbk)
ISBN: 978-1-032-74811-5 (pbk)
ISBN: 978-1-003-47102-8 (ebk)

DOI: 10.4324/9781003471028

Typeset in Times New Roman
by Apex CoVantage, LLC

Contents

Prologue

A timeless folk story dramatizes a core problem in our world today.

Once, two women claimed the same newborn baby and kept fighting, so the people took them to their village sage to resolve the issue. The elder listened, drew a line in the earth with a stick, and then told the first woman, "Hold the baby's arms," and to the second woman, "Hold the baby's feet." Then to both the sage said, "Whoever pulls the baby across this line is the true mother." The first woman agreed, while the other cried out, "No! That will hurt the baby, give him to her." Everyone immediately understood who the real mother was. (The story is most familiar to Westerners from the Bible, but there are many versions from other cultures.[1])

We often see parallel situations on the Internet today: many commentators are like the first woman, insisting on their convictions no matter what. We often have trouble understanding their beliefs because their positions seem wrong, or even perverse. Worse, many partisans are willing to kill innocents like the infant in the story – think lone mass murderers and jihadists.

In the story, the sage resolves the conflict through wisdom, knowing the true mother will not risk the infant's life, even if it means giving him up to the other woman. But where do we find such wisdom today?

The folk story itself provides an answer – in folk stories.[2]

People have struggled with difficult human problems throughout history. Wise storytellers put their insights and solutions into metaphorical tales. The narratives that rang true to people were retold to others. Over time, only the tales that made sense to many people in diverse cultures survived. This is a process of natural selection applied to narratives, and the results today are folktales with profound cross-cultural insights. (That selection process, I might add, is the original version of crowdsourcing, gathering the best insights from many generations and societies.)

The most dramatic examples of folktale wisdom come from medicine. Ancient narratives described treating fever with willow bark infusions and the 19th-century chemists who investigated the stories discovered aspirin. Recently, folk stories about Chinese wormwood curing malaria inspired efforts to identify the active ingredient. The result was artemisin, a vital antimalarial drug (and a Nobel prize). Equally important and useful **psychological** insights lie in folktales.

In this book I retell and discuss tales from around the world which are specifically about adults struggling to resolve conflicts between squabbling adolescents or competing clans. Folk stories about adults are startlingly different from more familiar tales about youth, such as "Cinderella" or "Snow White."[3] Tales about adults reflect the psychological tasks of maturity rather than youth. To identify these stories, my approach was simpleminded but systematic: I read through thousands of folktales published in English, picking out the ones depicting adults grappling with disputes. I then identified cross-cultural themes in the stories and tried to make sense of them.[4]

This approach highlights what is common to multiple cultures and historical times, and is thus old-fashioned, compared to the postmodern emphasis on local, contextualized, situation-specific factors.[5] Looking for themes shared across cultures, I might add, is the original form of meta-analysis, now common in contemporary science. In the latter, a researcher gathers multiple studies about a particular subject, evaluates the studies' methodological rigor, and makes conclusions using only research judged adequate. With folktales, the "research" comes from people repeating stories that seem especially true and forgetting the others.

Several prominent themes emerge from the stories, and a brief description of the motifs will serve as a preview or map for this book, like the guides that museums provide for visitors. First, folktales emphasize that conflict resolution depends upon storytelling, but the disputants must exchange **specific types of narratives**. There are of course many ways of classifying narratives – perhaps an infinity! We can simplify matters if we look not at what a narrative is about, i.e., its **content**, but what it is trying to do, i.e., its **function** or intention. The latter is something we must determine every time we see an item on the Internet. Is the material trying to tell us a fact about the real world, the one we all share? Or is it fictional, like a novel or fairytale? Could it be an ad – some kind of propaganda – trying to get us to do something, such as buy a product, or vote for a candidate? As the stories in this book illustrate, these narrative types are independent of culture.

These narrative types, I argue, reflect fundamental ways in which we understand the world, which we might call **modes of comprehension**. These modes are more general than the cognitive mental processes studied in contemporary psychology because comprehension modes also include how we organize our emotional and embodied experiences – in fact all aspects of human experience (hence the term "comprehensive" instead of "cognitive").

The concept of multiple comprehension modes has a long history in Western philosophy e.g., the focus on whether science and religion represent separate-but-equal ways of understanding the world. One of the more recent versions of this duality is Jerome Bruner's distinction between narrative and scientific reasoning.[6] Even earlier, Carl Jung introduced the notion of multiple comprehension modes in psychology with his typology of functions.[7] He proposed that people understand the world principally through four functions – thinking, sensation, feeling, and intuition. Someone relying on thinking often considers people who primarily use feeling to be irrational or erratic. Conversely, feeling-oriented individuals usually consider thinking types cold and uncaring. Respect for these type differences, and how they represent distinct but equally important ways of understanding the world, can help us resolve many of our conflicts.

Jung focused his career on exploring multiple modes of comprehension.[8] His early work, for instance, involved empirical, quantitative scientific research with the Word Association Test, detecting unconscious patterns of thinking. He subsequently explored psychoanalysis, becoming a close associate of Sigmund Freud, until their break. Subsequently, Jung suffered a personal crisis in which he experienced extraordinary visions. In grappling with such altered states of consciousness, Jung investigated the long history of people reporting similar experiences across cultures and began formulating his archetypal psychology. He expanded his explorations by looking into other cultures, such as those of India, China, Native Americans, and indigenous African traditions. But the foundation of his perspective remained respect for different modes of comprehension, each with its own validity.

Multiple comprehension modes are now widely accepted. In psychology, for instance, we have Howard Gardner's concept of multiple intelligences.[9] In contrast to the traditional notion of a single kind of intelligence, measured by IQ tests, we now have several differentiated types, e.g., verbal, mathematical, musical, emotional, interpersonal, and kinesthetic intelligences, among others. Postmodern commentators generalize the viewpoint and argue that each culture develops its own way of understanding the world, with all of them equally valid. Here we encounter the classic postmodern dilemma: if we have many, often contradictory, but equally valid ways of understanding the world, how do we choose one or another? Traditionally, we looked to truth for a guide, but now we must ask, does "truth" have any meaning today?[10]

Folktales, as we shall see, clarify the problem. They portray two basic paradigms of truth. The first we may call the **monolithic concept**. It holds that if something is true, it is true for all people since we all inhabit the same world. There cannot be two contradictory truths. The monolithic paradigm descends from monotheism – the belief that there is only one God for all people. This implies that there is only one truth e.g., what the one God says.

The second paradigm of truth is **multilateral**: we have many different and often contradictory truths, depending on what cultural beliefs we are committed to. This paradigm of truth is the latest edition of polytheism, the belief in multiple gods, which we can summarize as "Choose your god, choose your truth."

Fortunately, we find a third alternative in long-neglected stories of the ancient Greek Muses. The Muses were 12 daughters of Zeus and Mnemosene, goddess of memory, and each Muse was associated with a particular cultural discipline, such as Urania for astronomy, Clio for history, or Melpomene for tragic drama. More important, the ancient Greeks celebrated periodic competitions in the cultural disciplines, to honor the Muses.[11] These cultural competitions were analogous to the athletic Olympic games celebrating the Olympian gods. Often the athletic and artistic contests were held simultaneously, but there is some historical evidence that the Muses' competitions arose earlier than the Olympic ones.

We do not know how winners were picked in the Muses competitions, because Greek mythology says the Muses themselves did so and historical records say nothing. Here we can turn to the athletic Olympic Games for a model. The champion in each sport was the one who bested all others in their matches. Winning was decided based on the sport's traditions which defined what winning constituted, and presumably included rules about not bribing judges or sabotaging a competitor. That is, Olympic winners were those who were most **true-to** their sport, their discipline, with its rules and traditions.

By analogy with the Olympic competitions, we can imagine that the winners in the Muses' cultural contests were also those who were most true-to their discipline. For astronomy, this presumably meant that the winning contestant had the most accurate and complete observations or predictions of celestial movements, compared to any other contestant. For tragic drama, the winning play had to conform to established traditions of tragedy, e.g., the play was performed in public, and elicited a deeply moving, cathartic reaction in the audience.

Here we come to a third fundamental concept of truth – being **true-to a discipline**. A good example would be a medical diagnosis. In trying to figure out a patient's illness, a physician would follow usual procedures, such as talking with the patient, ordering appropriate tests, and thinking about various possibilities that could be causing the patient's problems. If the physician went through the process carefully and thoughtfully, her conclusions would be true-to the discipline of medicine, as understood then. She may be mistaken, especially if the case was a puzzling one. However, her diagnosis would be the best medical conclusion at the time. Juries work in a similar way: if the jurors followed the proper procedures, such as the instructions from the judge, tried to be impartial in hearing the evidence, and discussed the case among themselves as objectively as possible, their conclusion would be true-to the judicial discipline.

Not all the Muses' disciplines were cross-cultural. Astronomy and history would be, but ancient Greek tragic drama is unique to them – other cultures have their own dramatic traditions. Beyond the Muses' domains, however, many disciplines are cross-cultural, including one of the most familiar ones – cooking. Consider the difference between **what** we cook and **how** we do so. **What** people cook depends upon personal preference and cultural background, but **how** we cook is determined by physics. Cook meat at too low a temperature or for too short a time and we risk getting sick. The same applies to pottery – **what** pottery people make depends on their preference and culture, but if the potter uses the wrong kind of clay, and fires it at the wrong temperature, the result is not pottery but disappointment. **How** we make pottery (successfully) depends on physics.

In the same way, as I discuss later, our basic comprehension modes follow specific rules which are independent of culture. Those rules reflect fundamental constraints on how we understand the world e.g., how our brain works. A medical metaphor is useful here. The basic comprehension modes are analogous to the human skeleton, which has distinct types of joints. The structure of the joints determines what motions we can make. If we saw someone turn her head around 360°, for instance, we know that we are not dealing with a normal human, but a halluci-nation, a robot, or according to the movies, someone who is possessed by a demon. Turning our heads completely around is false-to human anatomy. In a similar way, different cultures have unique games, sports, and dances – but all those activities use the same basic bodily motions and follow the same skeletal rules. No game in any culture can involve rotating the head 360°.

Similarly, when a narrative violates the rules of a comprehension mode, e.g., that of the mythic mode, we know we do not comprehend the narrative correctly as a mythic story. That is, the story is not true in the mythic sense. Such a violation would be equivalent to seeing someone turning their head around 360°. The same applies to the factual comprehension mode. If an assertion violates the rules of the factual mode, as I discuss later, we know that it is false-to factual comprehension, i.e., it is not factually true.

These are grand claims to make, and most such theories generally arise from personal experiences. So, I recount what prompted me to pursue this long research project in Chapter 5. Briefly, it all began in my third year of medical school, when students traditionally switched from learning medical science in classrooms and laboratories, to learning its practice in clinics and hospitals. To complicate matters for me, medicine at the time was struggling with major transitions – an increasing focus on racial equity and cultural factors, worries about the cost of medical care and insurance, an explosion of medical technology, not to mention ethical and spiritual issues.

What helped my confusion was realizing that scientific knowledge and clinical practice involve completely distinct types of understanding. Medical science asks, "What do we **know** now?" The clinical setting asks, "What do we **do** now?" This was my introduction to diverse types of understanding. In retrospect, the point is obvious, and all practicing physicians learn it. But so was the concept of zero – once it was articulated. Yet only two cultures in human history used the zero (Hindus and Mayans). To complicate matters, I also began meditating to deal with medical school stresses and started experiencing altered states of consciousness. These included mystical episodes, out-of-body experiences, and dramatic visions. The latter I realized were the conclusions of fairytales whose protagonists were adults. I had never come across such fairytales, and this prompted me to investigate folktales from around the world. It quickly became clear that folk stories about adults have profound insights about human psychology.

A metaphor for this book is the San Francisco Golden Gate Bridge. Its soaring towers and cables are inspiring monuments to human insight, both beautiful and enduring – just like folktales The towers and cables on the bridge support a road-way, providing a link from San Francisco, isolated on a peninsula, to the American mainland. The roadway is analogous to my interpretations of the stories, translating their metaphors into practical psychological applications. Beneath the roadway is a complex system of steel beams, holding up the roadway and connecting its weight to the towers and cables. This engineering is analogous to the multimodal concept of truth and the fundamental logical characteristics of each comprehension mode.

In this anthology, I retell some two dozen folktales from around the world and interpret them in terms of analytical psychology, and recent developments in adult development, particularly cognitive and emotional maturation. I also base my comments on many further folktales, and years of experience doing psychotherapy with patients. At times it will seem that I am making too much of small details of one story. But this is the same problem that paleontologists face – from a few fragments of one jawbone, they reconstruct an entire, enormous dinosaur. But they base their interpretations on their experience with many other fossils of many different prehistoric creatures.

By now, most readers are anxious to get to the stories themselves. They are the stars of the show, and I merely the MC. So let us proceed to the first tale, which summarizes our contemporary situation in the world – our fundamental dilemma – while outlining solutions.

Notes

1 The story is common enough to have its own classification as tale type 926 in the Aarne-Thompson folktale index. (Aarne, 1961), (Ashliman, 1996–2002)
2 Good examples include: (Brody and Bond, 1992), (Forest, 1996), (Meade, 2001, 2012).
3 (Chinen, 1989, 1993a, 1993b, 1996)
4 By "folktales," I use a broad definition, namely "orally transmitted narratives," which include fairytales, myths, legends – really any narrative, including jokes and proverbs, which survive the narrative natural selection process. (McNeill, 2013)
5 (Helminiak, 2016), (Held, 2007), (Olson and Torrance, 1996)
6 (Bruner, 1986) This duality is related to what was earlier called "Verstehen versus Erklaren" in philosophy.
7 (Jung et al., 2012)
8 (Jung et al., 1989), (Owens, 2011)
9 (Gardner, 2011)
10 (Lynch, 2011), (Baggini, 2017), (Blackburn, 2005), (Allison and Fonagy, 2016), (Held, 2007)
11 (Allen, 2014), (Clarysse and Remijsen, 2012)

References

Aarne, A. and S. Thompson (1961). *The Types of the Folktale: A Classification and Bibliography*. Helsinki, Suomalainen Tiedeakatemia.
Allen, S. (February 6, 2014 (Updated: July 27, 2021)). "11 Notable Medalists in the Olympic Art Competitions." *Mental Floss* Retrieved 8/24/21.
Allison, E. and P. Fonagy (2016). "When Is Truth Relevant?" *The Psychoanalytic Quarterly* 85(2): 275–303.
Ashliman, D. L. (1996–2002). "Folklore and Mythology Electronic Texts: Child Custody Folktales of Aarne-Thompson Type 926." Retrieved 12/2/2020.
Baggini, J. (2017). *A Short History of Truth*, Quercus Hachette.
Blackburn, S. (2005). *Truth: A Guide*. Oxford; New York, Oxford University Press.
Brody, E. and L. Bond (1992). *Spinning Tales, Weaving Hope: Stories of Peace, Justice & the Environment*. Philadelphia, PA, New Society Publishers.
Bruner, J. S. (1986). *Actual Minds, Possible Worlds*. Cambridge, Mass, Harvard University Press.

Chinen, A. B. (1989). *In the Ever After: Fairy Tales and the Second Half of Life*. Wilmette, Ill., Chiron Publications.

Chinen, A. B. (1993a). *Beyond the Hero: Classic Stories of Men in Search of Soul*. New York, Putnam.

Chinen, A. B. (1993b). *Once Upon a Midlife: Classic Stories and Mythic Tales to Illuminate the Middle Years*. New York, Putnam Pub. Group.

Chinen, A. B. (1996). *Waking the World: Classic Tales of Women and the Heroic Feminine*. New York, Jeremy P. Tarcher.

Clarysse, W. and S. Remijsen (2012). "Ancient Olympics: Music and Musical Competitions at the Games." Published by: http://ancientolympics.arts.kuleuven.be/eng/TC015EN.html Retrieved 8/24/21.

Forest, H. (1996). *Wisdom Tales from Around the World*. Little Rock, August House Publishers.

Gardner, H. (2011). *Frames of Mind the Theory of Multiple Intelligences. New York, Basic Books*.

Held, B. S. (2007). *Psychology's Interpretive Turn: The Search for Truth and Agency in Theoretical and Philosophical Psychology*. Washington, DC, American Psychological Association.

Helminiak, D. A. (2016). "Advocating Truth but Respecting Diversity: Resolving the Contemporary 'Paradox'." *The Humanistic Psychologist* **44**(4): 355–65.

Jung, C. G., A. Jaffé, R. Winston, and C. Winston (1989). *Memories, Dreams, Reflections*. New York, Vintage Books.

Jung, C. G., H. Schmid-Guisan, J. Beebe, and E. Falzeder (2012). *The Question of Psychological Types: The Correspondence of C. G. Jung and Hans Schmid-Guisan, 1915–1916*. Princeton, Princeton University Press.

Lynch, M. P. (2011). *Truth as One and Many*. Oxford; New York, Clarendon Press.

McNeill, L. S. (2013). *Folklore Rules: A Fun, Quick, and Useful Introduction to the Field of Academic Folklore Studies*. Logan, Utah State University Press.

Meade, E. H. (2001). *The Moon In the Well: Wisdom Tales to Transform your Life, Family, and Community*. Chicago, Ill., Open Court.

Meade, M. (2012). *Why the World Doesn't End: Tales of Renewal in Times of Loss*. Seattle, Washington, Greenfire Press.

Olson, D. R. and N. Torrance (1996). *Modes of Thought: Explorations in Culture and Cognition*. Cambridge [Cambridgeshire], Cambridge University Press.

Owens, L. S. (2011). "Jung and Aion: Time, Vision and a Wayfaring Man." *Psychological Perspectives* **54**: 253–89.

Acknowledgments

Trace ancestry far enough, and everyone has genes from all over the globe – it takes a world to produce an individual. The same is true of a book – it combines the work of many individuals, from ancient writers to current colleagues and friends. Several people are particularly important to this book's publication. I would like to thank Katie Randall, my Editor at Routledge, who pushed the launch button on the project. I am also indebted to Karen Signell, for her years of friendship, enthusiastic encouragement, lively discussions and practical wisdom, starting in local cafés and continuing years later in cross country pandemic Zoom sessions. Gloria Gregg, therapist, teacher, musician and colleague provided startling, original insights about contemporary psychological, cultural and multicultural problems! William Barlak added his wealth of experience living in different cultures then teaching and counseling immigrants to America. Gina Atkinson's contributions included perceptive, detailed advice from her experience editing psychoanalytic publications, translating many of them into English. Most importantly, I thank the man with the shortest English first name, and the biggest heart, my husband, Roy Bergstrom, who wisely walked the dog when I started swearing at the computer!

Timeless Storytelling and Contemporary Wisdom

Chapter 1

Our Plight Today

"The Fisherman and the Djinn," Part I

Introduction

The first story in this book is ancient but it dramatizes how time-tested folktales have keen insights for us today. The story addresses one of our most troubling contemporary problems – the sudden, seemingly random eruption of murderous violence, from lone shooters to organized terrorists. The tale reveals the psychology behind these events and illustrates a surprising approach to solving them.

The original tale is quite long and convoluted, so I condense it and divide it into two parts which I will discuss in this chapter and the next.

The Story[1]

Long ago and far away, an old fisherman lived with his wife and grown daughters by the sea. Each day the old man cast his net four times, no more and no less, earning his livelihood from what he drew up from the sea. One day bad luck plagued him. The first three times he cast his net, he hauled up worthless rubbish. In despair, the old man prayed to God, asking for better luck on his next and last attempt. And sure enough, when he retrieved his net, he found a small copper bottle entangled in it.

The flask was sealed, and holy scriptures inscribed on its stopper. Out of curiosity, the old man opened the bottle. He found nothing in it, but a moment later, smoke poured from the flask, and a gigantic Djinn materialized. The fisherman shook with terror. The monster bowed to the fisherman, and said, "Mighty King Solomon, I salute you and thank you for releasing me from my prison!"

"I am not Solomon," said the fisherman. "The great king has been dead many centuries now!" The Djinn paused and then laughed. "In that case, prepare to die, little man!" The fisherman was horrified. "But you just said that I freed you from the flask!" he cried out. "What gratitude is this?"

"Solomon imprisoned me in this bottle because I rebelled against him," the Djinn explained, "and so for the first hundred years, I vowed that whoever released me I would make rich beyond all dreams. But no one came. In the next few hundred years, I promised that I would grant any wish to whoever freed me. And still

DOI: 10.4324/9781003471028-2

no one came. After several more centuries I became angry, and I swore a great oath that I would slay the man who freed me – on the spot. Now prepare to die, mortal!"

The fisherman pleaded for his life. "If you kill me, God will punish you!" But his pleas had no effect so he thought quickly, and exclaimed, "Very well, you can kill me, you ungrateful monster! But at least tell me the truth. How could a great Djinn like you fit in such a small bottle? You must have come from elsewhere. Why would you lie to me?"

The Djinn felt insulted. "Foolish man," he roared, "you do not believe me? I shall show you my magic power and then I shall kill you!" The Djinn turned into a cloud of smoke and poured back into the flask. Instantly, the old fisherman closed the bottle with its stopper.

A tiny voice came from the flask. "Let me out!" the Djinn screamed. "Never!" the fisherman said. The Djinn spoke more gently. "I will reward you richly if you release me!"

"You are a murderer," the fisherman replied, "and I shall throw your bottle into the sea and build my house on this spot to warn people never to fish here."

"No, no!" the Djinn cried out. "I was only testing you! Now that I know you are a clever man who fears God, I will reward you!" "You take me for a fool," the fisherman laughed. He lit his pipe, sat on the sand, and then smiled. "This reminds me of the story of the 'Ungrateful King,'" the old man mused. The Djinn said, "I have not heard that tale. Please tell it to me! But I cannot hear well in this bottle, so you must open the stopper first."

"I shall not release you," the fisherman laughed, "but I shall tell you the story." With that, he sat down next to the bottle and began his tale.

To be continued in Chapter 2.

Dreams and Folktales

The key event in this first part of the tale occurs when the old fisherman innocently opens the sealed flask he found, and the Djinn materializes from the bottle, and threatens to kill the old man. How are we to interpret this opening event?

If this were someone's dream, a common psychological interpretation would be that the Djinn, imprisoned in the bottle, represents a repressed, unconscious element in the person's psyche, such as a trauma that the individual could not deal with. The emotions elicited by the traumatic memory can be so intense, it threatens to overwhelm the individual – which the dream symbolizes as a threat of physical death.

Today, psychological interpretations of dreams may seem antiquated because many neuroscientists now consider dreams to be a normal part of everyday, neuro-physiological processes. This would explain why all known vertebrates have REM sleep. We humans, however, often wake up remembering one dream because it stands out for some reason. Out of the many dreams the sleeping brain produces each night, the awakening brain recognizes one is different and important. This is like the fisherman dragging up worthless things, but when he hauls up the sealed flask, he immediately recognizes the latter may be something valuable. So, he investigates further.

The same unconscious selection process occurs with a more familiar situation: sometimes we struggle to solve a problem during the day, sleep on it, and then the next morning think of the problem's solution. The unconscious brain produces something the waking one recognizes is meaningful, namely, how to solve a particular problem. A similar process occurs when we try to remember someone's name and cannot do so. Then some hours later, out of the blue, a name pops up, which we recognize is the correct one.

Folktales with enduring insights emerge in an analogous process. As mentioned earlier, in the narrative natural selection process, people spontaneously tell stories to each other, but only those that ring true to many people in different situations are passed on. The folktales contain insights about common human problems and solutions that worked. Timeless folk stories are thus equivalent to the dreams we spontaneously recognize to be significant, and thus worthy of a further look. Folk stories are like the dreams of human communities often with important messages for the group.

If we interpret the murderous Djinn leaping out from the bottle as a comment for a common community problem, what might it mean today? One parallel is readily evident today: in the middle of our everyday lives, an angry loner sometimes leaps out and proceeds to shoot innocent people at a night club or school. Or isolated, disaffected individuals join terrorist groups like Al Qaeda and ISIS and then massacre innocent civilians.[2] These murderous attacks seem inexplicable and unpredictable.

The story helps us understand such unprovoked violence when the Djinn explains the reason for his plan to kill his liberator. He was imprisoned in his bottle for so long, he became enraged and vowed to take out his anger on whoever liberated him. Most of us can empathize with the Djinn – to some degree. We too make angry promises to ourselves, such as, "I will get them for that," but we usually stop there as we cool down. The Djinn does not, but then he was stuck in a bottle for centuries, something no mortal human experiences. The Djinn represents an extreme, but understandable psychological reaction.

The Djinn's rage at his imprisonment is also a metaphor for a general societal process. When an oppressive government or institution collapses, liberating an entire people, the newly freed individuals often explode in what we might call *liberation rage*. The fall of Saddam Hussein in Iraq and Moammar Gadhafi in Libya, for instance, unleashed terrorist groups, including ISIS. Much earlier, when the French Revolution overthrew the oppressive monarchy, the Reign of Terror ensued, where hundreds of people were executed. The Russian Revolution repeated the pattern.

Here the Djinn reveals a surprising connection between democracy and terrorism: we often assume that after deposing a tyrant, democracy will flourish and all the people, too. We think that democracy is like a Djinn in movies and fairytales – once released the Djinn – or democracy – will grant people marvelous wishes.[3] What explains the other, dark – side of Djinns – and democracy?

When democracy gives everyone the right to speak their mind, people will assert their truth, and some will insist on theirs. Previously, only Kings and high priests presumed to do so. This is the *democracy of truth*: where everyone can insist they are right, and no one will yield – endless conflicts result. Previously, in such disputes only despots with soldiers could kill those who disagreed with them. Today, with widespread education – a result of democracy – anyone can gain murderous power: on the Internet, another benefit of democratic education systems, people can order guns or learn how to build bombs. This is the *democracy of terror*. An ordinary person can now do what only an absolute monarch – or a Djinn – could do before. This is the democracy of truth and terror, our contemporary predicament. Fortunately, as folktales like this one illustrate, we find solutions in the *democracy of wisdom* – the insights of "the folk," gathered over time in multiple cultures.

True-To an Oath vs. True-About the World

The Djinn insists on keeping his murderous oath, however ungrateful or irrational it might seem. Here the Djinn dramatizes an extreme example of a fundamental concept of truth – being **true-to** a promise. We say, for instance, a couple is true-to their marriage vows, a merchant to his contract, or a soldier to his oath of allegiance. This is the concept of truth as **faithfulness** to an oath or covenant. This concept of truth contrasts with a second paradigm of truth – being-true **about** the world. The fisherman demonstrates this familiar concept when he tells the Djinn that King Solomon has been dead for centuries, a fact the Djinn did not know.

Truth as faithfulness to a promise may seem less familiar in today's secular, scientific and technological society, compared to truth as fact. Surprisingly, truth as faithfulness – being true-to a promise – is the older concept of truth. In English, for instance, the word "truth" comes from "troth," meaning pledge or promise, as in "betrothed." The older meaning of "truth" is being true-to one's word.[4] The same applies to other Indo-European languages, and many outside that large linguistic clan.[5]

Clearly, there are many other concepts of truth, extensively discussed in philosophy. However, I will focus on only the concepts of truth that appear in folktales. Those concepts struck people as important and practical over time, and the stories containing them which were passed on, leaving out concepts of truth that seemed too abstract or irrelevant to everyday life.

The difference between truth as faithfulness and truth as fact, for example, has important political implications even today. As Jonathan Haidt observed in his research,[6] conservatives gravitate towards truth as faithfulness while liberals favor truth as fact. For example, conservatives emphasize loyalty to both people and principles, i.e., keeping promises to both. Promises made in the past require honoring the past, another key aspect of conservatism. And one of our earliest loyalties is to authorities like parents and teachers. Respect for authority is another virtue with conservatives. By contrast, liberals tend to favor truth as fact – a narrative being true-about the world. Factual claims are always open to new evidence and more knowledge about the world, even to the point of questioning widely accepted beliefs and authorities. Such curiosity fuels an interest in innovations and thus a focus on future developments, rather than the past.

Conservative or liberal, we all have commitments to principles, people and values. What happens when our commitments clash? The Djinn wants to keep his murderous promise, while the fisherman wants to survive. Analogously, many people today believe that abortion is murder because that position reflects the doctrines of their religion, and they have vowed to obey their religion. By contrast, secularists, committed to individual freedom, insist on limiting restrictions imposed upon a pregnant woman's choice. Whose oath should prevail?

Here a small detail in the story is instructive. When the Djinn first materializes out of the bottle, he bows to the fisherman, mistaking him for King Solomon, and thanks "Solomon" for freeing him after so long. The fisherman corrects the Djinn, saying that King Solomon has been dead for centuries. Only then does the Djinn announce his plan to kill the fisherman, his liberator. So, the vow the Djinn really follows is not to kill *whoever* liberates him, but something more like, "I vow to kill my liberator (*if it is safe for me to do so*)." His overt vow is not his real one. He keeps a secret exception to his vow, just like children crossing their fingers behind their backs to nullify a promise as they make it. Unfortunately, examples of these covert loopholes keep emerging in the news. Thus, we have fundamentalist leaders, whatever their faith, denouncing same-sex, premarital or adulterous sex, who are then caught doing exactly what they denounce.

So, what do we do when we strive to be true-to our vows, and they conflict with someone else's? The fisherman provides a suggestion.

Storytelling

The fisherman tricks the Djinn back into the bottle by asking the Djinn to reveal where he really came from, since the Djinn is obviously too big to fit in the bottle. To prove his claim and demonstrate his magical power, the Djinn miniaturizes himself and reenters the bottle. We might gloss over this event as a case of a clever human dealing with a powerful but foolish magical creature, but there is greater insight here. The Djinn wants to prove that he told the fisherman a factual truth about the world, namely he is so powerful, he can miniaturize himself. Such truth is important to the Djinn, just as it is to tyrants in general: they want others to acknowledge the objective truth of what they say. They want legitimacy. Power craves factual truth.

After tricking the Djinn into going back into the bottle, several versions of the fisherman's story have him throwing the bottle back into the ocean.[7] However, the original version from *The Thousand and One Arabian Nights* has a surprising twist. Instead of getting rid of the bottle and the Djinn, the fisherman does something extraordinary. He sits down and starts exchanging stories with the Djinn. This could be risky for the fisherman – he does not know if the Djinn can work deadly magic outside the bottle. The fisherman also does not gloat over the Djinn – the old man seems genuinely interested in hearing the Djinn's tales. The fisherman illustrates the psychology of maturity, rather than youth, and the virtue of wisdom instead of heroism. But how exactly does storytelling resolve deadly conflicts? The conclusion of the fisherman's tale provides an answer.

Notes

1 This version comes from *The Thousand and One Arabian Nights,* (Burton and Shumaker, 1977) but there are versions from other cultures, including one in the Grimms' collection.
2 (Diamond, 1996), (Gill, 2017), (McCann, 2010), (Moghaddam and Marsella, 2004), (Post, 2009), (Scarcella, Page and Furtado, 2016), (Schuurman, 2020)
3 President George W. Bush, for instance, invaded Iraq and Afghanistan in 2003, believing that both countries would quickly become flourishing democracies, and then inspire the rest of the Middle East to follow suit. Instead, murderous Djinns leaped out – civil wars, ISIS, and multiple terrorist attacks around the world.
4 (Oxford, 2020)
5 (Baggini, 2017)
6 (Haidt, 2006; 2012)
7 E.g., Bruno Bettelheim in his *Uses of Enchantment* (Bettelheim, 2010)

References

Baggini, J. (2017). *A Short History of Truth*. Quercus Hachette.
Bettelheim, B. (2010). *The Uses of Enchantment*. Knopf Doubleday Publishing Group.
Burton, R. F. and D. Shumaker (1977). *Tales from the Arabian Nights: Selected from the Book of the Thousand Nights and a Night*. New York, Gramercy Books.
Diamond, S. A. (1996). *Anger, Madness, and the Daimonic: The Psychological Genesis of Violence, Evil, and Creativity*. Albany, N.Y., State University of New York Press.
Gill, P., J. Silver, J. Horgan and E. Corner (2017). "Shooting Alone: The Pre-Attack Experiences and Behaviors of U.S. Solo Mass Murderers." *Journal of Forensic Sciences* **62**(3): 710–714.
Haidt, J. (2006). *The Happiness Hypothesis: Finding Modern Truth in Ancient Wisdom*. New York, Basic Books.
Haidt, J. (2012). *The Righteous Mind: Why Good People are Divided by Politics and Religion*. New York, Pantheon Books.
McCann, S. J. (2010). "Authoritarianism, Conservatism, Racial Diversity Threat, and the State Distribution of Hate Groups." *Journal of Psychology* **144**(1): 37–60.
Moghaddam, F. M. and A. J. Marsella (2004). *Understanding Terrorism: Psychosocial Roots, Consequences, and Interventions*. Washington, DC, American Psychological Association.
Oxford. (2020). Oxford English Dictionary Online. *https://www-oed-com.ucsf.idm.oclc.org/*.
Post, J. M., F. Ali, S. W. Henderson, S. Shanfield, J. Victoroff and S. Weine (2009). "The Psychology of Suicide Terrorism." *Psychiatry* **72**(1): 13–31.
Scarcella, A., R. Page and V. Furtado (2016). "Terrorism, Radicalisation, Extremism, Authoritarianism and Fundamentalism: A Systematic Review of the Quality and Psychometric Properties of Assessments." *PLoS ONE* **11**(12): e0166947.
Schuurman, B. (2020). "Research on Terrorism, 2007–2016: A Review of Data, Methods, and Authorship." *Terrorism and Political Violence* **32**(5): 1011–1026.

Chapter 2

Storytelling and Modes of Comprehension

"The Fisherman and the Djinn, Part II."

Story Recap

In the last story in Chapter 1, an old fisherman innocently released a Djinn from a bottle. The Djinn announced his plan to murder his liberator. The Djinn explained that he was imprisoned for centuries in the bottle and become so enraged that he vowed to kill whoever released him. The fisherman tried to persuade the Djinn to spare him, to no avail. Fortunately, the old man had an idea. "At least tell me the truth," the fisherman pleaded to the Djinn. "Where did you come from? You're much too big to fit in this bottle!" To demonstrate his magic, the Djinn reentered the bottle, and the fisherman quickly sealed it.

With the Djinn safely back in his prison, the fisherman sat down and began conversing with the murderous spirit. "Our situation," the fisherman said, "reminds me of the story of 'The Ungrateful King.'" "I do not know that story," the Djinn replied. "Please tell it to me, but I cannot hear well in the bottle, so you must release me first."

The fisherman laughed, and said, "I will not release you, but I will tell you the story.

Once upon a time, a King fell ill with a horrible disease, and none of his physicians could cure him. One day a doctor came by who recognized the ailment. The physician cured the King, and in gratitude the monarch honored the doctor above all other men in the land. This made the Vizier jealous, so he whispered to the King about how easily the doctor could poison the monarch and counseled the King to execute the doctor before the physician could murder him. Finally, the King heeded the Vizier's advice and ordered the doctor thrown into prison. All the good man's pleas to spare his life were fruitless, so he finally asked the King for permission to go home and put his affairs in order before he died. The King agreed. Just before the doctor was beheaded, he gave the monarch a book and said, "After you cut my head off, place it next to this book, and my head will speak to you." When the King put the lifeless head next to the book, the head said, "This book contains all the knowledge in the world." The King opened the book and looked through it, only to find its pages had no writing. Instead, they were poisoned, and soon afterward

DOI: 10.4324/9781003471028-3

the King died in agony. "Just so," the fisherman concluded, "God will punish you if you kill me!"

The Djinn spoke up from in the bottle, "Our situation is not like that at all. I was not really going to kill you. I was actually testing to see how clever and brave you are, just like in the story of the Prince and the Ogress."

"I have not heard that tale," the fisherman said, so the Djinn proceeded to tell it.

All that afternoon, the fisherman and the Djinn exchanged tales. Late in the day, the fisherman said, "I must return home now, so I will throw your bottle back in the ocean. Then you cannot threaten anyone else."

"Please release me!" the Djinn asked again. "I vow I will not harm you, and I swear this to God Almighty, on the Most Holy Name." The fisherman paused, and then said, "You would not dare break such an oath to God, since it was that Name, written on the bottle which imprisoned you. So, I will release you."

The old man took off the stopper, and the Djinn reappeared. Instantly, the Djinn kicked the bottle into the sea. "Remember your oath!" the fisherman stuttered, his knees starting to knock. The Djinn glared at the fisherman, but the Djinn kept his word. He told the old man about a secret lake where the fisherman should catch four fish – and only four – and then take them to the Sultan of that land. The fisherman did so, and one thing led to another until an enchanted kingdom was liberated. But that story is for another time.

Basic Types of Narrative

The fisherman's story ends with the fisherman releasing the Djinn and the latter rewarding the old man rather than murdering him. They resolve their deadly dispute. Unfortunately, the story does not clearly explain how they come to their resolution. The only clue is that it follows hours of exchanging stories with each other, rather than what we might expect – explicitly negotiating or bargaining for a resolution. In the process of storytelling, the fisherman and the Djinn use basic types of narrative found in other folktales around the world. Understanding how those types of narrative work, in turn, explains how storytelling helps us determine truth and resolve conflicts.

There are numerous ways of classifying narratives – perhaps an infinity! For simplicity, I will begin by focusing on the categories that "The Fisherman and the Djinn" illustrate.

Most of the stories that the fisherman and Djinn exchange are fairytales. Fairytales typically have a characteristic introductory phrase that tells us to suspend belief **and** disbelief. In Western fairytales, this is usually, "Once upon a time," while in Arabic stories it is commonly, "Once there was, once there was not."[1] Fairytales are about virtual worlds that may or may not exist. By contrast, factual narratives aim to describe the world that exists. The deadly dispute between the fisherman and the Djinn starts off with such a factual statement: when the Djinn mistakes the fisherman for King Solomon, the fisherman corrects him, and says that the King has been dead many centuries. The Djinn accepts the correction, and then announces his plan to kill the fisherman. Fisherman and Djinn assume they share the same real world.

These two categories, fact and fantasy are probably our most familiar types of narrative. We also usually understand them in terms of what kind of reality they refer to.[2] Factual narratives refer to the real world. Virtual narratives refer to a possible world, which may or may not exist. However, "The Fisherman and the Djinn" immediately brings up a problem with this way of classifying narratives. The Djinn is a supernatural being as are demons, ghosts, gods and God. Stories about them are traditionally called "myth." Are these stories fiction or nonfiction? What kind of reality does myth refer to?

Most westernized individuals no longer believe a supernatural realm exists, inhabited by goblins, angels or fairy godmothers. This is one reason "myth" today has come to mean "mistaken fact" or "imaginary tale." We talk, for instance, about the "myth of El Dorado," the (nonexistent) city paved with gold, or the "myth" of (the never-found) Bigfoot and the Loch Ness monster. People in the past, however, did believe in stories about Zeus or Osiris, enough to build elaborate temples, and offer costly sacrifices in them. And most people in the world today also believe in God or gods. To dismiss their beliefs as "false facts" without further thought is disrespectful.

We can bypass endless metaphysical arguments about whether gods, God, ghouls, or gremlins are real by focusing on our **experiences** of what we call "supernatural." We shift our question from, "Does the supernatural **exist** in the world?" to a different query: "What do we **experience** when we encounter what we call 'supernatural'"? This is the celebrated phenomenological shift, where we simply try to describe what we experience, without any judgments or conclusions about the underlying reality.

We can define "supernatural experiences" in a literal way: the supernatural involves whatever is beyond ("super") our **natural** or **usual** experience. This would include anything that amazes, astonishes, baffles or bewilders us. Stories involving such experiences we might call "**mythic** stories," to distinguish them from "myth," meaning, "false stories." Similarly, experiences of what is unfamiliar or incomprehensible to us would be "mythic experiences," to distinguish them from mistaken ones. More generally, we could call this the mythic **mode** of experience. Familiar examples of mythic narratives are ghost tales, horror stories and Halloween movies. Good ones give us shivers down the spine and not only terrorize us, but also baffle us – how could a serial killer be so cruel?

Mythic experience requires a more detailed discussion. Rudolf Otto, an early 20th-century theologian, described three central characteristics of mythic experiences, based on his study of dramatic examples, namely mystical revelations described in Hindu, Jewish and Christian tradition. The defining features of mythic experience are the *mysterium, tremendum* and *fascinans* – an experience of **mystery**, which makes us **tremble**, and yet is so **fascinating**, we cannot ignore it.[3] More recently, psychologists have focused on the experience of awe[4] as a key to mythic experiences.

Mythic experiences also include more everyday examples such as watching a breathtaking sunset, marveling at its beauty and magnificence. Or a grandparent holding their first grandchild for the first time, feeling awed by the miracle of life.[5] Mythic experiences are not always pleasant or positive. They can also be demonic and horrific.[6] For instance, most of us who watched the news of the 9/11 attack on the World Trade Center in real time reacted in a comparable way. As the planes hit the towers, and the skyscrapers started to collapse, we felt horrified, frightened, overwhelmed and even disoriented. Yet we were also unable to take our eyes off the live news images. We could not comprehend how anyone could deliberately kill thousands of innocent people while simultaneously committing suicide. This is the *mysterium, tremendum* and *fascinans* that Otto described: the event baffles us, makes us tremble in this case with horror, and yet we cannot turn away from the news. No encounter with God or a supernatural realm is required – just an encounter with something completely beyond ordinary human experience.

Some people later attributed the 9/11 attack to vast conspiracies, involving unknown plotters in the American government, staging the whole thing for unknown reasons. Conspiracy theories invoke mysterious people rather than a mysterious deity, but the experience of something unknown or inexplicable is the characteristic feature of mythic experience. In other words, many conspiracy theories are examples of mythic narratives and experiences. Of course, many conspiracy theories are also myth, meaning "false story."

Despite the range of mythic experiences, from mystical revelations to marveling at a sublime painting, a single core process operates – experiencing something unfamiliar or unknown. The fact that we have so many different forms of mythic experience can be summed up in a metaphor – mythic experiences are like birds. Today, scientists tell us that birds are really dinosaurs.[7] They are not merely **descended** from dinosaurs, but have the same core features, e.g., being warm-blooded, feathered, laying eggs and raising their young. In short, birds **are** dinosaurs. We do not think of birds as dinosaurs because they are so much smaller and innocuous, compared to *Tyrannosaurus rex*. In just the same way we overlook less intense mythic experiences because we expect dramatic examples such as God speaking to us, rather than just hearing a deeply stirring symphony.

Facts, Advertisements, Oaths and Home Stories

We can take the same approach with fictional and factual narratives, looking at what we experience with them. Our fictional experiences have one defining feature which fairytales exemplify. When we listen to a fairytale, we split our attention in two, attending to the characters and events in the virtual world of the fairytale, at the same time we remain aware that we listen to a real person tell a story. This doubled consciousness is the defining feature of what we might call the **virtual** mode of comprehension. We pay attention not just to a real situation, e.g., listening to someone tell a story, but to possible realities, i.e., the worlds in fairytales, fiction and imagination. Games provide another example of virtual comprehension.

Playing tennis or chess creates a virtual world, that of the game. When playing, we furiously try to score points against our opponent, but we also remain aware of the real world in which we play the game and so try not to injure the other player. We separate the virtual world of the game from the real one. We structure our experience with doubled vision, a kind of cross-eyed view. This is the phenomenology of the virtual mode of experience.

Factual narratives and the **factual mode of experience** have their own defining characteristics. Factual conclusions involve integrating multiple experience – our own and those from other people. Ideally, the result is a coherent and consistent account of the real world. Anyone who has served on a jury case will be familiar with this process. Jurors must consider all the evidence presented to the court, and decide which testimony seems reliable or not. The group eventually – hopefully – arrives at a coherent conclusion about whether the accused really did commit the crime or not. Integrating the experiences and observations of different people is the unique characteristic of the factual mode of experience.

A fourth basic type of narrative is illustrated by the Djinn's vow, which sets up the whole drama of the story: enraged by his long captivity in the bottle, he promised himself that he would kill whoever liberated him. Oaths, promises and vows are what we may call the **pledge type of narrative**. They can be short, such as, "I swear to tell the truth, the whole truth and nothing but the truth," or awfully long, e.g., "I will pay for this car over the next four years in monthly increments of so many dollars, and follow all the following clauses. . ." When we make such a commitment, we organize our lives around fulfilling it, integrating our actions, priorities and beliefs around our oath. We feel responsible to do so, and (usually) feel guilty if we fail or forget. We might call this the **faithfulness mode of experience**.

Note that faithfulness uses the same integration operations we apply to our factual experiences, except with commitment we focus more on our actions than our observations. The result is that factual conclusions and faithfulness use the same fundamental process – integrating our experiences. **What** experiences we integrate vary, but not **how** the integration occurs. An important implication of this is that science and religion, the two main examples of factual and faithfulness experiences, are siblings. This may explain their constant quarrels.

The Djinn illustrates a fifth basic type of narrative after becoming trapped the second time in the bottle: many of the stories he tells the fisherman are meant to persuade the latter to release him. These are **pragmatic** narratives, and we tell such tales when we want to produce a particular result. An excellent example in the story is the fisherman's demand to know where the Djinn really came from, since the Djinn was obviously too big to fit in the bottle. The fisherman already saw the Djinn emerge from the bottle, so the old man was not asking a factual question. He was trying to provoke the Djinn into going back into the bottle, using his doubt as a tactic. The modern version of a pragmatic narrative would be an advertisement, telling us a very short, entertaining story to get us to buy a particular car or vote for a specific candidate. Or we tell a sob story to the parking meter officer, so as not get a ticket. Using a narrative or experience to produce a particular effect is the defining feature of the **pragmatic type of experience.** After an argument with a coworker, we might go for a walk or eat an ice cream cone, because we know from experience either will calm us down.[8]

There is one last category of story which we might overlook, because that is its chief characteristic. These are the narratives we follow in everyday life, without reflecting on them. The fisherman gives us an excellent example. The story says that he always goes to the same seashore to fish, and always does the same thing, casting his net only four times. This is his morning work routine. He has done it so often, he probably could go to the location and fish with his eyes closed. We might call this narrative type, "**home stories,**" because we **live** in them, rather than **tell** them. They are the scripts we follow in our lives, typically unaware of them. With the corresponding **home type of experience**, we simply assume that what we experience is reality – we do not reflect on or question our experience. We might call this the WYSIWYG principle, from computer terminology – "What you see is what you get," i.e., if we experience it, it is real. As we shall see later, the home mode of experience is closely related to what we consider "self-evident truths."

Six basic categories of stories and modes of experience appear prominently in the fisherman's tale – and most people's lives. Not all cultures classify stories in this six-fold manner, but I think we can map their classifications of narratives into the six categories. The latter are analogous to the cardinal directions, North, South, East, West (as well as above and below.) Diverse cultures define directions in ways relevant to them. For Muslims, the direction of Mecca defines the most important one. For farmers in Asia the southwest is primary because the annual monsoons arrive from that direction, bringing life-sustaining rain. On their islands, Hawaiians define directions by whether they face the sea or the mountains, but when navigating on the ocean they switch to the cardinal directions, marked by the sun rising and setting, as well as by specific stars at night. In a comparable way, I argue that we can classify the different types of stories in terms of the six fundamental types of narrative and experience. The divisions may be arbitrary, but as we will see, they help us navigate our way through difficult conflicts.

The next story provides another example of these fundamental modes of experience, from a completely different culture. Even more important, the story explains how storytelling and the basic types of experience mediate resolution of conflicts.

Notes

1 (Bushnaq, 1986)
2 In philosophy, different types of reality are called modalities, which is "mode of reality" said very quickly. I shall return to this topic in later chapters.
3 (Otto and Harvey, 1923)
4 (Bonner and Friedman, 2011), (Keltner and Haidt, 2010), (Graziosi and Yaden, 2019), (Shapshay, 2018)
5 (Anderson, Dixon, Monroy, and Keltner, 2020), (Bonner and Friedman, 2011), (McPhetres, 2019), (Atchley, 1997) (Gordon, Stellar, et al., 2017)
6 (Gordon, Stellar, et al., 2017), (Diamond, 1996)

7 (Coghlan, 2018), (Feduccia, 2002), (Hutchinson, 1998), (Norell and Xu, 2005)
8 Two American philosophers, Charles Sanders Peirce, and William James were the first to formalize the pragmatic concept of narrative and experience and make it philosophically acceptable.

References

Anderson, C. L., D. D. Dixon, M. Monroy and D. Keltner (2020). "Are Awe-prone People More Curious? The Relationship between Dispositional Awe, Curiosity, and Academic Outcomes." *Journal of Personality* **88**(4): 762–779.

Atchley, R. C. (1997). "Everyday Mysticism: Spiritual Development in Later Adulthood." *Journal of Adult Development* **4**(2): 123–134.

Bonner, E. T. and H. L. Friedman (2011). "A Conceptual Clarification of the Experience of Awe: An Interpretative Phenomenological Analysis." *The Humanistic Psychologist* **39**(3): 222–235.

Bushnaq, I. (1986). *Arab Folktales*. New York, Pantheon Books.

Coghlan, A. (2018). "The Birds that Steal Fire." *New Scientist* **237**(3160): 4–4.

Diamond, S. A. (1996). *Anger, Madness, and the Daimonic: The Psychological Genesis of Violence, Evil, and Creativity*. Albany, N.Y., State University of New York Press.

Feduccia, A. (2002). "Birds are Dinosaurs: Simple Answer to a Complex Problem." *The Auk* **119**(4): 1187–1201.

Gordon, A. M., J. E. Stellar, C. L. Anderson, G. D. McNeil, D. Loew and D. Keltner (2017). "The Dark Side of the Awe: Distinguishing a Threat-Based Variant of Awe." *Journal of Personality and Social Psychology* **113**(2): 310–328.

Graziosi, M. and D. Yaden (2019). "Interpersonal Awe: Exploring the Social Domain of Awe Elicitors." *The Journal of Positive Psychology*: 1–9.

Hutchinson, J. (1998, 9/27/05). "Are Birds Really Dinosaurs?" created 11/21/95; revised 1/22/98. Retrieved 5/26/10, from http://www.ucmp.berkeley.edu/diapsids/avians.html.

Keltner, D. and J. Haidt (2010). "Approaching Awe, a Moral, Spiritual, and Aesthetic Emotion." *Cognition and Emotion* **17**(2): 297–314.

McPhetres, J. (2019). "Oh, the Things You Don't Know: Awe Promotes Awareness of Knowledge Gaps and Science Interest." *Cognition and Emotion* **33**(8): 1599–1615.

Norell, M. A. and X. Xu (2005). "Feathered Dinosaurs." *Annual Review of Earth and Planetary Sciences* **33**(1): 277–299.

Otto, R. and J. W. Harvey (1923). *The Idea of the Holy: An Inquiry into the Non-rational Factor in the Idea of the Divine and its Relation to the Rational*. London; New York, H. Milford, Oxford University Press.

Shapshay, S. (2018) "At Once Tiny and Huge: What is this Feeling We Call 'Sublime'?" Aeon.

Chapter 3

Comprehension and Transformation Today

"A Christmas Carol"

Introduction

The story in the last chapter, "The Fisherman and the Djinn," illustrated how story-telling can resolve even deadly disputes. Unfortunately, it did not show us exactly how this works. The current story does. The fisherman's story lays out all the parts of an IKEA furniture kit, so to speak, but does not tell us how to put the chair together. The present tale provides us instructions.

The story was written by Charles Dickens in 19th-century England, but it has resonated with so many people around the world, and been passed from generation to generation, it now qualifies as a folktale. (This is also probably how most classic folk stories arose in the first place: invented by a gifted storyteller, the tale spreads through time and space.) Although coming from a completely different culture and historical period, Dickens' tale depicts the same six basic comprehension modes we discussed with "The Fisherman and the Djinn." The cross-cultural convergence is striking, but perhaps more important, "A Christmas Carol" shows us how these basic comprehension modes bring about the deep personal transformations required for reconciling intractable and deadly disputes.[1] The same process occurs in successful psychotherapy, and life crises, especially at midlife.[2]

The Story[3]

Once upon a time, there lived a miser named Scrooge. One Christmas Eve, his nephew came to invite him to a Christmas Eve celebration. "Bah! Humbug," Scrooge replied, as he had for many years. And he said the same thing when a delegation came to ask him to donate money to the poor for Christmas.

When Scrooge went to bed that night, a specter appeared in his room. It was his long-dead business partner, Marley, who said, "I come to warn you, because you're the closest thing to a friend I had in life, and you're headed for my eternal doom." Scrooge muttered to himself, "I am having a bad dream. My dinner must have been spoiled."

Marley's ghost then screamed at Scrooge, which terrified the miser so much, he bowed down at Marley's feet. The ghost continued, "Three Spirits will visit you

DOI: 10.4324/9781003471028-4

tonight, and they will give you a chance to escape my damnation." The specter vanished, Scrooge reassured himself that it was just bad digestion, and went back to sleep. He awoke with a start to find a child, or rather an old man, or some combination of both, standing next to his bed. "I am the Spirit of Christmas Past," the Spirit said. "Take my hand." Frightened, Scrooge obeyed.

They flew over the nighttime city and landed outside a place Scrooge recognized – his childhood boarding school. He saw himself as a young boy eating alone on Christmas Eve after everyone else had gone home for the school break. A young girl came running in and cried out, "Dear brother, Father has changed, and he's not so hardhearted. You can come home for Christmas this year!"

In the next moment, Scrooge looked in on a Christmas party – one of many he enjoyed as an apprentice accountant. The youthful Scrooge laughed, danced, and played games with his fellow apprentices and the master's family. When the Spirit reached out for Scrooge's hand, the miser protested, "Ah, let me linger here a moment, I was so happy back then."

The Spirit did not heed him but took Scrooge to another time and place. Scrooge was a young man, sitting next to a beautiful young woman. She said sadly, "I release you from your vows, because we became engaged when we were both poor. Now that you're rich, I see that you love wealth more than me." As the woman arose and left, Scrooge grabbed the Spirit and cried out, "Show me no more!" He awoke to find himself struggling with his bedclothes.

A moment later, a great light shone from an adjacent room, where a gigantic, jovial man sat, surrounded by gifts and food. "Welcome," the Spirit cried out, "I am the Spirit of Christmas Present. Touch my garment," the Spirit instructed Scrooge. Immediately, the two flew over the city, stopping outside a small house. Scrooge recognized his clerk, Bob Cratchit, coming in from the cold with his crippled young son, Tiny Tim. The family sat down to a merry if meager Christmas Eve meal. Everyone laughed, sang and feasted, until the clerk raised a glass of wine, and said, "Let us toast my employer, because his money pays for all of this." The family began arguing. "He should pay you more!" "We should not toast such a miser!" "Remember," the clerk gently chided everyone. "This is Christmas, so let us make our toast anyway."

Scrooge asked the Spirit, "What will happen to the crippled child?" The Spirit replied, "Next year, I see an empty seat at the Christmas table, and an unused crutch in a corner." The Spirit waved his arm, and Scrooge found himself looking in on a Christmas party at the home of his nephew. Seeing the young man laugh, Scrooge exclaimed, "How he resembles his mother – my dear departed sister!" Then the nephew stood up, and said, "Let us toast my uncle, even though he never comes." The room fell silent, but quickly filled with protests. "Why toast such a miser!" "He gives no goodwill to anyone!" "Nevertheless," the nephew said, "the person he makes most miserable is himself!" The scene dissolved before Scrooge's eyes, and he found himself alone in his bedroom.

A shadow soon appeared in his room, or rather a shadow of a shadow. Scrooge could barely make out a human figure, shrouded in the darkness. The Spirit held out his hand, and Scrooge fearfully took it. "Of all the Spirits," Scrooge explained, "I fear you the most, Spirit of Christmas Future." The Spirit did not reply, but flew with Scrooge over deserted streets, pausing over a group of men, wishing each other a Merry Christmas.

"The old miser is finally dead," one man said. "There will be nobody at the funeral," someone predicted. "Unless they give lunch!" a third man quipped. The Spirit conducted Scrooge to a bedroom, where a man lay dead under a sheet. Three people squabbled with each other. "His burial suit is mine!" one person said. "Well, I claim the bed curtains," said another. "I'll take his silver snuffbox," declared the third thief.

Then the Spirit motioned for Scrooge to go to the dead man. "I cannot bear to see who that is," Scrooge said. "Take me away from here!" In the blink of an eye, Scrooge found himself in a graveyard. The Spirit pointed to a tombstone. On it was inscribed Scrooge's name, and nothing more – no words of grief or affection, not even the date of his birth or death. Scrooge desperately asked, "Fearsome Spirit, can I change this future you show me?"

The Spirit only pointed to the tombstone again. Overwhelmed with horror, Scrooge collapsed on the frozen ground, sobbing, begging for a chance to change, and vowing to do so. When he paused to catch his breath, he was back in his own familiar bedroom, and the Spirit was gone.

Morning light streamed through the window. Scrooge called out to a boy passing by, "What day is this?" "It is Christmas day!" came the answer. Scrooge rejoiced and asked the boy to go to the nearest grocery, and have the grocer deliver the largest goose he had to Cratchit's house. Scrooge gave the boy a good sum of money, exclaiming, "Keep the change!" Then Scrooge dressed in festive clothes he had forgotten he owned and made his way to his nephew's house. When the young man opened the door, everyone at the party was dumbfounded. Scrooge smiled hesitantly. "I decided to take you up on your invitation," he said. And that evening, for the first time in as far as he could remember, Scrooge had a Merry Christmas.

From that day on, Scrooge was true to his vow, giving generously to the poor, the sick and the unfortunate. Tiny Tim did not die, because Scrooge raised his clerk's salary. And so, it came true that God blessed everyone!

Home and Mythic Experiences

Scrooge starts his story believing that the business of man is business, as Dickens puts it so eloquently. Scrooge believes everyone should work hard, like he does, and pay their debts, especially to him. He does not question these beliefs, but simply assumes they are true – they are part of his home story. He lives in these beliefs and does not step outside of them to look at them. Thus, when Scrooge meets people who wish him "Merry Christmas!" he automatically gives his famous reply, "Bah! Humbug." And when townspeople ask him to donate to the poor, he says the same thing. He reacts without questioning or reflecting on his reactions. He operates in the home mode of comprehension, where he assumes that what he believes is true and what he experiences is real. This is analogous to the principle of WYSIWYG in today's computer terminology – "What You See Is What You Get."

Scrooge's home story conflicts with that of his culture, especially at Christmas time, when generosity to the poor and spiritual salvation take prominence. However, as the story reveals, the conflict is not just between him and his culture, but within himself – between the adult miser, and the youth who enjoyed life and fell in love.

When Scrooge goes home after work, Marley's specter materializes in front of him. Scrooge is momentarily astonished and bewildered – the hallmarks of a mythic experience. For a moment, his familiar home story cracks open, and he glimpses mystifying worlds beyond. Scrooge is faced with a decision. Is Marley's ghost real and thus a baffling and frightening experience, or just an illusion? Scrooge quickly decides the apparition is a hallucination, thus using the virtual mode of comprehension. He dismisses the ghostly encounter, thus protecting his familiar, materialistic worldview. He demonstrates the double vision characteristic of the virtual mode – he sees Marley's specter but classifies it as a virtual reality rather than an objective one.

Ignored by Scrooge, Marley's specter lets out a bloodcurdling shriek which terrifies Scrooge so much that he bows down at Marley's ghostly feet. Scrooge is overwhelmed with fear, awe and bewilderment. Scrooge is thrown from his familiar world into an unknown realm. This is a numinous experience, one of the most dramatic examples of mythic experiences. It often takes such a mythic moment to trigger the process of deep transformation.[4] Home stories can be so comforting, sometimes only a catastrophe can pry us out of them, such as the death of a child, being diagnosed with a dread disease, or a natural disaster.

Having attained Scrooge's undivided attention, Marley goes on to warn him that three Christmas Spirits will visit Scrooge to prompt him to change his ways. Marley is trying to help his old friend avoid a miserable fate in the afterlife, but Marley does not simply **exhort** Scrooge to change, he arranges intense experiences for the miser. Here Marley uses the pragmatic mode of comprehension. **If** Scrooge can relive his painful past, **then** he will be more empathetic with people suffering in the present; **if** he feels the terror of facing his own unwarranted death, **then** he will be motivated to change. Pragmatic comprehension focuses on actions and consequences – therapy interventions followed by therapeutic results. As we shall see, Dickens' tale is one of the first psychotherapy case histories, anticipating many of Freud's and Jung's insights.

The Pragmatic Mode and Transformation

The Spirit of Christmas Past begins the process and takes Scrooge back to three episodes from the miser's own history: when Scrooge was a young boy spending Christmas painfully alone at boarding school; later, as an apprentice accountant, enjoying the fellowship of his coworkers, especially at Christmas festivities; and finally, the fateful moment when he forsakes his fiancée for love of money. Scrooge recognizes the scenes from his past, so he does not – and cannot – say they are hallucinations. From these journeys into the past, we can now understand why Scrooge was so hardhearted and miserly – his father treated him in exactly that manner, abandoning him at boarding school during Christmas because it cost too much to bring him home. Scrooge himself subsequently abandons his fiancée – and love itself – to pursue his business career and wealth. Dickens was an astute observer of human nature but explaining Scrooge's past is not Dickens' goal – rather reawakening the past and having Scrooge re-experience the emotions he avoided all his adult life.

Revisiting these past emotional experiences is not a matter of regression, because he really experiences them with greater psychological strength, consciousness and the aid of the Christmas Spirits. Now the older Scrooge can feel sympathy for his younger self, abandoned at boarding school at Christmas, and for Tiny Tim, crippled and sickly but cheerful. Then when Scrooge visits his nephew's Christmas festivities in the present, the miser recognizes how much the young man resembles Scrooge's beloved, deceased sister, reminding him of both his love and grief for her. Now, however, the older Scrooge can bear his grief and does not flee from it – or his nephew. This is the pragmatic mode of comprehension at work – the right experiences, in small steps, can change us in deep ways.

After these festive gatherings, Christmas Present then introduces Scrooge to two harrowing characters – Ignorance and Want. However, Christmas Present and Christmas Past carefully modulate the intensity of Scrooge's experiences, so that the miser is not completely overwhelmed emotionally. The Christmas Spirits interleave positive episodes with distressing ones, so that Scrooge is able and willing to continue the journeys. Like a good sports coach, the Spirits push Scrooge through intensive practice sessions, emotional rather than athletic, but never to the point of trauma. Effective therapists do the same.

Christmas Future arrives and takes Scrooge on a journey to the deathbed of someone who died alone and mocked, and then on to a forgotten gravestone in a cemetery. The miser wants to turn and flee, to avoid seeing the name on the grave, but the Spirit forces Scrooge to face it – "Ebenezer Scrooge." Scrooge is overcome with horror and fear. He does not attempt to dismiss the experience as a hallucination or minimize it by saying something like, "Everybody dies, so what's the big deal?" Scrooge has changed significantly since the first Christmas Spirit visited him.

Coming face-to-face with our own death is a paradigm of mythic experience – an encounter with ultimate mystery, something beyond our normal experience. And the prospect of immediate death is frightening. Death, of course, is a natural event and does not require a supernatural explanation, emphasizing that the mythic type of experience is not tied to specific beliefs, such as in a god or God.

When Scrooge awakens the next day, he radically changes his view of the world. His motto metamorphosizes to "The business of man is man." Here Scrooge adopts a pledge narrative – to change his miserly ways, and become a better, more humane person. He commits himself to that goal, organizing his life around it, essentially undertaking a quest. Mythic experience often inspires us to change, but the latter requires perseverance and effort, as we all know from New Year's resolutions.

Dickens' insights are striking because the same sequence of comprehension modes occurs in other cases of deep transformation. Successful psychotherapy is a prime example. Observing the parallels between folktale transformation and the therapeutic change process in psychotherapy helped me identify the role of different types of narrative and experience in key personal changes. Insights from folk stories informed therapy practice, and vice versa.[5]

Psychotherapy and the Deep Transformation Process

Individuals often come to therapy because a chronic problem like depression or anxiety finally becomes too much to deal with – their home story wears out. Sometimes a traumatic event precipitates the process, such as being fired unexpectedly, or having a spouse die – their home story is shattered. The triggers vary but the effect is to push us beyond anything we have experienced before: the crises are mythic experiences, the way Scrooge's world collapses when Marley screams at him.

The first challenge a therapist faces is creating an environment where the client feels safe in exploring any emotions and thoughts, however forbidding or forbidden they may seem. Fundamental to success in this task is a caring and knowledgeable therapist – analogous to the Christmas Spirits helping Scrooge. Also required is the virtual type of experience (analogous to Scrooge's virtual excursions with the Christmas Spirits). The psychological process of double vision – characteristic of virtual comprehension – is essential here: the client may experience intense emotions in the session, reliving a past trauma, while remaining aware that he is in a safe place, reassured and grounded in the therapist's presence.

Most therapists try to understand the individual's situation by finding out how he or she got there – their history. This parallels how Christmas Past appears first and takes Scrooge into his long-forgotten past. The task for the therapist is piecing together evidence from the individual's past, which might be from memories, comments from family and friends, journals or photographs. This is the process of integration central to the factual mode of understanding. Understanding the past is often thought to be a major goal of psychotherapy, but it also can be a trap. In Scrooge's case, for instance, the miser could conclude from his visions of past events, "This is why I am so hardhearted – it was from childhood traumas! And now I am too old to change. (So do not bother me with requests for charity!)" The past becomes an excuse for the present, rather than a precedent to overturn.

Dickens does not make clear whether Marley's ghost and the Christmas Spirits are real, dreams or hallucinations. Other folktales answer the question – all three types of situations can be transformative for an individual, and the same is true for therapy. Virtual experiences can change us as much as real ones. The purpose of virtual experiences is pragmatic, changing a person, rather than factual, learning about someone. A striking recent example of this pragmatic approach comes from virtual reality therapy for phobias like a fear of spiders, heights, flying and a host of other fears. The process begins with a computer program generating a mildly distressing scene, such as seeing a picture of a small spider at a distance. When the individual can tolerate that image without feeling anxious, the computer generates progressively more distressing scenarios, for instance, confronting spiders that are ever closer and larger, but never so large and close that they are terrifying. (This is exactly what the Christmas Spirits do with Scrooge, introducing him to progressively more distressing experiences, alternating those with pleasant ones, using the proverbial spoonful of sugar to make the medicine go down.) When the individual can look at a large virtual spider up close without fear, the **lesson holds in real life.** The pragmatic process is the same for posttraumatic stress disorders but more difficult and dramatic.

Psychotherapy is like physical therapy. Just as the latter uses progressively more demanding physical exercises to restore a person's everyday functioning, psychotherapy uses ever more challenging emotional exercises for the same purpose. Intellectual insight is not sufficient for transformation. Emotional retraining is necessary and the Christmas Spirits provide that for Scrooge. There are many different schools of psychotherapy, and they each preferentially use different kinds of experiences to produce change – but they all use the pragmatic type of experience.

The result of Scrooge's encounters with the Christmas Spirits is that he gains a vastly expanded experience of the world. He no longer inhabits a constricted emotional universe, focused only on his own wealth. He can now empathize with other people's suffering, like Tiny Tim, remember how much he loved his long-dead sister, and extend that affection to her son. He experiences this expanded perspective as an "Aha!" moment when he awakens on Christmas Day, and intuitively accepts its truth. The same type of "Aha!" experience occurs in effective psychotherapy, when the individual's issues suddenly fall into a coherent whole, making sense perhaps for the first time.[6]

"Aha!" experiences are deeply moving but such inspiration requires deep commitment to actualize. We know, however, that Scrooge is capable of perseverance in a difficult endeavor – after all, Scrooge has made a fortune through discipline and perseverance, all the while suppressing his human emotions – no mean feat.

Descent and Return

"A Christmas Carol" highlights a specific sequence of comprehension modes in the process of deep transformation. We might call this the **re-forging process,** where we alter our fundamental life stories. When we talk about life narratives, it is easy to follow a literary metaphor, and say that we simply need to **rewrite** our life scripts. However, significant, and enduring life changes are much more arduous, and in the middle of the process we often feel hammered, melted down and hammered again – **reforged** rather than rewritten.[7]

Scrooge went on virtual journeys into the past to reclaim crucial parts of his life which he repressed or forgot. Then in his journey into the future, he descended into progressively more ancient comprehension modes, culminating with a mythic experience – an encounter with his own gravestone. This numinous, horrifying experience prompts him to reforge his life story, changing from miserly bean-counter to magnanimous benefactor. He promptly proceeds to do so when he awakens in everyday life the next morning.

The oldest example of this reforging process can be found in shamanic tradition. Typically, an individual becomes a shaman after he or she is called by spirits or gods. This is analogous to Scrooge's terrifying encounter with Marley, who sends him the three Christmas Spirits. The shamanic initiate next descends into the underworld, which for Scrooge were the emotions of his past, which he had pushed into the unconscious. The shaman-to-be meets supernatural beings in the underworld who inspire – or terrify – the candidate to begin the painful process of reforging their life, the way Scrooge encountered his own gravestone. The result is that the shaman-to-be gains healing powers and the ability to communicate with spirits with which he or she returns to a new life in the everyday world. For Scrooge, the healing powers involved raising Cratchit's salary so that Tiny Tim could be healed, and reconnecting with his nephew, his long-repressed love for his deceased sister – and his fiancée.

More recent experiences of reforging – were described by Emmanuel Swedenborg and William Blake, as well as Jung himself in his *Red Book*.[8] These archetypal accounts, highlight the content of the experiences, rather than the comprehension processes. Understanding the latter, however, helps us deal with reforging independent of the content of experience.

The next story help explains why folktales from different cultures portray the same reforging process. The key lies in the difference between what we experience and how we comprehend it, the content versus the comprehension mode.

Notes

1 The story is also typical of folktales from around the world particularly about successful men at midlife who suffer a crisis, learn wisdom, and become an elder, as I discuss *In the Ever After* and *Beyond the Hero*.
2 I discuss this at greater length in *Beyond the Hero*. See also (Clarke, 2009)
3 Here I can only recount the highlights of Dickens' masterful story.
4 (Russo-Netzer and Davidov, 2020)
5 I discuss this in further detail, including case vignettes, in *Once Upon a Midlife*, *In the Ever After*, *Beyond the Hero* and *Waking the World*.
6 But such insights can be mistaken. (Jopling, 2001). Cf. (Allison and Fonagy, 2016), (Laukkonen et al., 2021), (Levine, 2016)

7 (Russo-Netzer and Davidov, 2020)
8 (de Resende and Martinez, 2020)

References

Allison, E. and P. Fonagy (2016). "When Is Truth Relevant?" *The Psychoanalytic Quarterly* **85**(2): 275–303.

Clarke, J. H. (2009). "The Metapsychology of Character Change: A Case Study of Ebenezer Scrooge." *Journal of Spirituality in Mental Health* **11**(4): 248–263.

de Resende, P. H. C. and M. D. Martinez (2020). "C.G. Jung's Katabasis: From Ancient Myths to Modern Visionaries Experiences." *Jungiana Online* **38**.

Jopling, D. A. (2001). "Placebo Insight: The Rationality of Insight-oriented Psychotherapy." *Journal of Clinical Psychology* **57**(1): 19–36.

Laukkonen, R. E., D. J. Ingledew, H. J. Grimmer, J. W. Schooler and J. M. Tangen (2021). "Getting a Grip on Insight: Real-time and Embodied Aha Experiences Predict Correct Solutions." *Cognition and Emotion* **35**(5): 918–935. https://doi.org/10.1080/02699931.2021.1908230

Levine, H. B. (2016). "Psychoanalysis and the Problem of Truth." *The Psychoanalytic Quarterly* **85**(2): 391–409.

Russo-Netzer, P. and J. Davidov (2020). "Transformative Life Experience as a Glimpse Into Potentiality." *The Journal of Humanistic Psychology*: 2216782093748.

Chapter 4

Why Comprehension Modes Are Cross-Cultural

"When You Really Listen to a Story"

Introduction

This story from India provides another illustration of how we use the basic modes of comprehension, this time in the context of everyday life. Perhaps more important, the Hindu tale helps explain why these modes occur across cultures.

The Story[1]

A celebrated storyteller came to a village to recount the classic Hindu story, the Ramayana. One woman in the village wanted very much to go and insisted that her husband come with her. He refused, but she kept nagging until he reluctantly agreed. At the first performance, the husband sat way in the back, and since it was an all-night performance, he soon fell fast asleep. When that night's storytelling was finished, people shared sweets, as was the tradition, and somebody put one in the husband's mouth even as he slept. He woke up and returned home with his wife. On the way, she asked him what he thought of the Ramayana, and he said, "It was very sweet." "You listened to the story!" the wife exclaimed, thinking that he had not simply fallen asleep, as she had feared.

The next night, the two went to the performance to hear the continuation of the Ramayana, and the husband sat at the back again, leaning against the wall. He started snoring. A young boy climbed on his shoulder to be able to see the performance, but the husband was sleeping so soundly he did not awaken. At the end of the story, when the husband awoke, he rejoined his wife. "How did you like the story?" She inquired. "It was very heavy," he replied, shaking his aching shoulders. "That's exactly how the story goes!" she said, impressed that he understood the saga.

The third night, the husband and wife went again to the story, and he fell asleep, lying on the ground in the back of the audience. Just before the storytelling ended, a dog came by and urinated near the man, so that some drops flew into his mouth. He awoke quickly, as his wife rejoined him and asked, "What did you think of the story tonight?" He replied, "It was salty." "Salty?" she explained. "What do you

DOI: 10.4324/9781003471028-5

mean?" She pestered him with questions until he confessed, he really had fallen asleep all three nights.

The next night, during the conclusion of the great epic, the wife insisted that her husband sit at the front of the audience. He soon became absorbed in the story, listening to every word the storyteller uttered. Then the tale came to point where the monkey-god Hanuman accidentally dropped a precious ring into the ocean. Hanuman started wailing and wringing his hands.

Engrossed in the story, the husband jumped up, exclaiming, "Hanuman, don't worry, I'll get it for you." He dived onto the stage, but when he stood up, he held a ring, just like the epic described. Everyone was astonished and realized that the man must be particularly blessed by Hanuman and Rama. So, he lived in honor and contentment with his wife the rest of their days.

Content and Comprehension

This humorous story deals with two narratives – first is the *Ramayana*, a classic epic in India, retold over many generations. Its contents – characters, events, and often even the exact wording – are fixed by tradition. The second tale describes how the husband and wife understand the same story in different ways and thus misunderstand each other. The result is humorous, but the same situation occurs frequently on the Internet today, where partisans of different persuasions read the same story, come away with completely different interpretations, and become ever more polarized. Fortunately, this ancient tale from India can help us out in the situation: it shows how the inadvertent use of different comprehension modes can generate disputes, whereas an understanding of the modes can resolve them.

This situation with comprehension modes is analogous to Jung's typology of personality. Jung argued that individuals tend to favor one out of four principal means of gaining information about the world – through sensation, thinking, intuition and feeling. Individuals who favor thinking tend to dismiss those who rely on feeling, and vice versa. This often leads to disputes, but awareness of the different means of learning about the world – and their unique strengths and weaknesses – helps resolve such conflicts. In a similar way, awareness of the distinctive strengths and weaknesses of each comprehension mode helps us understand apparently opposed viewpoints, as the story illustrates.

The story begins with the wife very much wanting her husband to attend the *Ramayana* performance. In traditional Hindu culture, the *Ramayana* was regarded as a sacred story, recounting the drama of Rama, the avatar or incarnation of the great god Vishnu. This traditional attitude uses the mythic mode of comprehension with the story, emphasizing mysterious, eternal, and ultimate questions like the meaning of life, and the correct way of living. The same reverence can be found in most cultures with their Scriptures, e.g., Buddhist sutras, the Hebrew Torah, the Christian Gospels, and the Muslim Koran.

However, the husband is not the least bit interested in hearing the *Ramayana*. Clearly, he does not consider the epic to be sacred or otherwise important. He has undoubtedly heard the story many times from childhood onward and such repetition makes any story routine and even boring. He treats the *Ramayana* as something so familiar, he does not give it a second thought. He understands the epic as part of his familiar **home story**, not a separate, sacred narrative. He is like a custodian at Notre Dame Cathedral in Paris: most visitors are awed when first arriving at the famous site and experience the place to be mysterious and wondrous – mythic. A janitor who works there every day, by contrast, is likely to have a completely different experience – he uses the home mode of comprehension, not the mythic one.

Another reason for the husband's indifference about the *Ramayana* is more common today: many people regard traditional religious tales to be pure fiction, i.e., superstition. They are "myths" in the sense of "false stories," as we discussed previously. Treating the stories in this way means we comprehend them in the **virtual** mode, like a fairytale, and for many people, that means it is barely worth listening to. By contrast, the *Ramayana* was often regarded as a true, **factual story** about the distant past when the gods walked the earth and interacted with humans. In this time-honored view, Hanuman, Rama, and the other characters of the story are historical figures. This is analogous to how many Westerners regard the Bible to be historically true, applying the factual mode of comprehension to its narratives.

Another traditional belief about the *Ramayana* is that listening to the story is a meritorious, religious act which helps erase a person's negative karma, from past sins. This illustrates the **pragmatic** mode of comprehension: people listen to the *Ramayana* intending to produce a specific result, namely their personal redemption. Something equivalent today would be one spouse trying to get the other to church, synagogue, or mosque in the hope of redeeming them, or at least make them more cultured. An even better example of the pragmatic approach would be the storyteller in the tale. Traditionally, he would be an itinerant professional, traveling from village to village, telling stories to earn a living. The tales are pragmatic means to an end for him, namely, surviving economically.

After the first night of storytelling, the wife asks the husband what he thought of the saga. He says that it was sweet. Here he refers to his immediate experience, since he just awoke and ate something sweet. That is the only reality he attends to. This is the home mode of comprehension – if something is present in our experience, we do not question it, look beyond it, or reflect on it. We simply take it for granted. His wife, by contrast, assumes that he is talking about listening to the *Ramayana* epic, and this would involve thinking of two separate things at once. The first is the world of the *Ramayana*, i.e., the situations and characters described by the epic. The second is the real world where the storyteller recounts the tale, and the audience listens. This double attention is characteristic of the virtual mode of comprehension.

The confusion continues two more nights, until the husband says, "It was salty," to describe his experience of that night's storytelling. The wife quickly realizes he is not talking about the epic, nor has he been all along.

To make sure her husband pays attention to the *Ramayana* the final night of the performance, the wife insists that they sit in the front of the audience. This will make sure her husband stays awake and involved in the drama. (This strategy reflects pragmatic comprehension.)

Once seated in the front row, the husband becomes so engrossed in the story, it is as if he were living through the epic along with the protagonists. He responds to Hanuman's distress about Rama's ring falling into the ocean by volunteering to retrieve it. Then he leaps into the "ocean" described in the story. Most of us have experienced something similar, though less intense, becoming so absorbed in a movie or novel, we enter its virtual world and temporarily forget about the real one around us. Fans watching a football game on TV, for their part, often start yelling at the coach or referee. This is the home mode of comprehension where we comprehend what we experience in the moment as reality.

What happens next in the story is the surprise of the tale – after leaping onto the stage, the husband really does retrieve a ring, just like the one described in the *Ramayana*! The audience is naturally shocked and mystified. They witness something beyond their normal experience and understanding, which is characteristic of the **mythic** mode of comprehension. For some in the audience, the moment of perplexity would be quickly replaced by an explanation – they assume that the storyteller had previously planted the ring, since he knew from experience that someone would jump on stage looking for it. Such an interpretation reflects the pragmatic mode of comprehension – the storyteller arranged a trick to generate astonishment and awe.

According to the tale, however, most of the audience regarded the event to be miraculous, i.e., mysterious, inexplicable, and mythic. Furthermore, from then on, the villagers treated the husband as someone chosen by the gods, approaching him with reverence. They apply the mythic mode of comprehension to the husband himself.

Choosing Content and Comprehension Modes

"When You Really Listen to a Story" dramatizes how the **content** of a narrative or experience is independent of how we **comprehend** it. Husband and wife both hear the same story – the very same words from the storyteller. But with any content of a narrative or experience, we must also determine whether we will treat it as fact, fiction, propaganda, myth and so on. We must decide **how** we will understand that content, i.e., what mode of comprehension to use. Many of our disputes arise from adopting competing comprehension modes. By itself, using different modes is innocuous, but problems arise when we reject other approaches and insist only on one (usually our own favorite mode). Perhaps the most common example today involves people seeing the same news item on television and one person taking the narrative to be a scientific report, using the factual mode of comprehension while another classifies it as "false news" i.e., as a virtual narrative. Both people assume that their take on the story is the truth, and that there is only one truth, namely through the comprehension mode they prefer. Identifying conflicting comprehension modes helps in resolving disputes.

and distinguishing between modes requires separating content and mode of understanding.

In psychology, one of the earliest distinctions between content and comprehension can be found in Freud's distinction between the overt content of an experience or action, and the unconscious process behind that content. When someone gets us angry, we often take it out on the first person we meet, such as a clerk at the grocery store. Overtly, we express anger at the hapless cashier for no good reason, but what is really going on is that we shift the target of our anger from the real culprit to someone who cannot retaliate against us. This is the process of unconscious displacement. Analogously, with the process of psychological projection, we may dislike a coworker, because he always tries to take credit for team successes. However, more objective observers think the converse, namely that we try to take credit, while the coworker does not: we project our fault on to the innocent colleague. The process of projection is often habitual or characterological, but the content of the projection can vary. However, underlying all the psychological processes are the comprehension modes, the fundamental ways in which we understand the world.

A concrete way to differentiate the content of a narrative from the comprehension mode we use can be found in old-fashioned bookstores with physical books on shelves. We can shelve the same book in many different sections: one person, for instance, might put the Bible, Torah and Koran in the religious studies sections. Another person might be tempted to put them on the literature, history or fantasy shelves. Conversely the same comprehension mode can apply to many different books. For instance, do-it-yourself books operate in the pragmatic comprehension mode, trying to teach us how to do various tasks, which can range from fixing the plumbing, to naming the constellations at night. The same comprehension mode can apply to virtually an infinite number of books.

A metaphor is helpful here. **What** we count depends upon our culture and situations. An agricultural society focuses on bushels of wheat, number of cattle or acres of land, whereas a postindustrial entrepreneur enumerates stocks and bonds, or how many people follow her Internet posts. **How** we count, however, is independent of **what** we count and involves addition, subtraction, multiplication, division – the rules of arithmetic. If we disobey those rules, our calculations will be incorrect, and we will have endless disputes over who owes how much money. Similarly, what we experience frequently – the content of our experiences and concerns – depends upon our culture, situation, and personal preferences. However, the comprehension modes themselves are independent of our culture, or preferences.

Perhaps the clearest example of the independence of content and comprehension mode comes from two dramatic experiences virtually all people have encountered at some point in their lives. The first example is *jamais vu* (French for "never seen"). Here we enter a situation we **know** we have been in before, such as taking friends to a famous monument. However, on this occasion the monument seems unfamiliar to us, as if we have never encountered it before. The resulting experience is eerie and uncanny – it is an example of the mythic mode of comprehension. That sense of mystery and wonder is independent of the content of experience, e.g., the monument we might be visiting at the time. We can also experience a similar sense of mystery and wonder with a beloved artwork or meeting an old friend – under the right circumstances. (Similarly, staring at a familiar object, like a lamp, for a prolonged period can make it seem uncanny, and even eerie.)

Most of us have also encountered the converse of *jamais vu* – the experience of *déjà vu* ("already seen"). For example, we might go to another famous monument we know we have **never** visited before and yet experience it as something familiar, as if we had been there many times previously. In this case, we use the home mode of comprehension, applying it to the experience of a new location. Another *déjà vu* experience is coming to an unknown place and yet feeling as if we "arrive home" for the very first time in our lives. The sense of familiarity and fulfillment that we typically feel when at home is something we can experience in many other situations. *Deja vu* and *jamais vu* have been reported from cultures around the world, involving varied objects of attention. **What** we experience as mysterious or familiar depends on our individual choice, history, and surrounding culture. **That** we can experience mystery, or a sense of the familiar, is true of everyone, because the two experiences arise from fundamental human modes of comprehension.

Narratives typically give clues to what their intended comprehension mode is. As we discussed, the most direct examples are introductory phrases, like "Once upon a time," telling us we deal with a virtual narrative, or "I swear to tell the truth, the whole truth and nothing but the truth," indicating an oath or promise. Even more commonly, we change our intonation when speaking. We use an authoritative tone and speak louder when we tell someone what to do, which is a very basic example of the pragmatic mode. We may also use nonverbal clues, like winking to listeners, when we tell a tall tale.

Most languages also use "grammatical moods," to indicate what comprehension mode is intended. For example, the indicative grammatical mood indicates we describe or indicate something about the objective world, i.e., we use the factual mode of comprehension. When we ask questions, by contrast, we use the interrogative mood. We make no assertion about the world, but simply consider a possible situation – using the virtual mode of comprehension. For its part, the subjunctive mood expresses wishes, hopes, or desires. These statements involve possibilities rather than real situations and are further examples of the virtual comprehension mode. The mythic type of narrative typically employs archaic language. Religious scriptures, for example, are often recited in ancient, even extinct languages, like Latin or Pali.

From Media and Material to Modes of Comprehension and Truth

The difference between content and comprehension is related to Marshall McLuhan's discussions about communication media.[2] He distinguished the **media** of communication from its **material**. Media involves how a message comes to us, such as by television, gossip, and now its latest form, the Internet, a combination of both. The material is the content being conveyed – what the communication is about. The content could be anything from a weather report to hilarious videos of cats. Whatever the subject matter, however, specific types of media produce distinctive effects on us. Reading a written story, for instance, is usually much less engaging and vivid than watching a video of the same material. McLuhan's important insight was that the characteristics of a particular **media** are independent of the **content** conveyed. The effect of a media can be so powerful it does not matter what content is being communicated. Social media dramatizes the point today: making anonymous comments to equally anonymous readers encourages netizens to post astonishingly crude or hateful comments – no matter what the topic.

Jung anticipated this concept of media, distinct from content, with his typology of thinking, feeling, sensation and intuition. Thinking types prefer receiving information about the world in the form of ideas and thoughts, independent of the content; feeling types gravitate towards emotion, whether the subject matter involves people, politics or algebra; sensate types value sensory perceptions; and intuitive types prefer intuition. Thinking, feeling, sensation and intuition are different media by which information about the world comes to us, irrespective of the subject matter. By contrast, most other personality classifications typically focus on what **contents** of experience a person favors. Some individuals, for instance, need high stimulus situations, such as extreme sports, or intense interpersonal interactions. Others prefer quiet introspection, or making something tangible, such as a cookie or a clock. This is analogous to how some people prefer certain genres of books over others, e.g., romance fiction, or historical accounts. And many people have a preferred media of communication, e.g., social media on the Internet, videos, or books.

Modes of comprehension add a third step to McLuhan's analysis. An inbox – physical or electronic – illustrates the point. A narrative arrives in the inbox in various ways – as an email, a physical memo, a telephone call, and so on. This is the **media** by which a narrative comes to us. **What** the narrative is about constitutes the **material**, the content of the narrative, such as a polite request to do something, a joke from a friend, or a newsletter. We have an infinite variety of material, but a limited number of media.

Whatever the media or content, we must decide what to do in response. Do we let a communication sit in the inbox? Or must we act on the message immediately? Our response, in turn, is determined by how we understand the narrative, e.g., whether we take it to be factually true, fictional, an advertisement, and so on. Thus, the three elements in responding to a narrative are the media, material, and mode of comprehension. The material is limited by culture and personal preferences, but can include an infinite number of topics. The media include a finite number of communication methods, which depend upon technology: long ago, we had only oral communication, then written, and now video and virtual reality. What comes next is anyone's guess! The mode of comprehension, finally, is determined by human capacities, determined more by neurophysiology and genetics rather than culture or technological development.

Our story provides illustrations of each. The media of the Ramayana event is oral storytelling, as opposed to a written scroll or television program. The material involves events of the Ramayana tale. The story includes many classical archetypes, commonly found in mythology, e.g., the hero, Rama, who is the avatar of the great god Vishnu; the villain, who is also supernatural, namely a demon; the kidnapping of Rama's wife and so on. As Jung pointed out, archetypes are repeated patterns of human experience, expressed in mythology, dreams, and now literature and other media. Archetypes involve the content of a narrative or experience, the material or content of them.[3]

The third component, comprehension modes, is dramatized by the husband leaping on stage to retrieve Rama's ring, lost in the ocean, and then actually finding a ring. Most of the audience experiences the event as wondrous, miraculous, astonishing. They understand the event in the mythic mode of comprehension. Others comprehend the event as part of the storyteller's stage performance using the pragmatic comprehension mode, planting the ring beforehand to evoke a sense of wonder and awe.

The six basic comprehension modes are ancient, emerging in time-tested folktales from around the world. Yet as the next narrative dramatizes, we use the same comprehension modes in today's high-tech culture and they can help us navigate through postmodern complexities and dilemmas.

Notes

1 (Ramanujan, 1993)
2 (McLuhan, 1964)
3 Archetypes are an example of recurrent motifs in folklore, comprehensively listed by various scholars. (Aarne and Thompson, 1961) (Ashliman, 1996–2002). Motifs and themes, however, are usually expressed verbally, while archetypes are presented visually.

References

Aarne, A. and S. Thompson (1961). *The Types of the Folktale, a Classification and Bibliography*. Helsinki, Suomalainen Tiedeakatemia.

Ashliman, D. L. (1996–2002). "Folklore and Mythology Electronic Texts: Child Custody Folktales of Aarne-Thompson Type 926." Retrieved 12/2/2020.

McLuhan, M. (1964). *Understanding Media: The Extensions of Man*. New York, McGraw-Hill.

Ramanujan, A. K. (1993). *Folktales from India: A Selection of Oral Tales from Twenty-two Languages*. New York, Pantheon Books.

Chapter 5

Ancient Modes and Modern Doctors

A Medical Joke

Doctor Jokes

An irreverent joke dramatizes how modern medicine uses the six basic modes of comprehension we have discussed. Good jokes, I might add, are like folk stories: jokes which "ring true" to many people in diverse audiences are passed on and endure from generation to generation and culture to culture. Bad stories – and bad jokes – are simply forgotten. The following joke is unusually insightful and contains accurate insights about how different specialties in medicine today operate. It also illustrates the distinct roles of comprehension modes in contemporary, high-tech situations.

> *Internists know everything but do nothing.*
> *Surgeons know nothing but do everything.*
> *Psychiatrists know nothing and do nothing.*
> *Family doctors know a little, do a little, but comfort a lot.*
> *Pathologists know everything and do everything – but too late.*

Although the joke involves stereotypes of the different medical specialties, it nevertheless contains pearls of truth – doctors in different specialties approach patients in distinctive ways. And those approaches correlate with the six basic modes of comprehension we have been discussing.

Internists are usually considered to be the most cerebral of physicians. They often can cite recent research reports to justify clinical decisions, e.g., which antibiotic to use with an infection in a particular patient. Internists tend to wait and observe, gathering as much evidence as they can, before making diagnoses and starting treatment. In short, they focus on the objective, factual mode of comprehension.

By contrast, surgeons prefer acts over facts. Particularly in trauma situations, they cannot wait until all the diagnostic tests come back. They must act on whatever information they have, and decide on their next move, based on the results of their previous actions. They do not look up research reports so much as how the patient is doing. They operate in the pragmatic mode of experience, emphasizing immediate action and consequences. They often cannot afford to think ahead more

DOI: 10.4324/9781003471028-6

than two or three steps, e.g. in dealing with someone bleeding badly from a gunshot wound. Moreover, surgeons learn their craft in a pragmatic way, by **doing** surgery, not by reading about it. They learn by direct experience, not research reports.

Psychiatrists focus on subjective meanings, and unconscious patterns of emotion and behavior. These are mini-worlds – malleable, constantly in flux, and separate from the larger reality. Psychiatrists work with the virtual mode of comprehension – the stuff of fairytales, novels and imagination in general. Dealing neither with facts or actions, psychiatrists know nothing and do nothing – as far as internists and surgeons are concerned! To non-psychiatrists, unconscious meanings and dreams are just like fairytales – not to be taken seriously.

Family doctors are usually thought of as not knowing very much, and not being able to do very much, except to refer patients to specialists. Their unique skill, however, is making patients feel comfortable and safe, creating a home experience. This is especially important for patients dealing with serious illnesses. Family doctors operate in the home mode of experience (which is one reason their practices are often called "the medical home" of a particular patient).

Finally, pathologists are often called the final or ultimate diagnosticians since they conduct autopsies and learn the true diagnosis which may have baffled all previous doctors. They thus know what treatments should have been used – but too late. Pathologists also deal with death and dead bodies, traditionally the realm of the mythic, of ultimate questions and answers. So, if they do not use the mythic mode themselves, they personify it.

Learning about Modes

Although short and amusing, the medical joke sums up lessons it took several years for me to learn during medical school. The first two years of medical school traditionally focused on learning the basics of medical science, from biochemistry to physiology. (Most medical schools have changed the curriculum to emphasize contact with patients early on, and not just book learning.) Medical science focuses on the objective, factual mode of comprehension. In the third and fourth years of medical school, students traditionally move on to hospital wards and clinics, and work directly with patients. The change was disorienting for me, and for a time I felt incompetent and started to doubt if I was cut out for the profession. On hospital rounds, I would often look out the window and see gardeners working, envying them since they knew their profession well. Then I discovered an experimental computer program trying to teach clinical reasoning. As I played with the program, I gradually realized that clinical work with real patients required a completely different kind of thinking from the objective factual mode emphasized in medical science. The question was not "What do we **know** now?" but "What do we **do** now?" Instead of gathering all the available evidence and putting it together, the focus of the factual mode of comprehension, the emphasis of clinical reasoning was on taking action, often without adequate information. This is the pragmatic mode of comprehension. In retrospect, what made it difficult to learn and accept pragmatic thinking was my assumption that there must be only one correct way of reasoning, namely the objective, factual mode of comprehension.

What complicated matters was that I had started meditating to deal with the stresses of medical school, and then began having altered states of consciousness, ranging from out of body experiences to ecstatic, mystical states. What was I to make of these? I also began to have vivid images, especially while jogging along the beach, which I realized were the endings of fairytales. So, I sat down to write them out, and found that they were strange – they all featured adult protagonists at midlife and beyond. Yet the fairytales I was familiar with had **young** protagonists. I thought I must have created a new genre, so I submitted them to a dozen publishers, to no avail. I then switched strategies – I figured that there must surely be folk fairytales about adults, so I planned to look them up, retell and analyze a few of them, and then get mine published. However, as I started finding more and more examples of fairytales about adults, I quickly realized that my own stories were like cubic zirconia jewelry, compared to the real diamonds, emeralds, and rubies in authentic folklore. I switched from trying to write my own fairytales, to finding, understanding and reviving the tales that had been handed down over generations. Thus began my journey into narratives, and the different modes of comprehension they reflected.

Serendipity and Logic

While at a party, I talked to a philosophy graduate student and briefly mentioned my work with types of stories and modes of comprehension. He off-handedly commented that it sounded a little like modal logic, but, unfortunately, we did not have time to discuss it further. I knew nothing about that branch of logic and quickly went to look it up, which took some time, because this was before the Internet, and research required roaming among physical library bookshelves. To my surprise, I found that modal logic does indeed parallel the different modes of comprehension.[1] More important, I realized there were logical aspects to those comprehension modes, which led to many surprising and practical applications to contemporary problems.

However, logic usually seems intimidating. This is because logic is like a skeleton – logic represents the fundamental structure, the bare bones, of how we organize our experience. And dealing with skeletons – like logic – can be gruesome. As any viewer of the popular TV series "Crime Scene Investigation" knows, obtaining a skeleton is a macabre process – boiling the dead body until just the bones remain. Skeletons are important, however, because the way our bones are put together determines how we can move our bodies, and thus what actions we can take. As mentioned in the Prologue, we cannot turn our heads 360°, so if we saw someone do that, we know we do not deal with a normal human, but with some kind of illusion, an alien creature, or someone who is possessed by a demon, at least according to the movies. In a similar way, comprehension modes follow certain rules. For example, if someone said that they have a friend that no one else could ever see, we know that their experience could not be factual. The latter assumes that other people can perceive objective facts. If no one else can, we are dealing with the equivalent of someone turning their head 360°. The invisible friend could be imaginary, hallucinatory, a trick, a deception – but not a factual observation.

The next story, another from India, gives us an extraordinarily clear summary of how each mode of comprehension works. The story uses striking visual metaphors to convey the rules that each comprehension mode follows.

Note

1 (Chinen, 1984)

Reference

Chinen, A. B. (1984). "Modal Logic: A New Paradigm of Development and Late-Life Potential." *Human Development* **27**(1): 42–56.

Part II

Comprehension Modes in Operation

Chapter 6

Comprehension Operations
"The Turtle Tower"

Introduction

We cannot call this brief Hindu narrative a "story." Nothing changes, unlike a normal story. Yet the tale provides striking visual metaphors for how each mode of comprehension organizes our experiences. That understanding, in turn, helps us identify and use comprehension modes more effectively when trying to reforge the fundamental scripts we enact.

The Story[1]

Ancient sages say that the world we live in is an immense tower. Our everyday life is the very top, but it rests upon a hidden platform. That platform, in turn, is held up by enormous pillars, resting upon the backs of great elephants. Those gigantic animals themselves stand upon an even larger turtle swimming in the cosmic ocean.

Structures of Experience

This brief narrative gives us a snapshot of how comprehension modes work. It is analogous to a schematic diagram explaining how a particular device, such as a watch works. It shows us the structure of the different comprehension modes. The mini-story is unusually abstract, leaving out local cultural details. This makes the story more relevant to multiple cultures including our own.

We begin at the top of the Turtle Tower with everyday life, where we go about our usual business, following routines and scripts. We do not ask questions or wonder what more there might be in life. This is the home mode of comprehension. In it, we take for granted that what we experience is reality. To use computer terminology, we follow the WYSIWYG principle: "What you see is what you get." We might call this the principle of **presence** – what is present in our experience (we assume) is present in the world. We take our immediate experience to be reality. The principle of presence applies to any content of experience, e.g., thoughts, emotions, images, somatic sensations. This is clear with dreams. While dreaming, we

DOI: 10.4324/9781003471028-8

are rarely aware that there is a real world beyond the dream. What we experience during a dream, whether that is an action, emotion, or sensation, we experience as reality.[2]

The Turtle story portrays a giant platform holding up everyday life. We can interpret the platform to be a theatrical stage. When we watch a production on such a stage, we have two types of experiences – becoming engaged in the world of the drama, on one hand, and being aware of watching the play as part of an audience. This is the virtual mode of comprehension in which we use a kind of "cross-eyed" consciousness, where we have two things in mind at once. This separation of possible and real worlds is the central characteristic of the virtual mode of comprehension – the domain of fairytales, fiction, theater, imagination and self-reflection. We might call this the principle of **divergence**, to distinguish it from the characteristic feature of the home comprehension mode, namely presence.[3] The twofold attention of divergence also occurs in playing games, such as tennis: while playing, we focus on hitting the ball, so it flies accurately, but we are aware that we are playing a game, and so we do not aim the ball at the other player's head, intending injury.

The platform/stage of the Turtle Tower is supported by great pillars. Building pillars requires gathering stones, judging the strength of each, discarding those that do not meet the requirements, cutting the blocks carefully, and putting them all together correctly, so they stand on their own. Integrating all these actions illustrates the principle of **convergence**, the characteristic feature of the objective mode of comprehension. But there are two types of convergence.

Scientific research illustrates the first type, namely, making factual conclusions. The scientist records observations and conducts experiments, judging which are reliable. She must then put the evidence together with previous findings from other scientists, integrating all the data into a coherent, consistent story, e.g., a scientific paper. Her conclusion must be able to stand on its own, just like a well-made pillar, meaning that other people hearing the same evidence would likely come up with the same conclusion.

Juries ideally use the same process of convergence with one important difference. Jurors are free to use their emotional and intuitive reactions to witnesses, e.g., in evaluating how trustworthy a witness might be. (Scientists are not supposed to.) However, the jurors' experiences must be corroborated by other evidence such as another person having the same reaction to the witness. Convergence of subjective experiences can be evidence. The same applies to eyewitness testimony – which as we know from a variety of experiments is notoriously unreliable. So, any one person's report must be corroborated by further evidence.[4]

Successfully building a pillar also requires many people committing to the same goal. This may be a short-term commitment for day laborers, or an open-ended one for the architect who promises to continue until the project is complete. Their promises to work on the pillars illustrate a second type of convergence, namely the commitment mode of comprehension, where we organize our actions and lives around fulfilling an oath or promise. The result is faithfulness, remaining true to the vow and its goal. That objective may vary from building a pillar, to fulfilling a business contract, being faithful to a marriage vow, or keeping a covenant with God. The objective varies, but the logic of convergence is the same. [5]

The dual nature of convergence – faithful or factual – can be seen in the double meaning of the word, "objective." On one hand, we use "objective" to mean "a goal," what happened to him e.g., "Our objective is to reach the mountain summit." We commit to that goal and strive to achieve it. On the other hand, we have "objective truth," which we assert describes reality, independent of any specific individuals i.e., we integrate observations from any reliable witness.

The word "fact" reiterates the two types of convergence. "Fact" comes from the Latin word "facere," meaning "to make." But so does the word "feat." Facts and feats are both things we make or achieve. This easily leads to the confusion that we create facts and thus we create reality, i.e., there is no reality independent of us. To be more precise, we should say that we create factual **conclusions,** but we do not create the facts themselves.

Identifying the fundamental process of convergence links two apparently different domains – fact and faithfulness, and their most common forms today, science and religion. Facts and faithfulness use the same convergence operation, but **what** they integrate differs. Science integrates observations, religions integrate actions, values, and beliefs. But both focus on the process of convergence – when everything seems to fall into place. Metaphorically, fact and faithfulness are siblings – which may explain much of their constant bickering.

Elephants and the Turtle

The fourth level of the Turtle Tower consists of enormous elephants, who carry the pillars upon which the platform and everyday life rest. Elephants are extremely intelligent animals and can learn complex sequence of events, which is why they were once used in circus acts to perform tricks, and for logging operations in countries like India and Burma, not to mention their historical use as war animals.

Elephants learn their skills through repeated sequences of events, illustrating the principle of **consequence.** We learn the same way. Most of us discover, for instance, that if we talk only about our troubles at a party, people will move away. Observing such regular sequences of events is the core of the pragmatic mode of comprehension. This is the principle of consequence: "If A happens then B happens," e.g., "If I eat too much chocolate at night, then I will not sleep." Once we learn the sequence, we can turn it into an intention: "I will not eat chocolate at night so that I can go to sleep without problems." Consequence organizes our perceptions, and not just our intentions and actions, e.g., if there is a bright flash of light on a stormy day, we normally expect to hear thunder.[6]

The Turtle Tower explicitly places the elephants on a level below the pillars. The position is accurate – the pragmatic mode of comprehension, which the elephants symbolize, underlies the objective comprehension mode represented by the pillars. The pragmatic mode makes the objective one possible. The former is more fundamental than the latter. Consider, for instance, trying to identify a strange looking animal in the neighborhood. We move closer to get a better look and observe how it reacts to us. We listen to see if it makes any distinct noises, and we look around to determine if there is anybody looking for their exotic pet. These experiences specifically involve sequences of events and integrating these sequences in a coherent manner leads us to a factual conclusion, "Bob's chinchilla somehow got loose!" The objective mode of comprehension builds upon the underlying pragmatic mode. The latter is more basic than the former. The story emphasizes this point with a small detail.

The elephants are the first animals to appear in the Tower. As intelligent as elephants are, they do not build pillars, platforms, or other permanent structures. People do. The fact that the elephants are located beneath the platform and the pillars (that humans construct) suggests that the pragmatic mode of comprehension is more basic or "primordial" compared to building pillars. However, "primordial" is not to be confused with "primitive." "Primordial" means "elemental" which is not to be confused with "elementary."[7]

Back to the Turtle

At the base of the Tower is the Turtle, swimming in the cosmic ocean. The Turtle constantly moves into unknown horizons – the vast cosmos. At the same time, he carries his shell with him – his portable home. He dramatizes the core principle of **transcendence** – moving **from** a familiar world, his shell home, **toward** unknown horizons.[8] Transcendence is the characteristic feature of the mythic mode of comprehension, involving an encounter with mystery, the unknown and uncanny.

Although not explicit in the narrative, we can imagine the Turtle withdrawn into its shell for protection, on the seashore or at the bottom of the ocean.[9] Ensconced in its shell, the Turtle makes a good symbol for the home mode of comprehension, where we assume that our immediate experience is all of reality, and do not inquire about what might be beyond. This is the principle of presence, again. The top of the Turtle Tower is everyday life, the domain of the home mode of comprehension. And we find the home mode again at the bottom of the Turtle Tower. This suggests that the home mode is our usual, everyday one, while it is also the most basic level of human comprehension. Other stories will reiterate the theme, linking the home mode of comprehension with "necessary" and "self-evident" truths.

The reforging sequence of comprehension modes is one of many formulations for the process of deep transformation. Another viewpoint comes from Hegel's dialectical philosophy. He described the fundamental logic of significant change as a sequence of three phases: first, we have a thesis, e.g., where a narrative is asserted; second, an antithesis spontaneously arises, contradicting the original narrative; and finally, a synthesis emerges, in which thesis and antithesis are integrated in a greater whole. Note that Hegel focuses on the **content** of a narrative or experience, in contrast to the **media** by which we encounter the material or the **mode** by which we comprehend it. Hegel's dialectic logic underlies Jung's view that significant psychological change comes from holding a tension of opposing psychological tendencies long enough for a synthesis of the two to emerge, such as male and female, or divine and mundane.[10]

Hegel's dialectic provides an overview of key steps by which deep conflicts can be resolved. As we shall see in subsequent stories, the reforging sequence of comprehension modes portrays more details of the process. And a major theme is that mythic experience typically provides a new, integrating synthesis, which becomes the inspiration and motivation for profound changes.

The importance of mythic experience in deep transformation is one of Jung's major contributions to psychology and psychotherapy. Rather than dismiss or explain away mythic experience, including mystical ones, Jung recognized its central role in the deepest changes we can make in our lives. "Archetypes," "archetypal," and myth are central concepts for Jung and a theory of multiple comprehension adds a new perspective on them.

"Archetypes" are recurrent themes in mythology, dreams, literature and imaginal experiences e.g., the archetypes of the Great Mother, the Hero or the Sage. "Archetypes" are a classification of the **content** of our experience. We have many different ways of categorizing such content, as illustrated by the extensive lists of recurrent motifs in folklore, enumerated by various scholars.[11]

On the other hand, "archetypal" is often used in the sense of "an archetypal experience" or "an archetypal story," and usually means something deeply moving, astonishing, memorable. An individual meeting the United States President in person might feel flustered and a little awed by such a powerful figure. The experience is archetypal, i.e., mythic. Archetypal experiences often involve archetypes, but not always. A spectacular sunset, for instance, may deeply move and inspire someone witnessing it. The experience is archetypal, but if we start calling a sunset an archetype, then the word starts losing its impact and meaning, like addressing everyone as Lord or Lady.

Conversely, we can experience an archetype as something ordinary. Machu Picchu, for instance, is an archetype of a sacred site. When people first arrive at the mountain sanctuary, almost everyone is awed and sometimes even overwhelmed by it – they have a numinous experience, an archetypal experience. This involves the mythic mode of comprehension. However, an engineer tasked with protecting the monument from so many tourists would take a pragmatic perspective, thinking of what specific measures could be taken to prevent subsidence or landslides. This is not a mythic or archetypal experience but simply practical and literally down to earth.

A metaphor may help clarify the differences between the meaning of "archetype" and "archetypal." An archetype is a classification of repeated themes in mythology, dreams, imagination and human experience in general. Archetypes are analogous to basic features of a landscape, such as a mountain, lake, valley and so forth. This is geography, a classification of the features we encounter as we travel. With the science of modern geology, we now understand how these basic geographic features arise. And one of the most powerful forces involve the movement of the tectonic plates upon which the continents rest. The separation of the North American tectonic plate from the Eurasian plate, for instance, occurs right under Iceland. The split between the two tectonic plates allows molten rock, magma, to rise from deep within the earth, generating the numerous volcanoes and earthquakes of the island. And where tectonic plates collide, one typically moves under the other, pushing up mountains, like the Himalayas.

The hidden geological processes shaping the surface features we see constitute a kind of "tectonic logic" for geography. In an analogous way, the Turtle Tower reveals the fundamental processes governing our comprehension, a kind of "tectonic logic" for how we understand the world. The levels of the Turtle Tower constitute the basic features – the geography – of human comprehension. The distinct comprehension modes are like basic geographic features, i.e., mountains, deserts, oceans, etc. The fundamental processes of each level, e.g. divergence, conversions, transcendence, are the processes which shape those features of our understanding. With comprehension modes, we do not have tectonic plates physically moving toward or away from other plates. We deal with experiences that can move apart, diverging from each other to create a virtual reality. We can also integrate experiences, so they come together to generate our factual conclusions and our enduring commitments in life. Experiences can also move toward something beyond, something unknown in the process of transcendence.

The "Turtle Tower" illustrates the characteristic operations of each comprehension mode, using striking visual metaphors. I have discussed the Turtle Tower moving from the top level to the bottom, but we could have done the reverse, starting at the bottom and moving up. The levels remain the same, no matter which direction we travel. (Moving downwards is *katabasis* as we discussed in the last chapter – returning to older, primordial levels of comprehension. Moving upwards, conversely, is *anabasis* – moving upward or outward, expanding our world.)

The next story portrays the comprehension modes in completely different metaphors, using a developmental framework. This is the Navajo Story of Emergence. However, the striking cross-cultural parallels between the Navajo tale and Turtle Tower reiterate that comprehension modes deal with something basic about human understanding.

Notes

1 (Ramanujan, 1993)
2 Visual diagrams are also useful in conveying how comprehension modes work, what "operations" are involved. We can diagram the principle of presence as: ◉ Here the square is a narrative, or more generally, an experience (think of a TV screen). The dark circle is what we take to be reality (think of a globe, representing the world). In the diagram, the dark circle is completely enclosed in the square – what we take to be reality is completely within our immediate experience. We do not look beyond it or question it. We can also summarize the principle of presence in an exclamation, "This!"

3 We can diagram divergence as: ▢◁●○ Here the rectangle represents a narrative or an experience. The arrows indicate how the narrative refers or points to a real world (the dark circle) or the virtual one (the white circle). We keep in mind both worlds. Divergence can be summarized verbally as "This or That," where we hold both in mind the same time.

4 We can diagram convergence as: ▢→● where the rectangles represent various observations which converge upon the dark circle, representing a real situation. Convergence can be summarized verbally something like this: "If we have evidence A, evidence B, and evidence C, then we have fact F." Conversely, "If we have fact F, then we will find evidence A, evidence B, and evidence C.

5 We can use the same diagram for convergence in the commitment mode of comprehension, as well as the factual mode of comprehension: ▢→● Here the rectangles represent intentions, actions and beliefs which aim to bring about a specific goal, represented by the dark circle.

6 We can diagram the logic of consequence as: —▢—○— In this case the rectangle represents an action, and the arrow pointing to it represents our intention to do it. The circle indicates the result we expect from our action – the consequence we hope for.

7 $1+1 = 2$ is elementary, $e = mc^2$ is elemental. The former is fundamental in arithmetic and mathematics. The latter equation requires complex mathematics to understand, but it reveals fundamental structures of the universe.

The different levels of comprehension are analogous to levels of cultural complexes, described by Singer (Singer, 2006, 2019).

8 We can diagram transcendence as: ■◁○ An example of the process is seeing a picture of a saint. We usually interpret a picture to be a portrait or representation of the actual saint, represented by the circle. In this case the circle is empty because we may be unsure if the saint actually looked like that, or really existed. The curved arrows pointing outward represent the experience of something unknown, mysterious, in contrast to the familiar portrait. We can summarize transcendence by "There!?" in contrast to presence, "This!"

9 This Hindu story puts the Turtle at the bottom of the world and parallels the stories of Native American depicting the world resting on a cosmic Turtle.

10 (Jung, Adler and Hull, 2014) Hegel's dialectic also underlies fundamental principles of alchemy, as Jung interpreted them: alchemical transformation occurs only when the vessel that holds the substances can contain powerful opposites, for long enough for a synthesis of them to occur. (Franz, 1980)

11 (Aarne and Thompson, 1961), (Ashliman, 1996–2002), (Littleton, 1965), (Nguyen et al., 2012)

References

Aarne, A. and S. Thompson (1961). *The Types of the Folktale, a Classification and Bibliography*. Helsinki, Suomalainen Tiedeakatemia.

Ashliman, D. L. (1996–2002). "Folklore and Mythology Electronic Texts: Child Custody Folktales of Aarne-Thompson Type 926." Retrieved 12/2/2020.

Franz, M.-L. v. (1980). *Alchemy: An Introduction to the Symbolism and the Psychology*. Toronto, Inner City Books.

Jung, C. G., G. Adler and R. F. C. Hull (2014). *Collected Works of C.G. Jung. Volume 20; General Index*. Princeton, NJ, Princeton University Press.

Littleton, C. S. (1965). "A Two-Dimensional Scheme for the Classification of Narratives." *The Journal of American Folklore* **78**(307): 21–27.

Nguyen, D., D. Trieschnigg, T. Meder and M. Theune (2012). *Automatic Classification of Folk Narrative Genres*. KONVENS.

Ramanujan, A. K. (1993). *Folktales from India: A Selection of Oral Tales from Twenty-two Languages*. New York, Pantheon Books.

Singer, T. (2006). "The Cultural Complex: A Statement of the Theory and its Application." *Psychotherapy and Politics International* **4**(3): 197–212.

Singer, T. (2019). "The Analyst as a Citizen in the World." *Journal of Analytical Psychology* **64**(2): 206–224.

Chapter 7

The Development of Comprehension Modes

"The Navajo Story of Emergence"

Introduction

There are many versions of this Navajo story, depending on the storyteller, where the story was told, and when. I use this version[1] for two reasons – it was the first I came across, and it is also one of the simplest. Even so, the story is overwhelming because of its length and detail, so I will recount and discuss it in smaller bite-sized segments.

The story describes the journey of the Navajo People from the First World, through a series of worlds to the present one, the Fifth World. It presents a structure of the cosmos that is analogous to the Turtle Tower in Chapter 5. However, the Navajo tale explicitly begins at the bottom and moves upward to our current reality. The Navajo tale also parallels a story from modern Western psychology – the saga of cognitive development in early childhood and later.

From the First to the Second World

The First World was dark and cramped, with only a small area of land, surrounded by burning pitch. The People lived there in misery, but one day Dragonfly got an idea. He made himself some wings and flew into the sky. The other People followed suit. Locust found a crack in the sky, and everyone squeezed through it. They discovered a large, brighter new world, and rejoiced in their good fortune. This new home was the Second World.

As soon as the People entered the Second World, the Birds quickly confronted them. "This is our world," they told the People. "You must leave because there is not enough food for your people and ours." The People begged to stay, saying they only ate grass and leaves, so the Birds relented. "But you must not come to our homes across the water," they warned. In time, the People ate everything up in their sanctuary, and impelled by hunger, they gathered in a great cloud. They invaded the Birds' homes and the Birds counterattacked, killing countless of the People. The People fled into the sky, where they found a crack through which they escaped into the Third World.

DOI: 10.4324/9781003471028-9

We begin with the First World which is a sealed stone cavern where the People live. For the People in the First World, what they see is all of reality and they have no concept of anything beyond their small cavern. This is the principle of **presence** i.e. what is present in their immediate experience they assume is all reality. It is characteristic of the home mode of understanding, the earliest and most basic comprehension mode to appear in human development. (The home mode is represented in the Turtle Tower, as we discussed in the last chapter, with the Turtle at the base of the Tower withdrawn into its shell.) A paradigmatic example of presence and the home mode of comprehension is the infant nursing. Nothing exists beyond the immediate experience of suckling – the infant is enclosed in the reality of the moment, the way the People are enclosed in the First World. As adults, we have an equivalent experience when we become absorbed in an experience, say, watching the ending to "The Game of Thrones" or a Super Bowl. We become engrossed in the drama and in that moment, nothing else exists in the world for us. We momentarily climb back into a small, sealed stone cavern.

At some point, Dragonfly has the notion that there must be something beyond the First World. She has a new concept – an unknown world lies beyond their familiar home. In flying up to the stone sky, seeking a way beyond, Dragonfly illustrates the process of **transcendence**, moving from the familiar into the unknown. It is the fundamental process of the mythic mode of comprehension. (The equivalent in the Turtle Tower would be the Turtle at the base of the Tower, swimming in the cosmic sea, and constantly entering new domains and mysterious horizons.)

Transcendence arises in early infancy: infants quickly distinguish familiar from unfamiliar – for example, staring longer at a stranger's face, compared to mother's or father's. They instinctively gravitate towards the unfamiliar and unknown, which typically generates fascination and sometimes fear.[2] The infant's curiosity and anxiety represent early forms of transcendence which ultimately evolve into adult mythic experiences. This does not mean that mythic experiences – which include many religious ones – are infantile. They are primordial, not primitive.

The Emergence Story depicts the mythic mode of comprehension emerging after the home mode. The reason is that transcendence involves a more complex logic, compared to presence. We can articulate the experience of the home mode simply as "This!" – something is present in our experience. Transcendence, on the other hand, involves what is unfamiliar and mysterious – "not-This." Here we add the operation of **negation**, an extra logical step compared to simple presence. The story in the next chapter will elaborate on this point.

After the exhilaration of entering the Second World, the People encounter the Birds, who demand that the insects leave. The newcomers manage to persuade the Birds to let them stay. Their successful plea is an example of the pragmatic mode of comprehension where we say or do something to achieve a specific goal. The fundamental process here is **consequence**. The process of consequence is much more basic than language. Infants quickly learn that when they smile, people are more likely to play with them. Even as adults, learning by action and consequence continues. From experiences of doing the wrong thing, for instance, we learn what will get a spouse or partner mad, and most people stop doing those things.

In the Emergence Story, the People at this point do not learn enough about actions and consequences – they eat up all the food in their domain, and then invade the Birds' territory, heedless of the consequences. The Birds react by driving the People out of the Second World. This is the first in a series of hard lessons the People will learn about actions and consequences, the core of the pragmatic mode of comprehension.

From the Second to the Third World

The People fled into a new world which was larger and brighter than the Second World. This Third World was the home of many people, including birds, animals, and humans. All creatures initially looked alike, but everyone gradually began to change, taking on the appearances they still have today. With so many people, food soon became scarce, and everyone started fighting and stealing from each other.

All the people gathered in a meeting to figure out what to do. They now called themselves the First People, and agreed they needed a leader to settle their disputes. But they argued over who that should be. The mountain people suggested Mountain Lion, the plains dwellers wanted Wolf, the forest residents nominated Hummingbird, and the valley people insisted on Bluebird. Everyone finally agreed on a test – the four candidates would each go on a quest, and whoever brought back the most useful things for all the People would be chief.

Wolf returned first with morning light, spring rain and young corn. The people were so delighted they made him chief. Then Bluebird arrived, bearing summer rain, soft corn and blue sky, followed by Mountain Lion, bringing evening light, autumn rain and ripe corn. Everyone agreed these gifts were as valuable as Wolf's, so they made Bluebird and Mountain Lion chiefs, along with Wolf. Hummingbird arrived last, bringing northern lights, corn and beans, and a bowl to store them in. The people decided he should be a fourth leader.

This episode of the Navajo story has many bewildering events. But they do have an underlying commonality, and that is a focus on sequences of actions and consequences, events and effects. This focus is characteristic of the pragmatic mode of understanding and the People continue to struggle with it. For example, upon arriving in the Third World, the People eat everything up, repeating what they did in the Second World. Fortunately, the People recognize they must do something different in this new world. They decide to choose a leader to help them solve their problems and especially foresee consequences of possible actions.

The People specifically decide that their leader will be the one who goes out into the world and brings back the gift most useful to the People (a very pragmatic attitude). It is not a matter of fighting for the top spot in a hierarchy (which may or may not help the People). And what the candidates bring back for the People are specifically sequences of events, such as morning light followed by the blue sky of day and then evening light. The initial gifts are not enduring objects which might be more useful, such as food or magic objects, which are more usual in quest stories. This suggests that there is something special and significant about all these ephemeral gifts.

We can interpret the Third World as a metaphor for a specific state of consciousness in which we comprehend the world in terms of sequences of events, rather than enduring objects. That is, we use the pragmatic mode of comprehension rather than the objective one. William James described one example of this consciousness as "a blooming, buzzing confusion," and attributed it to the young infant.[3] (Another apt metaphor comes from the Turtle Tower: gigantic elephants stand on the back of the Cosmic Turtle. Elephants are highly intelligent and can learn complex sequences of events, as we discussed before. But elephants do not make and carry objects with them, such as tools or jewelry, nor do they build permanent structures, like houses. They live in a world of events and effects, more than enduring objects.)

It is hard for human adults to imagine experiencing the world chiefly in sequences of events, except by using specific techniques to alter everyday consciousness. Many meditation techniques, for instance, seek to experience the world as a flux of constant change, rather than a collection of enduring objects. Psychedelics often have a similar effect, changing normal perceptual experiences of the objective world into a kaleidoscope of constantly changing experiences. The Third World described in the Emergence story is an apt metaphor for such a world organized in terms of sequences rather than objects, i.e., with the pragmatic comprehension mode.

In the story, Hummingbird brings back objects – corn, beans and a pot in which to store them. His gifts point to the next mode of comprehension to emerge, illustrated by the Fourth World.

The Fourth World

After the First People chose their four leaders, everything went well in the Third World – until food again became scarce. So, the leaders called a council of the First People, in which everyone decided to seek a new world. They put on wings and flew into the sky. There they met First Man, First Woman, First Girl and First Boy. These mysterious helpers led the People through a passage into the Fourth World above. In this even larger and brighter world, the People discovered the Pueblo People with their fields of corn, beans and squash. First Woman told the People to apprentice themselves to the Pueblo tribes so they could learn how to grow food.

Coyote and Badger appeared at this point. Coyote suggested they steal the food, rather than work for the Pueblo People. Badger warned against that, but the People took Coyote's advice, only to fail repeatedly – the Pueblo People kept careful watch over their fields. So finally, the People went to work for the Pueblo tribes, learned how to plant and harvest, and then started their own fields and settlements.

In the Fourth World the People meet the already-established Pueblo culture who are farmers. They grow their foods, unlike the People, who are hunter-gatherers.

The transition from hunter-gatherer culture to agrarian culture was a major development in human history. With agriculture, civilization literally began – the construction of cities and the emergence of governments. But the rise of agriculture also required shifting from the pragmatic mode, typical of hunter-gatherer culture, to the objective mode of comprehension.

To succeed in agriculture, farmers must organize their activities, follow strict seasonal schedules, and ignore distractions. They integrate their actions around their objective, namely a successful harvest. This is the principle of convergence, characteristic of the commitment mode of comprehension. Heroic quests are the most familiar example of the commitment mode, and we usually do not consider farmers to be dramatically heroic. Yet they are: they commit themselves to an objective, namely growing enough food to feed family and community and remain faithful to their quest. Farmers repeat this quest every year, so they seem more humdrum than heroic.

Coyote suggests that the People skip the bother of farming and simply steal food from the Pueblo People. He reflects the pragmatic comprehension mode focused on immediate actions and outcomes, ignoring long-term consequences, characteristic of hunter-gatherer cultures. Badger, on the other hand, advises patient labor and learning, reflecting the commitment comprehension mode. He reflects the mentality of settled agricultural societies, like the Pueblo People.

Coyote's advice does not work, because the Pueblo People protect their crops. So, the People finally apprentice themselves to them. The two parties make a contract, a pledge – in exchange for their labor, the People learn the practice of agriculture from the Pueblo farmers. Contracts and promises are paradigmatic examples of the commitment mode of comprehension as we discussed previously. This is the faithfulness comprehension mode.

Agriculture also provides a metaphor for the factual mode of comprehension, another example of the objective mode. Farmers must collect a multitude of seeds – just a few will not do. They must also sort the seeds, throwing out the rotten ones that might spoil the rest. Farmers must follow proper procedures, such as planting their seeds at the right time, weeding their crops, and protecting them from anyone that might eat them before harvest. (The equivalent in the Turtle Tower are the pillars, whose construction requires integrating the activities of many workers around a shared objective.)

Scientists do something similar. They collect a multitude of observations, because only a few are rarely useful. Scientists must also determine which observations are reliable, and which are not. They must follow up evidence to see where it might lead – unexpected observations often lead to novel discoveries. They must also tend to their evidence, making sure they do not record their observations erroneously, or miscalculate statistics. And of course, scientists must not fabricate evidence, which would be equivalent to a farmer knowingly selling pebbles to another farmer instead of seeds. Agriculture illustrates the core logic of the objective mode of comprehension – convergence – which lies behind both the factual and faithfulness modes of comprehensions.

The capacity for convergence and the objective mode of comprehension develops early in childhood. The first step is the infant learning to integrate multiple separate actions to achieve a goal. This may seem to be simple, for instance, reaching out and grabbing an object. However, the action requires coordinating eyes, arms and hands – simultaneously. Learning to walk is an even more complex process of integrating movements and perceptions of the body.

Integrating actions also underlies the experience of enduring objects. When playing with a ball, for instance, an infant learns that the ball will not fit in his mouth, unlike the corner of a blanket; if he pushes the ball, it will roll away; if he ignores the ball, and then returns to it later, the ball will have the same properties. The infant integrates all these sequences of events into the experience of a ball which exists whether he plays with it at the moment or not. Convergence converts the flux of embodied experiences into the reliability of an enduring object and ultimately the objective world.

Coyote and Trouble

After the People learned how to farm, all went well in the Fourth World. Then one day, Coyote gambled with Water Monster. Coyote won by cheating and as his prize took home Water Monster's magnificent coat. Coyote discovered Water Monster's babies in a pocket of the coat, but Coyote said nothing and kept the children. When Water Monster discovered his babies gone, he became angry and started a great flood throughout the Fourth World. The People were forced to flee to higher ground, but the waters followed them. So, they desperately dug a hole in the sky, and escaped into the world above.

The Fifth World was a small island surrounded by water. However, Water Monster's flood entered the Fifth World, threatening to drown everyone. The People finally discovered that Coyote had Water Monster's babies and gave them back to their father. The floodwaters receded, sparing the People. But their problems were not over – there were other monsters in the Fifth World which they had to defeat. The Fifth World was also a small island in the middle of the sea, which they enlarged, creating the present world we all live in.

In the Fourth World Coyote causes trouble, as he usually does in Native American tales. Coyote gambling with Water Monster is the first mention of a game in the Navajo story. Games are examples of the virtual mode of understanding and involve the creation of a virtual world, separate from the larger one. Keeping secrets, as Coyote does next, is another example of the virtual mode – we have the world of the secret, separate from the real world. The virtual mode involves the process of **divergence**, where we have two things in mind at once: for Coyote this is knowing that he has Water Monster's babies, while pretending that he does not, and furthermore, claiming he has no idea why Water Monster might be causing the disastrous flood.

Significantly, Coyote plays his games and keeps his secrets **after** the People learn about agriculture. In psychological development, the virtual mode develops after the objective one. From infancy, of course, children "play" with objects, e.g., pounding, twirling, or throwing whatever they can grasp. In the process, they experiment with objects, learning what actions lead to which consequences. This is the pragmatic mode of comprehension in action. (It is also the infant's version of science – conducting experiments to learn about the world. The experimental method in science is primordial, but not primitive.) The older child, by contrast, takes an object and transforms it in imagination – a spoon can become a spaceship, a pillow might turn into an exotic but comforting creature. Play is no longer about discovering an object's properties, but rather creating an entirely new object – which exists in its own world, separate from the larger reality. Divergence develops after convergence. We understand imaginary or virtual objects, only after we have learned about the enduring objects of the objective world.

When Water Monster realizes his babies are missing and that Coyote has them, Water Monster becomes enraged, causing a terrible flood that threatens to drown all the People in the Fourth World. The People manage to escape to the Fifth World, discover Coyote's secret, and return Water Monster's babies to him, stopping the continuing flood. Unlike all the previous new worlds, the Fifth World is a barely habitable place. The new world is no Eden, like the previous worlds initially seemed to be. The people must fight to survive in the new world, and labor to expand it. The result of the People's efforts is the present world. The Navajo story is surprisingly postmodern here. However, instead of claiming as many postmodernists do, that we create our world *ex nihilo*, the Navajo story more modestly says that we take a previously existing world and reshape it to our needs – with much effort.

Living in the current Fifth World the People are not aware of the many levels beneath everyday life. In the same way, we take our present world for granted – not aware of the long developmental history, and the multiple modes of comprehension sustaining our experience of the world.

Migration and Metamorphosis

The Emergence Story recounts the People's migration from the cramped First World through progressively larger, brighter, more complex worlds, until arriving at the present Fifth World. The journey parallels the actual history of the Navajo, who originated as an Athabascan tribe in northern Canada, and subsequently migrated progressively southward, into warmer, sunnier climates. That is, the story is not simple fantasy, but metaphorical history, encoding an actual collective experience of the Navajo people.[4]

However, we can also interpret their story as a metaphor about the development of comprehension modes from early childhood. The larger, clearer, more differentiated realms the Navajo discovered reflect increasingly complex comprehension modes. Note the Emergence Story describes changes in the world, not in how the Navajo perceive the world. They project their evolving psychological abilities onto the physical world. Jung pointed out that medieval alchemists did something similar – they depicted evolving psychological states in terms of evolving physical states, because descriptions of the physical world were familiar and at hand, whereas descriptions of psychological phenomena did not yet exist. In hearing the Emergence Story, the Navajo could relive their collective history – and thus re-experience in a small way the emergence of more complex comprehension. Jung argued that medieval European alchemy provided an analogous experience – alchemical imagery was a metaphor for the different phases of deep transformation.

The Navajo Emergence Story is not the only origin story to recapitulate the basic development of human comprehension. Three other stories portray the same developmental sequence using different metaphors as we shall see in the coming chapters. One story is ancient but the other two are modern. Before discussing the three tales, we must ask a question: Why are there parallels between the structure of human comprehension and the structure of the cosmos in creation stories?

I suggest that the structure of our comprehension governs the structure of the cosmos – how our minds operate determines how we see the universe. (This is Immanuel Kant's fundamental and revolutionary philosophic insight.) Another way to put this is that the comprehension of creation mirrors the creation of comprehension.

The next tale comes from Polynesia, and describes the creation of the world by Ta'aroa, the primary deity. Using completely different metaphors, this Tahitian story presents the six basic comprehension modes we have discussed and visually depicts how each operates. The story also depicts how the comprehension modes unfold in a sequence, paralleling cognitive developmental psychology.

Notes

1　(Newcomb, 1967)
2　(Scherer, Zentner and Stern, 2004) (Young, 2011) (Markovits, 2014)
3　(Moll and Tomasello, 2010)
4　This is an example of the collective unconscious, on a clan level (Singer, 2006, 2019)

References

Markovits, H. (2014). *The Developmental Psychology of Reasoning and Decision-making*. Hove, East Sussex, Psychology Press (Taylor and Francis).
Moll, H. and M. Tomasello (2010). "Infant cognition." *CB/Current biology* **20**(20): R872–R875.
Newcomb, F. (1967). *Navaho Folk Tales*. Santa Fé, N.M., Museum of Navaho Ceremonial Art.
Scherer, K. R., M. R. Zentner and D. Stern (2004). "Beyond Surprise: The Puzzle of Infants' Expressive Reactions to Expectancy Violation." *Emotion* **4**(4): 389–402.
Singer, T. (2006). "The Cultural Complex: A Statement of the Theory and its Application." *Psychotherapy and Politics International* **4**(3): 197–212.
Singer, T. (2019). "The Analyst as a Citizen in the World." *Journal of Analytical Psychology* **64**(2): 206–224.
Young, G. (2011). *Development and Causality: Neo-Piagetian Perspectives*. New York, Springer.

Chapter 8

Structures of Creation and Comprehension

"Ta'aroa Creates the World,"
and "The Big Bang"

Introduction

Two stories show how the fundamental operations of comprehension modes unfold from the simplest to the more complex. First is the ancient Tahitian creation tale and the second, an analogous story for modern physics. The Tahitian story of how Ta'aroa created the world is unusually succinct and surprisingly abstract, revealing the link between comprehension modes and basic logical operations. As will become evident, the two stories also parallel the Navajo Emergence story and the Hindu Turtle Tower.

The Story

In the beginning, there was no sun, no moon, no land, no sea, no beast, no tree. There was only Ta'aroa enclosed in his shell. For a long time, he remained alone in silence, until one day, his shell broke open, and he stepped out. Climbing upon his shell, he cried out, "Who is above there? Who is below there?" There was no answer, except the echo of his voice. "Who is in front there?" he continued, "Who is in back there?" Still, no one replied.

So Ta'aroa commanded, "Rock, come here!" But there was no rock to obey. Ta'aroa then called out, "Sand, come here!" but there was no sand to heed him. Ta'aroa became vexed. He picked up his shell and threw it into the air, so that its dome formed the sky. After a moment of rest, he took off another shell that covered him, and made it into rock and sand. Still angry, he took his spine and made it into a mountain range, using his ribs for the foothills. He cast his organs into the air, so they became clouds, bringing life-giving rain. His flesh became the earth, and his arms and legs, the strength of the earth. He took his fingers and toenails to make the scales and shells of the sea creatures. His feathers became trees, vines and shrubs, and his intestines, eels, lobsters and shrimp. And his blood rose like steam and became the redness of sunset, sunrise and rainbows.

Finally, Ta'aroa created the gods, including Tu, the first, who helped him create humankind. The result is the world as we know it now. Somewhere in the world, Ta'aroa's head remains unchanged – he still lives, the creator and sustainer of the earth.[1]

DOI: 10.4324/9781003471028-10

The Logic of Comprehension Modes

Ta'aroa begins his story with just himself, contained in his shell, and nothing else in the cosmos. He is aware only of the world within his shell and has no concept of anything beyond. His situation is analogous to the People in the First World of the Navajo story where they live in a small, sealed, stone cavern. As far as the People are concerned, what they see is all of reality. The same is true for Ta'aroa, enclosed in his shell. This is the principle of presence, where we assume that what is present in our experience is all of reality.

The next event in the story is that Ta'aroa's shell breaks open and he steps outside, encountering an unknown new world. Moving from his familiar shell world to face unknown horizons is the process of transcendence, the defining characteristic of the mythic mode of comprehension. Ta'aroa stepping out of his shell parallels the People breaking out of their First World and entering the larger, mysterious, unknown Second World. At this point, Ta'aroa is also analogous to the Turtle at the base of the Tower, sticking his head out of his shell and swimming into unknown domains of the cosmic ocean.

Transcendence involves distinguishing between the known and the **not** known, the familiar and the **not** familiar. Here we come to a fundamental aspect in the logic of transcendence – **negation**. The home mode focuses on "This!" while the mythic mode focuses on "Not-This." Mystery is what we do **not** understand, what we have **not** previously experienced.

We can summarize Ta'aroa's two perspectives: he experiences "This!" when facing his familiar shell-world, and "Not-This," when turning and facing the unknown world outside. For brevity, we can rename "Not-This" to "There?"

The Structure of the World

After breaking out of his shell, Ta'aroa asks, "Who is above there?" and "Who is below there?" This means that he now distinguishes two basic directions in the outside world. The difference arises from a sequence of experiences: for instance, Ta'aroa turns his head one way, and sees his familiar shell-world, then turns his head another way, and sees the unknown world. Observing such sequences is the principle of consequence or conditionality, the fundamental feature of the pragmatic mode of comprehension, e.g., "If I look to my right, I will see the right half of my shell and beyond it, an unknown world;" "If I look down and right, I will see the top of my shell." We can summarize the sequences as "If this experience, then that experience." More simply, "If this, then **that**." The nebulous "There?" in the mythic mode becomes a specific "That" in the pragmatic mode.

In the next step of his creation story, Ta'aroa creates the physical world from parts of his body. This might seem like a gory and even bizarre event, but other ancient beings in mythology do the same thing, e.g., Pan Ku from China, and Ymir, the primordial frost giant in Norse mythology. The meaning of the gruesome theme in Ta'aroa's tale becomes clear if we focus on how children learn about the objective world, as we discussed previously. When a young infant pushes a ball, and it rolls away, she will follow it if she can see it. If it rolls behind another object and disappears, the very young child will not pursue it: out of sight is out of existence. If she can see the ball again, she will go up to it, push it, and see it roll away again. After several such experiences, she learns that even when she cannot see the ball, it is still there, and it still has its own characteristics, such as rolling when pushed. She integrates multiple momentary perceptions into the experience of an object that exists independent of her. And all those momentary perceptions are embodied experiences. Metaphorically speaking, she takes parts of her body – or bodily perceptions – and integrates them into the experience of an independently existing object.

This example of convergence involves integrating different observations about the ball and the result is a factual conclusion. But there is another type of convergence involved here, too. If the child has never encountered a ball before, she will usually experiment with it, pushing it to see what happens, pounding it, and so forth. She has a goal in mind, namely, to find out what this unknown object is. And so she coordinates multiple actions around that objective. This is convergence as a feat, achieving a goal, the process fundamental to the faithfulness mode of comprehension.

In the next step, Ta'aroa creates people – both gods and humans. What distinguishes people from everything else Ta'aroa has created so far – mountains, trees and so on – is that people have their own subjective, inner realm, separate from the material world. In dealing with people, we thus have two things in mind at once, their inner, subjective reality, and their material reality as a body in the world. The former is a virtual world, and the latter the objective one we all share. This is the process of divergence, the logic of the virtual mode of comprehension.

At the end of Ta'aroa's narrative, we have the familiar world we live in now. For the most part we have forgotten about how Ta'aroa created the world, and simply take the world we see for granted. This is the home mode of comprehension once more. What we experience is sufficient for us, so we do not ask questions or reflect. After Ta'aroa creates everything, however, his head remains somewhere in the world. It is the last remaining part of the original Ta'aroa – he survives in the world he created. His continuing presence in the world presumably means that he can start creating new aspects of the world. So however confident we might be that we understand the whole world, we must always be open to something completely new and surprising, and this includes new modes of comprehension.

I turn now to a creation story from our current modern, Western scientific tradition. This is the tale of the Big Bang and how it created the universe as we know it. The story, of course, is subject to revisions based on new evidence, but it is the current best thinking about how the universe was formed. I bring it up to emphasize one point: the basic structure of the Big Bang story parallels that of Ta'aroa's creation story, the Hindu Turtle Tower and the Navajo Emergence story.

The Big Bang

*In the beginning there was only the **singularity** – no heaven or earth, no space or time, not even a void, because that is something. The singularity contained all there was to be in the universe to come – the vast expanse that would hold galaxies, the planets they would contain, and their inhabitants.*

*From the singularity, space and time emerged: in a fraction of a second, the universe expanded from an infinitesimal point to millions of miles wide, and then beyond. This is the second phase of the universe – **inflation**.*

*The expanding universe contained a cloud of energy, roiling with incomprehensible power. In this maelstrom, particles materialized only to vanish, becoming energy again. There was no enduring matter, just a constant flux of ephemeral particles, like one's breath condensing in cold air into tiny water droplets, and then evaporating again. However, all was not chaos, because the primordial particles in the universe followed rules, such as gluons turning into the strong nuclear force, and back again, but not becoming the electromagnetic force. We may call this the **flux** phase of the universe.*

*As the universe expanded it cooled, and some particles endured, no longer destroyed in the energy maelstrom. This is the way a cloud in the sky cools, so that droplets of water begin to persist, and then join other droplets, finally falling as rain. In a similar way, quarks combined with other quarks to form protons and neutrons, which combined again to form atoms of hydrogen and helium. We might call this the **consolidation** phase of the universe.*

The process of consolidation continued. Atoms formed vast clouds in space, which gravity pulled into ever denser clouds. In some, the compression of gravity became so great that hydrogen atoms started to fuse with each other – giving birth to stars. The stars in turn fused larger and larger atoms together, forging all the different elements. The atoms combined to form dust, which combined to create pebbles, and then rocks, boulders and eventually planets. This is the way raindrops fall to the earth, and become streams, which combine into rivers, and then lakes or seas.

Given the right conditions and sufficient time, life arose, eventually leading to intelligent life, at least on one planet, and that life eventually invented stories about how the universe came to be, like this one.[2]

Parallels

The universe begins with a singularity, from which everything will arise. A singularity is the simplest, most basic possible structure of the universe. Here the Big Bang parallels Ta'aroa's tale, which starts off with Ta'aroa in his shell – and nothing else. Everything in the world will arise from Ta'aroa. This is the principle of presence: what Ta'aroa sees is all that exists or will exist. Similarly, everything that will exist is contained in the original singularity.

In the inflation stage of the Big Bang, space-time unfolds from the singularity. This corresponds to the second step in Ta'aroa's story when he breaks out of his shell and faces a vast, unknown new world. Here we have the principle of transcendence. The singularity might be summarized as, "This!" Space-time is something new, distinct from the singularity, which we might call simply, "Not-this" or "That." This is the logic of transcendence and negation, illustrated by the expansion phase of the universe.

As the singularity expands, space-time unfolds. The generic distinction between "This" and "Not-this" becomes differentiated into "Here" and "Not-here," as well as "Now" and "Not-now." These are the fundamental distinctions of space and time. This step in the Big Bang is analogous to Ta'aroa's asking, "What is above?" and "What is below?" – he establishes the primary directions in his unfolding universe.

The next stage of the Big Bang is flux, where the primordial universe is filled with a maelstrom of high energy, in which particles form and then vanish. The particles, however, follow rules, e.g., if we have a gluon, then it can turn into the strong nuclear force, but not the electromagnetic force. This is the archetypal logic of sequence: "If x, then y." We see the same logic in Ta'aroa's tale when he commands Rock and Sand to come to him. He assumes that **if** he commands them to come, **then** they will obey.

The next episode in the story of the Big Bang is the consolidation phase: particles combine with other particles to form enduring matter. Thus two "up quarks" and one "down quark" combine to form a proton which endures, while one "up quark" and two "down quarks" combine to form a neutron which also becomes a stable particle. The consolidation process is iterative, so protons and neutrons combine to form atoms, which in turn join to form molecules. The principle here is convergence, characteristic of the objective mode of comprehension.

This is equivalent in Ta'aroa's story to him creating the material world from his body. As we discussed that process provides a metaphor for how we integrate fleeting, embodied experiences into enduring objects. The Big Bang follows the same process, except the integration involves particles and energy rather than embodied experiences. Enduring material objects are the result in both cases – the material world in the first case, and human experience of that world in the other.

Most physicists end the story of the universe here, but we can extend it further, because many scientists believe that given the right circumstances and enough time, life spontaneously emerges. And life illustrates the logic of the virtual mode. A living organism creates its own world, following its own rules, within the larger material one. A simple example would be a bacterium living in a pond. It separates itself from the larger world with a boundary, the cell membrane, takes in energy and nutrients, transforming them into its own internal structures. It creates its own virtual world. The process is iterative. As biological organisms become more complex, they evolve a nervous system, which creates models of the world. The model constitutes another kind of virtual world involving information rather than nutrients. For a mouse, the model might involve a mental map of its environment and where food often can be found. As animals evolve bigger brains, these models become progressively more complex, until we get language and eventually narratives like this one. Ta'aroa illustrates the same process of creating virtual worlds when he creates other gods and humans – who each have their own inner, virtual worlds.

Why the Parallels?

Ta'aroa's creation story and the Big Bang parallel each other because the same unfolding logic shapes both, and that logic proceeds from simple to more complex. We understand ever more complex aspects of nature as our comprehension modes evolve. Thus, any creation story, like the Big Bang or Ta'aroa's, moves from the simplest to the more complex aspects of the world in parallel with the development of our cognitive capacities.

We can put this another way: **stories of creation mirror the creation of stories**.

We still have a fundamental question – a mystery, really. Why should human modes of understanding – including logic and math – accurately explain nature? As the Nobel physicist, Eugene Wigner, dryly asked, how do we explain "the unreasonable effectiveness of mathematics in the natural sciences?"[3] One common answer is that our cognitive processes evolved through evolution, and only those creatures whose logic matches the world would survive. Ultimately, however, we are left with an enduring mystery – like Ta'aroa's head somewhere in the world.

In this section, Part II, we have focused on how comprehension modes work, exploring their deeper logic. In the next section I turn to stories which illustrate how using comprehension modes helps resolve disputes and prompts deep transformation.

Notes

1   Adapted from (Teuira, 1928).
2   Although we have not discovered evidence for it yet, many scientists assume there is life elsewhere in the universe.
3   (Russ, 2011)

References

Russ, S. (2011). "The Unreasonable Effectiveness of Mathematics in the Natural Sciences." *Interdisciplinary Science Reviews* **36**(3): 209–213.
Teuira, H. (1928). "Ancient Tahiti." *Bernice P. Bishop Museum Bulletin* **48**: 339–340.

Part III

Comprehension, Truth, and Transformation

Chapter 9

Comprehension Modes and Transformation

"Why the Platypus is Special"

Introduction

This tale from the Wiradjuri people of Australia presents a seemingly simple example of how the skillful use of comprehension modes helps us change fundamental beliefs, and thus resolve seemingly intractable disputes. Each comprehension mode plays an essential role in this reforging process.

The Australian story is significant, because aboriginal Australian culture has a continuous 40,000-year cultural history, stretching back to the original human culture. The story presumably reflects fundamental ways people have resolved conflicts since the dawn of humanity. Yet, as will quickly become apparent, the story has practical applications to our contemporary disputes.

The Story[1]

Long ago, in the Dreamtime, all the birds gathered. "Only we can fly," one bird said, "so we come closest to the Creator in Heaven. We must be the Creator's favorite!" All the birds murmured and agreed. "But what about the Emu," someone asked, "because he cannot fly." This disturbed the birds, until the Emu replied, "I have feathers and lay eggs, just like all of you, so I am part of the bird clan." So, all the birds welcomed the Emu into the best clan. "We forgot about the Platypus and his kin," one bird piped up. "They lay eggs, like we do, and have a bill like the ducks." The birds conferred with each other and agreed that the Platypus should join their clan. They sent an invitation to the Platypus, who was quite flattered but did not know what to do.

"I will think about your offer and consult with my family," the Platypus replied, asking them to wait a few days.

Meanwhile, all the land animals gathered. "We are the strongest of all creatures," the kangaroo said, "so, we must be the Creator's favorite!" All the animals agreed when a voice piped up, "What about the Platypus?" "Well," a wise old Koala replied, "the Platypus may spend most of his time in the water, and lay eggs, but they all have fur and nurse their young, just like we do. So, they must be one

DOI: 10.4324/9781003471028-12

of us." The land animals sent an invitation to the Platypus to join them, the most important clan of animals. The Platypus was even more perplexed at this invitation coming on the heels of the earlier one from the birds. He told the land animals he would have to talk it over with his family.

While this was going on, all the water creatures assembled. "We swim to the depths, and know the foundations of the world," an ancient fish observed. "So, we must be favored by the Creator." "We must invite the Platypus," a water snake added, "since he spends most of his time in the water, and the entrance to his home is underwater." All the creatures of water agreed and sent an invitation to the Platypus to join their clan. For the third time, the Platypus demurred and told the water clan he had to talk it over with his family.

When the Platypus conferred with his family, however, they could come to no conclusion about which clan to join, or what to do about the invitations. So the Platypus went to see his cousin, the Spiny Anteater. They talked for a long time and came up with an answer. The next day, the Platypus asked all the creatures of air, land, and water to gather near his home the next morning, when he would tell them his answer.

All the animals gathered at the designated time, each sure that the Platypus would join their clan, since theirs was the best. "I'm flattered," the Platypus began his address to the assembled creatures, "that all of you have invited my family to join your clans." He paused. "But I realize," the Platypus went on, "that I cannot join any one of your clans." The animals were astonished at the Platypus' answer and started to mutter and fidget. The Platypus continued, "I am like each clan in some crucial way, yet different in others. And I think the Creator arranged this to remind us that we all came from his hands. So, no clan could be better than the other, and the Creator must have placed my family among all of us, as a reminder of this, so we would respect each other and honor our differences."

There was a long silence after the Platypus finished speaking, but then a murmur began, as the creatures talked among themselves, and realized the wisdom of the Platypus' answer. Gradually, the creatures began applauding, clapping wings, paws, and fins, to show their appreciation for the Platypus' insight. Then all the clans and creatures departed, wiser than when they had arrived. And that is why, to this day, the Platypus is special: no one hunts the Platypus, and anyone seeing one is sure to have good luck on that day.

Converging Stories

For the ancient Australians, resolving disputes was crucial, because in their often-harsh environment, cooperation between nomadic bands was essential for survival – if one group fell on hard times and could not find food or water, they could rely on aid from other groups they encountered. Selfishness or holding grudges could be fatal. Ironically, their ancient quandary is our contemporary one today, made much worse by our technology: we can ruin the entire planet for everybody. Fortunately, the Australian tale explains how stories generate conflict and how storytelling can resolve it. Understanding the process boosts our chances of doing so with our problems today, too. The story is explicitly about a dispute within a social group. However, we can also interpret the story as a metaphor for transformation in both social and psychological domains, as further stories will confirm.

At the beginning of the tale, the animals simply go about their everyday business. They follow familiar routines and beliefs, not questioning or reflecting on them. This is the home type of experience where we simply enact our home stories and take things for granted.

At some point, someone raises a question. The tale does not specify the query involved, but it could be something like, "Who am I similar to?" or "Who are my people?" A common stimulus for such questioning is encountering someone from a completely different religious, cultural or ethnic background. Whatever the specific question is, asking it breaks the individual out of habit. The questioner now attends to two things at the same time, namely, her familiar, everyday routine, and a new possibility, raised by the question, "Who am I like?" This "double attention" is characteristic of the virtual mode of comprehension: we pay attention to the real world we are in, but also to possible alternative worlds we can imagine or create.

Once we ask questions about our home story and recognize new possibilities of how we can live, we must decide what to do with those alternatives. In the story, the animals start recognizing similarities between themselves and group themselves into three categories – creatures of the air, earth and water. But no one quite knows where to put the Platypus.

Classifying animals into three clans based on their similarities and differences is a factual claim, reflecting the objective mode of comprehension. The factual belief soon becomes a commitment – "It is important to me that I am part of the Bird Clan," and "I will be loyal to my Clan." Here the birds make a vow to each other, which is the defining feature of faithfulness, another form of the objective comprehension mode. That central commitment to the clan, in turn, provides organization and structure for all their experiences and actions. The animals now feel a sense of obligation, e.g., "I must defend any other bird in danger!" Or "I ought to overlook that bird's rudeness, since we are one Clan." Loyalty to a group, like to a sports team, often becomes a claim for its superiority to all other groups. Commitment to a group then become exclamations such as, "Our Bird Clan is the best of all animals! That is why we must be loyal to each other."

Each clan tries to recruit the Platypus to their cause, because he has features of each of the three clans, and if he joined any single one, that would prove their superiority to all other Clans. This is the pragmatic type of experience, focused on intentions and consequences. "If we get the Platypus to join our Clan, then everyone has to admit we are the best clan!" (This is the original version of a celebrity endorsement, e.g., a famous athlete or movie star agreeing to be the public face of a shoe brand.)

When each Clan successively invites the Platypus to join the "best Clan," namely their own, he demurs, saying that he must consult with his family and his cousin the Spiny Anteater.[2] Here the Platypus is clearly thoughtful and reflective – he consciously uses the virtual mode of comprehension to consider the situation. Moreover, in postponing his answer to the Clans until all of them ask him, the Platypus makes all the Clans wait. He thus enforces a timeout in the competition between the groups. This helps cool down their increasingly vociferous dispute. Such a timeout is a familiar technique used by mediators dealing with stubborn opponents – or therapists working with families. The technique, in turn, depends on the pragmatic comprehension mode, where we do or say something intending to produce a specific effect in other people. In this case, the Platypus makes all the Clans wait for his replies to calm them down.

The Platypus is the exception to the clan classification the other animals have adopted: he has key defining features of each clan, yet not all of any single one. He belongs to a very special category, namely, "None of the above." (Indeed, when Western scientists first encountered the body of a platypus, they were befuddled, and initially assumed it was a hoax, stitched together from different animals.) The Platypus is mysterious, transcending our familiar categories, and that is the defining characteristic of the mythic mode of experience.[3]

Insight and Transformation

The Platypus explains his unique situation: the Creator made him like all the different Clans and yet unlike them all, to remind all creatures of their shared origin in a great mystery – the Creator and Creation. Reference to both confirms the shift to the mythic type of comprehension and to what is literally "super-natural," beyond nature.

Note what the Platypus does **not** do: he could go one step further and claim that his unique connection to the Creator makes him special, e.g., favored by the Creator. This would make his Clan, tiny though it may be, the best of all, the most important, nearest to the divine. The Platypus says the opposite: he represents the common **ground** of all creatures, what they all share, not what makes one Clan better than another. Where the other animal Clans think in terms of hierarchy, and fight over who will be at the top, the Platypus thinks in terms of foundation – what supports and sustains everything. In the story, that is ultimately the mystery of the Creator. We typically associate mythic experiences with something grand, awesome and overwhelming, like the gigantic prehistoric crocodiles, birds and kangaroos the ancient Australians historically encountered when they first arrived on the island continent. Compared to the megafauna, the Platypus seems lowly and ordinary indeed – much like the dirt on which the prehistoric giants walked. However, the Platypus still represents a mystery, something that does not fit into our usual understanding of the world.

As a result of the Platypus' explanation, all the animals are transformed. They spontaneously recognize the truth of what he says and give up their claims of clan supremacy. Here the Platypus plays the role of a seasoned therapist or analyst, who makes an interpretation that sums up the main issues a person deals with, integrating them all in a wider, new, more inclusive perspective. This is an "Aha!" moment which we experience as something self-evidently and even indubitably true – a paradigmatic experience of truth. We could be mistaken when we have such a powerful insight – experiencing something to be true does not make it so.[4] And insights in psychotherapy are sometimes mistaken. However, in psychological experiments, "Aha!" experiences are more often accurate than ordinary insights.[5] How then can we judge which "Aha!" insights are true or not? I will return to this important question with stories that highlight the problem.

On the way to their epiphany, the animals move through a sequence of comprehension modes, starting off with their familiar, unreflective home story. One of the animals then wonders how he or she is a like or different from all the other animals, shifting out of the home mode into the virtual mode of comprehension. The other animals follow suit. They all can then consider different possibilities of how they relate to each other. The animals choose to classify themselves into three groups, which reflects the factual mode of comprehension. They then commit themselves to their individual Clan, shifting from the factual mode into the commitment one. Their new commitments generate their ongoing conflict. Here the story illustrates the **forging sequence** of comprehension modes. (Here I use "forging" in the sense of a smith's activity, i.e., heating, melting and hammering a metal repeatedly, to strengthen it. I do not use "forging" in the sense of "forging money" or "forging artwork.") The forging sequence commonly generates disputes: fierce disagreements do not arise out of nowhere but evolve through a sequence of comprehension modes that progressively intensify and solidify disputes.[6]

Fortunately, the Platypus interrupts the dispute. He then reminds all the animals of an ancient experience they all share, namely how the Creator created them in the Dreamtime. The Platypus thus invites everyone into the mythic mode of comprehension, where they find a deep commonality in the mystery of creation. This is not merely an intellectual experience for the assembled animals, because the Platypus embodies and evokes that mystery. For the ancient Australians, the Platypus can serve the same function as the crucifix and gospel for Christians, the eight-spoked wheel and sutras for Buddhists, and the Torah for Jews. All function as physical links to ultimate mystery, not simply representing, but **evoking** the experience of transcendence. This is particularly relevant to Aboriginal Australian culture because the Dreamtime was not simply a long-ago event, but an ongoing one, which everyone could access by cultivating trances through specific rituals, music and dances.

In reminding all the animals about the Creator, the Platypus illustrates *katabasis*, the descent into deeper, older, more primordial experiences. The effect is to dismantle – to dissolve – the old structures and make way for the new.[7]

The next story comes from yet another tradition, but it also reflects indigenous tradition. The tale is Native American and illustrates the same comprehension modes involved in deep transformation and resolving difficult conflicts.

Notes

1 (Ellis, 1991)
2 The Spiny Anteater is the only other creature in the same biological classification as the Platypus, namely monotremes. The two constitute a tiny clan of their own. And only Australia has both creatures.
3 The Platypus is also an undifferentiated creature with all the characteristics that define the differentiated animals – laying eggs, nursing their young and living in water. He is a good metaphor from the natural world for the alchemical *prima materia*. Paradoxically at the same time, he represents a link to the Creator and Creation, and the power of transformation – what Jung called the transcendent function of the psyche, which can hold deep, conflicting psychological impulses long enough for an even deeper, integrating perspective to emerge (Franz, 1980), (Rozuel, 2019), (Marlan, 2020)
4 (Danek and Wiley, 2017), (Topolinski and Reber, 2010), (Charlton, 2007).
5 (Danek and Wiley, 2017), (Laukkonen, et al., 2020), (Topolinski and Reber, 2010)
6 The reforging sequence is an example of *anabasis*, the move upward and outward, in initiation rituals, and in alchemical symbolism. It is part of the youthful, heroic drama, seeking victory over adversaries.
7 The reforging sequence parallels Jung's interpretations of medieval alchemical texts about transforming material substances as metaphors for deep psychological transformation. That is, the transformation processes described in alchemy have the same structure or logic as deep psychological transformations. And both have the same deep logic of the reforging sequence of comprehension modes. Another way to put this is that change processes, whether psychological or physical, follow the same deep structure, which shapes all our experience. This is another example of Kant's transcendental categories of understanding. Jung explicitly credited Kant as an important influence (Bär, 1976)

References

Bär, E. (1976). "Archetypes and Ideas: Jung and Kant." *Philosophy Today (Celina)* **20**(2): 114–123.

Charlton, B. G. (2007). "Scientific Discovery, Peak Experiences and the Col-oh-nell Flastratus! Phenomenon." *Medical Hypotheses* **3**: 475–477.

Danek, A. H. and J. Wiley (2017). "What about False Insights? Deconstructing the Aha! Experience along Its Multiple Dimensions for Correct and Incorrect Solutions Separately." *Frontiers in Psychology* **7**: 2077–2077.

Ellis, J. A. (1991). *From the Dreamtime: Australian Aboriginal Legends*. Victoria, Australia, CollinsDove.

Franz, M.-L. v. (1980). *Alchemy: An Introduction to the Symbolism and the Psychology*. Toronto, Inner City Books.

Laukkonen, R. E., B. T. Kaveladze, J. M. Tangen and J. W. Schooler (2020). "The Dark Side of Eureka: Artificially Induced Aha Moments Make Facts Feel True." *Cognition* **196**: 104122–104122.

Marlan, S. (2020). *C.G. Jung and the Alchemical Imagination: Passages into the Mysteries of Psyche and Soul*. London, Routledge.

Rozuel, C. (2019). "Unearthing Gold from the Mud: Alchemy and Organizational Tensions." *Journal of Management, Spirituality & Religion* **16**(2): 178–198.

Topolinski, S. and R. Reber (2010). "Gaining Insight Into the 'Aha' Experience." *Current Directions in Psychological Science* **19**(6): 402–405.

Chapter 10

Levels of Comprehension
"The Wolverine Grudge"

This Native American tale provides another example of transforming the fundamental values and convictions we follow in our lives. Those beliefs cause some of our most dangerous and intractable conflicts today. The insights of the Native American story are directly relevant to our contemporary problems.

The Story[1]

Once three brothers lived together with their wives and children, moving through the land with the seasons. Two of the brothers were conscientious and well respected. The third one always caused trouble, so the band often threw him out, but always took him back, since he was kin. One winter's day, the brothers decided to go hunting, and found a Wolverine's track. The troublesome brother said he was tired and would go back to camp and rest while the others went on. A few hours later, the two brothers returned, weary but triumphant, carrying a dead Wolverine with them. Back at the camp, they roasted the animal. "You remember the taboo," one brother said to the wayward one, "Yes, yes," the contrary brother replied, "a man cannot eat any Wolverine meat unless he hunted it himself. But I don't believe in such old superstitions." The brothers argued but the troublesome one eventually ate some of the roast.

After the meal, everyone told stories, drummed, sang songs, and then fell asleep. In their sleep, the three brothers started arguing with each other. "You sang the story wrong!" they accused each other. "You broke the Wolverine taboo and now we will all have bad luck!" The argument woke everybody else up. They stared in astonishment at the brothers yelling at each other while asleep. They had never seen such a thing! They tried waking the brothers, to no avail. Worse the men started hitting each other, all the while asleep.

"Let us throw them into the snow to wake them," one of the wives suggested. But that did not work, either. "When I was a child," an old woman spoke up, "I saw this happen. When a Wolverine is killed, another takes its place, and if someone has broken a taboo, the new Wolverine will cause a grudge, so that people start fighting for no reason. We must find the Wolverine and chase it away."

DOI: 10.4324/9781003471028-13

The family started looking and came across fresh Wolverine tracks. The creature had eaten all the game caught in the family's hunting traps, and then destroyed the snares. But the Wolverine was nowhere to be found. The band returned to their camp and saw the three brothers still arguing in their sleep, lying in the snow. "The Wolverine must be near them," the wise woman reasoned. And between the men, she saw the Wolverine's snout – the creature had burrowed under the snow right near the brothers. "Quickly, get me some hot tallow," the old woman said. Then she took it with her, crept carefully up to the Wolverine, and poured the hot tallow on its snout. The Wolverine quickly retreated, burrowing deep into the earth, and never bothered them again. The men woke up, and life was peaceful again -- until the next time the contrary brother made trouble.

Conflict, Comprehension and the Contrary

In a very compact drama, this story introduces a crucial point – conflicts arise at different levels of comprehension, and each level requires a different approach for resolution. The drama begins when the troublesome brother challenges the taboo that a man who did not hunt a Wolverine should not eat its meat. The tale makes clear that this brother always caused such trouble, and the family group frequently threw him out, taking him back when things cooled down.

The troublemaker brother fulfills a significant role found in many different Native American traditions. This is the contrary or *heyoka*, who takes inspiration from Tricksters in Native American folklore like Spider, Coyote, or Rabbit.[2] The contrary is supposed to do the opposite of convention, which means breaking rules and traditions just like the brother does in the story. However, contraries and Tricksters do not cause trouble out of maliciousness or stupidity, but specifically to make people reflect on their lives rather than follow familiar routines. In other words, they try to shock people out of the home mode of comprehension, to consider new possibilities in life and society.

Doing the opposite of convention often means violating common sense. Thus, *heyokas* walk backwards instead of forward, even for long distances. They wear heavy clothes in summer and little in winter, despite the discomfort, and they make fun of holy rituals, enduring the inevitable social backlash. The role is not taken lightly and is considered a sacred calling, often announced to the individual (male or female) by dreams of the Thunder Beings. Native American stories also warn that refusing to follow the calling results in terrible misfortunes for the person. The contrary role thus requires commitment and perseverance – the faithfulness mode of comprehension. Indeed, the contrary can be as heroic as any traditional warrior and perhaps even more so, because of the social condemnation they encounter.

In the story, the troublesome brother forces his family to think outside their traditions by challenging the Wolverine taboo everyone took for granted. Before breaking the prohibition, however, the *heyoka* brother announces his intention, prompting his brothers to plead with him not to do so. The Coyote brother does not act impulsively, hungrily grabbing some of the Wolverine meat after the hunt.

He consciously chooses his forbidden action. The brothers argue back and forth, trying to convince each other of their position. However, it soon becomes clear that neither side has any intention of changing their convictions. They now operate in the faithfulness mode of experience, defending familiar positions they are already committed to. The contrary brother intends to remain true to his vow to be the contrary, while the other two brothers, remain committed to the welfare of their family group.

Wolverine Grudges Today

Arguments like the brothers' are a familiar situation in real life, particularly with political or religious discussions. The disputing parties may start the conversations by genuinely suspending their convictions and interests. But discussions commonly become heated, and then turn into arguments, where everyone defends their long-established positions.

In the story, something extraordinary happens – the brothers fall asleep and start arguing, and then begin physically fighting, apparently interacting with each other as if they were conscious, even landing punches accurately. Sleep-fighting is like a combination of sleep talking and sleepwalking – two everyday actions, but now undertaken without consciousness or voluntary choice.

Bizarre though sleep-slugging might seem, it is common in real life. These situations range from chronic disagreements between siblings, to road rage. In both instances somebody "pushes our buttons," and we react immediately, following familiar scripts. Stimulus-response is the psychology behind sleep fighting. The patterns may be learned from experience, such as not trusting authorities, or instinctual, such as primates (including us) fearing snakes. Organizing our experiences in terms of regular patterns, such as cause and effect, or event and action, is characteristic of the pragmatic mode of comprehension. We say something to a person, hoping our words will produce the effect we desire. And conversely, someone who knows us well says something to us, and we react in the way the speaker anticipated.

When sleep fighting occurs on a community level, the disputes often spin out of control. The Protestants and Catholics in Northern Ireland during the "Troubles" provide one example, as do the Palestinians and Israelis in the Middle East. Conflicts at this level of experience require different approaches for resolution, which the story quickly explores.

When the brothers start sleep fighting, the families no longer try talking or reasoning with them, because neither work. This is obvious in the story, but in real life, it is surprising how often we **do** try to reason with people who are sleep fighting! The wise response to such a quandary is what the family does in the story, which is to try to wake up the brothers, first by yelling at them, then shaking them, and finally throwing them out into the snow. (The latter is the proverbial "cooling off" period, commonly used in couples therapy, union negotiations, and international disputes.) The family shifts to the pragmatic mode of comprehension, taking actions intending specific results. As the family tries to physically wake up the fighting men, we can interpret their action in symbolic terms – they try to make the quarreling siblings conscious of the script they are enacting.

Unfortunately, all the family's efforts fail. Then an old woman remembers a similar, long-forgotten situation from her childhood – a man violated the Wolverine taboo, eating some of its meat although he did not participate in the hunt. So, when a new Wolverine took the place of the dead one, the successor held a grudge, because of the taboo violation. The successor Wolverine caused the men to fall asleep and hit each other. The solution, the wise woman remembers, was to find the Wolverine and chase it away.

The sleep fighting men illustrate a phenomenon understood in many cultures as being "possessed" by a spirit or demon. The person's actions are controlled by a supernatural being. This is something beyond most people's everyday experience – it is mysterious, baffling, unnerving, i.e., mythic.

Featuring a Wolverine as a villain, rather than, say, a bear, also has symbolic significance. Wolverines are known for their cunning, voraciousness and ferocity even to the point of foolishness – Wolverines will even attack bears, ten times their weight. Wolverines are also solitary, nocturnal and smell bad – which is the reason they are often called the skunk bear. In Jungian terms, the Wolverine is an archetype of the "shadow," unconscious and uncontrolled elements in ourselves we would rather not see. Wolverines embody human nature at its worst – selfish and antisocial, cunning yet irrational. The shadow, and the unconscious in general, remain beyond our usual, natural experience. They belong to the realm of perplexing, seemingly inexplicable and "supernatural" experiences, the domain of the mythic mode of experience.

The tribe (presumably) did not have an explicit language for psychological matters such as we do today. But they did have the ability to use metaphors – a capacity that all people have. So, they described what they experienced with metaphors, using phenomenon they were familiar with, such as animal behavior. Animism was the language they used for psychological matters. Hence, the family attributed the sleep-fighting to a Wolverine with magical spiritual powers.

Note that the old woman's memory of the previous Wolverine incident is about a single event. It is anecdotal, not scientific or statistically valid, as are most historical accounts, including psychotherapy case studies.[3] Anecdotal evidence is important for pragmatic reasons – if they guide us to successful outcomes. Scientific accounts are objective not pragmatic.

Fortunately, the band heeds the old woman's advice and looks for a Wolverine. They find it hiding under the snow among the sleep-fighting men. She pours hot tallow on its snout and drives it away. In the context of the story, tallow is a valuable substance with many uses. Pouring it on the Wolverine snout is thus a kind of sacrifice, like making valuable offerings to animal spirits to appease them. Moreover, using melted tallow would also remind the Wolverine that the people know how to use fire, one of the few things the animal would fear. The old woman's solution is thus a curious mixture of the pragmatic and the mythic modes of comprehension. She recognizes the mysterious power of the Wolverine but relies on concrete actions with practical results. This is a characteristic of wisdom, one of the hard-earned benefits of later life. Her remembering a long-forgotten incident solves the problem in the present and is an excellent example a descent into the past to recover vital lost information.

Because the contrary defiantly breaks the Wolverine taboo, his tribe learns how to counter the resulting curse. This could then generalize to challenging other taboos about other animals, not to mention encouraging the tribe to listen to the old woman more often. This is a classic tale of the contrary's apparent mindless defiance of the taboo resulting in greater knowledge for all the family group.

In the next chapter, I return to another ancient Greek story, that of Orpheus' descent into the underworld. He recapitulates the reforging sequence – the *katabasis* – we discussed in the last two stories with "Why the Platypus Is Special," and "The Wolverine Grudge." Orpheus unfortunately fails in his descent to obtain his goal, retrieving his beloved Eurydice from the realm of the dead. And the reason brings us to a question we have left out so far, the nature of truth.

Judging truth is essential for significant transformation: if we give up a familiar home story, what new narrative should we follow? False beliefs and experiences generally do not foster deep transformation in psychotherapy or in political and cultural disputes. Instead, they help us dig ourselves deeper into a hole. From Orpheus' failure in this *katabasis*, we learn the crucial role of truth.

Notes

1 (Hitakonanulaxk, 1994)
2 I discuss Tricksters and contraries at greater length in *Beyond the Hero*.
3 (Miller, 1998)

References

Hitakonanulaxk (1994). *The Grandfathers Speak: Native American Folk Tales of the Lenapé People*. New York, Interlink Books.
Miller, R. B. (1998). "Epistemology and Psychotherapy Data: The Unspeakable, Unbearable, Horrible Truth." *Clinical Psychology (New York, N.Y.)* **5**(2): 242–250.

Chapter 11

Truth and Transformation

"Orpheus' Descent into the Underworld"

Introduction

The story of Orpheus' descent into the underworld has been retold for centuries
in paintings, dramas and music. It thus qualifies as a folktale. After his beloved
Eurydice died, Orpheus made his way into the land of the dead to rescue her. Along
the way he encountered gatekeepers, who effectively required a specific task for
anyone to proceed further. Their challenges provide poetic new metaphors for how
the basic comprehension modes function. In stories like "Why the Platypus Is Special," "The Wolverine Grudge," and "A Christmas Carol," the protagonists succeed
in reforging their lives. This is the significance of Orpheus – he fails. And why he
does so highlights the importance of truth in deep transformation.

The Story

*The son of Apollo and a mortal woman[1], Orpheus was the most magical of mor-
tal musicians. Apollo himself gave Orpheus a lyre and when Orpheus played his
music, it would calm ravenous beasts. Orpheus married Eurydice, the love of his
life, but a serpent bit her and she died. Orpheus was inconsolable and vowed to
bring her back from the dead.*

*Orpheus descended into the dark, perilous underworld, and soon came upon the
deadly River Styx. Crossing was possible only with the ferryman Charon, but he
forbade the living to pass and turned Orpheus away. The young man simply picked
up his lyre and sang, enchanting Charon so much that the boatmen willingly took
Orpheus over the poisonous River. On the far side, Orpheus met the dead – ghostly
shadows, constantly lamenting what they had lost in the earthly realm when they
died. For a moment, Orpheus was tempted to talk to Achilles and Odysseus and other
great heroes of old, to hear their stories of glory, but Orpheus pressed on with his
quest to save Eurydice. He ignored the whispers, pleas and stories of the specters.*

*At the entrance to hell, Orpheus met the savage, three-headed dog Cerberus,
who let no living being enter. With his sublime singing, Orpheus charmed the beast
and thus entered the underworld. Orpheus continued his descent and next encountered the Three Judges of the Dead, who weighed the virtues and vices of all souls.*

DOI: 10.4324/9781003471028-14

The Judges barred Orpheus from descending deeper into the underworld because he was still living. Then he sang to them so beautifully, they let him pass.

Finally, Orpheus came to Hades, the King of the Dead. Orpheus sang so movingly that the grim god gave him permission to take Eurydice back with him – a boon no mortal had ever received before. Hades imposed only one condition – Orpheus could not look at Eurydice until they had both returned to the land of the living. On the long journey back, Orpheus resisted the urge to look behind him and make sure that Eurydice was still following. When Orpheus finally stepped into open sunlight, he joyfully turned to Eurydice. Alas, she had not yet completely left Hades, and before his very eyes, she vanished. Orpheus knew he could not return and ask Hades for a second chance. So, he had to live without his beloved Eurydice, finding what comfort he could in his music.

Grief, Ghosts and Goals

Orpheus' tale begins with a blissful life, married to his beloved Eurydice. His home story is his ideal one. When Eurydice dies from a snakebite, Orpheus' familiar world collapses. He is thrust into a completely unfamiliar reality: how can he live without Eurydice? What else could there be in life for him? For a moment, he faces the unknown, which is the essence of mythic experience. He faces a double mystery – first, that of death, and second, that of undeserved tragedy and suffering. In response, he vows to retrieve Eurydice from the from the land of the dead. He will deal with her death by reversing it. This is a classic heroic quest, typical of a youth who commits himself (or herself) to overcoming an adversity or adversary. Heroic protagonists then center all their concerns and actions around achieving that goal in the faithfulness mode of comprehension.

It is useful to contrast Orpheus with Scrooge in "A Christmas Carol," because it illuminates why the former fails to transform his life, and the latter succeeds. When Marley first appears, Scrooge is startled and frightened but quickly dismisses his experience as a hallucination from indigestion. But then Marley screams at Scrooge which terrifies the miser so much he can no longer explain away his mythic moment. His terror opens him to new experiences and thus the possibility of change. By contrast, in embarking on his quest, Orpheus seeks to reverse the tragedy that befell him and effectively ignore it.

On his descent into the underworld, the first challenge comes from Charon, who ferries only the dead across the River Styx, enforcing the boundary between the human world, and the realm of the dead. To ancient Greeks, the dead were insubstantial and immaterial shadows of who they were when alive – like our contemporary image of ghosts. Most of the dead spend their eternity wandering in the underworld, lamenting what they lost in life. The specters illustrate the virtual mode of experience: the dead are aware of their current situation, but also the earthly life they had and sorely miss. They have two things in mind at the same time, just as we do when watching a movie: we are aware of being in a movie theater, at the same time we may be absorbed in the world of the movie.

Charon carries Orpheus across the River Styx because Orpheus enchants him with sublime music. Orpheus, in short, breaks a rule of the underworld, namely that no living person could enter it. However, Orpheus was accustomed to skirting laws of nature with his magical music. He could calm slavering beasts, inspire gods to pause amid an argument and even overrode the Sirens' deadly, seductive singing, with his magical music.

Orpheus also pays little attention to the ghosts. Yet the dead have many stories to tell him, which might benefit him greatly. Most of the dead suffered bereavement and undeserved tragedy in real life. They could tell him how they coped – or not. This, of course, is a great boon of the virtual mode of experience – we can learn vicariously from other people's stories.

Note that Orpheus had no one to guide or advise him on his underworld venture. By contrast, Scrooge had the Christmas Spirits, arranged by Marley, to take the miser on virtual journeys, specifically intended to help Scrooge change his ways. (Similarly, Dante had Virgil to guide him on a descent into the underworld.) Orpheus is left to his own devices.

Orpheus next faces Cerberus, the three-headed dog, who will not allow any living person to pass. In mythology around the world, it is often a supernatural dog like Cerberus that guards the underworld. We might think a more terrifying, dangerous creature would be a better choice – like a dragon or demon. The cross-cultural choice of the dog suggests that the choice of animal is symbolic.

One of the chief characteristics of a dog is loyalty – attachment to a particular person. That "human companion" is the center of the world for the dog. The same is true when we love someone deeply, the way Orpheus loved Eurydice. We integrate our lives around the beloved – so much so in Orpheus' case, he dares to enter the realm of the dead to rescue Eurydice. Such commitment to a specific objective or goal is characteristic of quests, promises, vows and covenants – and the objective mode of comprehension. Giving up such a central commitment – which gives meaning to our lives – inevitably feels like death, dramatized by Cerberus devouring any living person he encounters. And Cerberus has two reasons to devour Orpheus: the young man is not only alive, but he also pursues his quest to retrieve Eurydice and refuses to give up that organizing center of his life.

Psychologically, if we do not give up our commitments or attachments, we cannot move on to any new life. This is the difference between re**storing** an old life narrative and re-**storying** it. Orpheus does not seek change – he wants to return to his familiar old life with Eurydice. Orpheus is like Captain Ahab in *Moby Dick*, and Don Quixote in the Spanish classic: the protagonists continue their commitment to their objectives, no matter the cost to themselves or others. Scrooge, on the other hand, is open to moving on to something new after Marley's ghost screams at him.

Judgments and Hades

Passing deeper into the underworld, Orpheus next encounters the Three Judges of the Dead. A familiar theme in mythology, these Judges – the number depends on the culture of the mythology – determine the moral worth of the deceased. In judging a person's actions, we usually adopt the pragmatic mode of experience, scrutinizing the intentions and consequences of their actions. Orpheus avoids being judged by enchanting the Three Judges with his marvelous music. If they do not scrutinize Orpheus' actions, he does not need to do so either. He therefore does not consider the consequences of his quest. If he succeeded in bringing Eurydice back from the dead, for instance, would not everybody want to rescue their beloved? And if they tried, what chaos would ensue? Nor does Orpheus consider if Eurydice wants to come back with him. He focuses only on his goal – retrieving her – and its consequences for himself. Scrooge does the opposite. On his journeys with the Christmas Spirits, the miser witnesses his past actions and their consequences, not just to himself, but to people around him. Even more important, he experiences the emotions accompanying those events, including empathy and compassion for other people. He thus comes to judge himself and finds his life wanting in concern for others.

The Judges of the Dead do not simply judge a single action and its consequences – they evaluate a person's whole life, symbolized by "weighing" a person's soul. Was the person consistently kind and generous, for instance, with a few lapses into selfishness? Or were they always insensitive, demanding and selfish – with a few moments of kindness? The Judges evaluate a person's virtues and vices, which are repeated patterns of behavior. Attention to such patterns of actions and consequences, intentions and results, constitutes the core of the pragmatic mode of comprehension.

After enchanting the Three Judges, Orpheus descends further into the underworld and finally encounters Hades, King of the Dead. Hades was the most intimidating of the Olympian gods because he almost never responded to prayers and pleas – unlike the other gods, from Zeus to Athena. Hades, in fact, had no temples dedicated exclusively to him. He usually had a small shrine in the larger temples dedicated to Athena, Zeus, Apollo and other more popular gods. Presumably, no one wanted to face Hades alone, so feared he was – just like death itself. Hades personifies the experience of the utter unknown and ultimate mystery, which lies at the core of mythic experience.

Orpheus does not experience Hades as something numinous, mysterious or overwhelming. This is because he is so intent on retrieving Eurydice, he reacts to Hades in terms of how it helps or hinders success on his quest. His commitment to rescuing Eurydice precludes a mythic experience that would open him to something completely new in his life.

Hades agrees to let Eurydice return to Earth with Orpheus on one condition – Orpheus cannot look back at her as she follows him until he is out of the underworld. Orpheus fails at the last moment and loses Eurydice. In looking **back** at her, Orpheus dramatizes the objective of his quest – to **turn back** time and return to everything he had before Eurydice died. He seeks nothing new, learns nothing new, and thus gains no new life story.[2]

In short, Orpheus descends into the underworld **but does not experience it**. He is like a tourist who stays on the tour bus, never getting out to talk to the locals, eat with them, or feel the sun on his face. He is a spectator. Orpheus is like someone in psychotherapy who comes to many intellectual insights about themselves but has no emotional, embodied experience of them – and thus makes little change in their lives.

Another way to put this is that Orpheus cheats. The underworld guardians expect him to fulfill certain tasks before moving on, but he uses his magical music and skips them. Moreover, even if he did carry out the tasks successfully, a new question arises: what if all his new experiences and insights were false – self-deceptions or hallucinations? (The same question arises with Scrooge and the Christmas Spirits.)

The analogous situation also arises in psychotherapy. How do we identify a true insight, as opposed to a false one, e.g., a false memory? Intuitively, we expect that true insights are confirmed by corroborating information, but even more significantly, by positive changes in the individual's life. False insights, like false learning, do not usually help individuation and maturation. Untrue or irrelevant insights are at best distractions and sometimes effective ways of resisting progress.[3]

Here we run into troubling questions: if we have multiple modes of comprehension, do we also have multiple types of truth? Surely judging truth for a factual conclusion differs from the same task for a mythic experience? And if we have multiple ways of judging truth can different people come to contradictory conclusions, with everyone being correct? This is the postmodern dilemma.

To address these questions, we must go back to foundational stories in Western culture, which raise core issues about truth. For that, I turn now to the *Book of Exodus*, the paradigmatic expression of monotheism.

Notes

1 In some versions, Orpheus is the son of the Muse Calliope and a human King. In any event, Orpheus is half divine or closely linked to a divine musician.
2 "Turn back" is the root meaning of the word "reflect," which now also means "to think about." Reflection is another meaning of Orpheus turning to look at Eurydice. With self-reflection, we split our awareness between what we experience and our reflection on that experience. This means that we enter the virtual mode of experience. By reflecting on Eurydice, Orpheus puts her into a virtual realm – she becomes a specter again.
3 This is not always true. Jung, for example, argued that medieval European alchemy provides helpful metaphors for the psychological processes required for deep transformation. In fact, alchemy is factually false as chemistry. But the archetypal images are helpful to many individuals.

Chapter 12

Monotheism and Monolithic Truth

Moses Part I

Introduction

The Book of Exodus in the Hebrew Bible is one of the foundational narratives of
Western civilization. It is traditionally considered the original example of monotheism, but perhaps more importantly *Exodus* also illustrates two distinct concepts of
truth, which are highly relevant to our current postmodern disputes.

The Story[1]

*Long ago, Moses answered God's call to lead his people out of Egypt. God worked
miracles, sending plagues to Egypt, and parting the Red Sea, so that his people
escaped safely. Once free, the Israelites entered a wilderness, and soon ran out of
food. They began to murmur against God and Moses, saying, "Better to live under
the Pharaoh, than die of hunger in this desert." So, God caused manna to fall from
heaven, feeding everyone. The people journeyed on, but soon had no water and
again whispered against God and Moses. God then caused water to flow from rock.*

*After many weeks, Moses led the Israelites to Mount Sinai. There in the desert,
he followed God's instructions, and asked all the people whether they would make
a covenant with Him: if they worshiped only Him as their God and obeyed Him,
He would make them His special people, and lead them to the Promised Land. The
people agreed, and God told them how to prepare for his appearance atop Mount
Sinai. The people purified themselves, and stood away from the mountain, lest they
be struck dead by God's glory.*

*Thunder, fire, lightning and earthquake surrounded Mount Sinai. With the
sounding of mighty trumpets, and in an awesome voice, God declared, "I am the
Lord your God who brought you out of the land of Egypt. You shall have no other
gods before Me." God then pronounced the rest of his Commandments.*

*The people withdrew in terror, and begged Moses to intercede for them, fearing
to face God directly. Moses agreed and approached the summit of Mount Sinai.
There God told him more of the laws that His people were to follow – laws about
property and theft, marriage and murder, servants and sabbaths. Moses wrote them
down, returned to the people, and recounted God's laws to them, concluding by asking if the people agreed to follow them. The people promised. Moses then inscribed*

DOI: 10.4324/9781003471028-15

God's laws down in the Book of the Covenant, read it to the people, and asked if they agreed once more. All the people assented again.

Then Moses went up the mountain and stayed with God for 40 days. There God told Moses many more laws that the people were to follow. Moses wrote them down, and they were extensive and detailed: If a man stole an ox, he must return it with another, and if he could not, because he had disposed of the stolen ox, then he must give five oxen to the owner. The Ark of the Covenant was to be made of acacia, two and half cubits long, and a one and a half cubits wide and high. . . . Finally, God gave Moses two stone tablets on which He Himself wrote the 10 Commandments.

Moses was gone so long, people despaired he would ever return, and so at the urging of Aaron, Moses' brother, the people molded a golden calf, which they worshiped as a god. Then God saw what they were doing.

To be continued. . .

From Liberation Limbo to Divine Covenant

After their liberation from Egypt, the people of Israel wander in the wilderness, contending with thirst and starvation. They begin to doubt both Moses and God, moving from deliverance to doubt: "Maybe we should have stayed in Egypt, where at least we had food and water!" This is a common response to liberation – **limbo**. It is the complement of liberation **rage**, which we discussed in Chapter 1 with "The Fisherman and the Djinn." (Recall that when the fishermen released the Djinn from the prison-bottle, the Djinn was so enraged from his long imprisonment, he had vowed to kill whoever liberated him and thus prepared to murder the old man.)

The dilemma of liberation limbo is as problematic today as liberation rage. Disenchanted with traditional authorities, such as religion or established political elites, people seek new alternatives. But which should we choose? Encountering people who hold to foreign religions, unfamiliar ideologies, or alien gender roles and sexual norms is the modern equivalent of the ancient Israelites meeting many peoples worshiping different gods. In this situation, fervently embracing traditional ways is comforting and tempting. The result is what the poet Yeats described in his poem "The Second Coming": "The best lack all conviction while the worst are full of passionate intensity." We are torn between wandering in limbo and forging ahead, certain we know the way whether we do or not.

In *Exodus* limbo ends for the Israelites at Mount Sinai, when God appears to them in thunder, lightning, earthquake and trumpets blaring from the heavens. In a personal appearance, God asks the people to worship only him.

Monotheism and Monolithic Truth

These events are usually interpreted in terms of monotheism – the assertion that only one true God exists.[2] That claim is a **factual** one, describing something about the world we all share. And if a factual claim is true, it is true for everybody since we all share the same world.

A metaphor is useful here: factual truth is like a gigantic stone monolith, such as the one in the movie "2001: A Space Odyssey." Where the monolith stands, nothing else can – the monolith displaces any other claim for truth. If it is true that it is sunny where we are, that fact excludes other claims about the same place, e.g., "it is raining," or "it is cloudy." The monolithic nature of factual truth parallels monotheism – just as there is one God for all, there is one reality for everybody, and thus one objective truth, too. Today many secularists do not believe in one God, or any god, but they still believe in one objective reality for everyone, e.g., described by science. They follow the **monolithic model** of truth.

The monolithic model of truth readily leads to intolerance. If our religion or ideology is factually true, then it is true for everyone. Those who reject our beliefs are therefore mistaken or perverse. In the former case, we can correct their error. In the latter, we can persecute them. Science and scientists generally follow the monolithic paradigm of truth, but rather than persecute people who reject science, it is more common to patronize them.

In contrast to monotheism, polytheism can be simplified as, "Choose your god, choose your truth." Truth is whatever your god tells you. And with many gods, there are many truths. Today, we do not talk so much about multiple gods, as multiple truths, all of which can be equally valid even when they conflict. This is postmodernism which does not look for a single awesome monolithic truth, but multiple, lesser ones. Metaphorically, with postmodernism and polytheism, we have a multitude of stone statues, like the *moia,* the enigmatic statues of Easter Island. Depending on which statue we stand next to, we have a different perspective on the world. We might call this the **multilateral** metaphor for truth, to contrast it with the **monolithic** model.

Here *Exodus* has a surprise for us. A close reading reveals that God never explicitly claims that he is the only God that exists.[3] The Bible describes him as the "God of Israel," and not the "God of all people in the world." Instead of claiming to be the one true God, God asks the people to agree to a Covenant with him alone and to worship no other God. In return he would make them his chosen people. Several details of the event are significant. First, God asks the people to make a Covenant with him **three** separate times. This emphasizes that he wants a voluntary agreement. The initial request for a Covenant comes **before** God appears in divine glory atop Mount Sinai. Were he to ask **after** he appeared in an overwhelming supernatural event, the people would presumably feel awed, cowed, and pliable. Agreement in such a state would not be fully voluntary. Presumably this is why God asks for consent a second and third time – the way parliaments normally pass legislation in first, second and third readings, to prevent hasty, ill-considered decisions. God asking for a Covenant three times is a detail that many fundamentalists overlook today when they impose their religion or ideology on unwilling people: God did **not** impose the Covenant on his people. He asked for voluntary agreement – three times.

When God asks the Israelites to pledge their loyalty to him alone, and to forsake all other gods, he asks them to be true to him alone. Whether or not other gods exist becomes irrelevant. An everyday example of such an exclusive commitment is traditional, monogamous marriage. When we marry someone, we promise exclusive loyalty to that one person. Moreover, it does not matter whether other alternative spouses exist, and we also assume that other couples are free to marry. We do not insist that there can be only one marriage in the world, namely mine. We recognize that other people may commit themselves to different people and principles, which would define a different set of truths for them.

Applications and Implications

Truth as loyalty inevitably runs into a problem – when people come from different religious or ideological communities, they usually have different fundamental commitments, which often generate conflicts between them. *Exodus* dramatizes this problem when Moses leads his people to Canaan, and they proceed to conquer it. How are we to judge the conflict between the Canaanites' desire to keep their homeland, and the Israelites' to inhabit the Promised Land? Postmodernism throws up its hands here and says we cannot judge the conflicting claims.

Adopting a covenant specifies what being true-to the oath involves. This means that truth-as-faithfulness defines truth for an individual or community abiding by the commitment and not for everybody in the world. Being true-to an oath gives us multiple truths, depending upon which covenant we promise to follow. This is the multilateral paradigm of truth, again, where we have different truths for different people, in contrast to the monolithic model.

For most people, the multilateral situation is unsatisfactory. Fortunately, we have another important concept of truth, which does let us be true-to a commitment. This concept of truth comes from ancient Greece, the second pillar of Western tradition, besides biblical tradition. Ancient Greeks were polytheistic, so we might assume that we end up with the familiar postmodern problem of relativism and intractable conflict. But an overlooked ancient Greek tale has a surprise for us just as *Exodus* did.

Notes

1 Various authors. (1979) The Holy Bible: New King James Version, Thomas Nelson. (Bible, 1979)
2 (Frevel, 2013)
3 God does say that the world is his, but this could be said by a paramount god in a pantheon, like Zeus, powerful enough to force other gods to obey him.

References

Bible (1979). *The Holy Bible, New King James Version*. Thomas Nelson.
Frevel, C. (2013). "Beyond Monotheism? Some Remarks and Questions on Conceptualising 'Monotheism' in Biblical Studies." *Verbum et Ecclesia* **34**: 1–7.

Chapter 13

Disciplined Truth

"The Muses"

Introduction

The Muses are often overlooked in discussions of Greek mythology, especially compared to the Olympians like Zeus and Athena. The Muses function more like the chorus in ancient Greek tragedy – a collective voice, playing a secondary role compared to the principal deities.

One reason for the neglect of the Muses is that they deal with the arts such as dancing, music or drama. Especially today, these fields are often considered entertainment or hobbies. (Astronomy and history, the domains of Urania and Clio, respectively, would be exceptions.) This ignores how the arts descend from ancient, essential human endeavors, critical to the survival of early human groups. In tribal cultures, for instance, dancing and music were used in collective celebrations, and generated experiences of group solidarity. These community events also could produce altered states of consciousness, fostering conflict resolution and generating visions.[1] Today such ancient sacred tribal dance rituals often seem to have devolved into rave parties.

A close look at stories about the Muses reveals a new paradigm of truth, which has features of the two types we discussed in Chapter 1 – truth-as-faithfulness, and truth-as-fact. Perhaps more important, the Muses' new concept also resolves the problems that postmodern perspectives on truth give us.

The Birth of the Muses[2]

Long, long ago, the Titans ruled the world with Cronos as their king. He feared a prophecy that one of his offspring would overthrow him, just as he had overthrown his own father. To prevent this, Cronos swallowed all his children as soon as they were born. Finally, his wife, Rhea, outwitted him: she gave birth to Zeus, and saved him by giving Cronos a stone wrapped in blankets, completely fooling her husband. Zeus grew up in secret, and when fully grown, overthrew Cronos and established himself and his siblings, as the rulers of the world – the Olympian gods.

After his victory Zeus sought someone to celebrate his triumph over the Titans but found no one up to the task. So, Zeus lay with Mnemosyne, the goddess of

DOI: 10.4324/9781003471028-16

memory, and from their union came the nine Muses. The lovely sisters became a heavenly host, praising the gods and celebrating their victory with the most beautiful song, dance and poetry. From then on, the Muses graced all the festivities of the Olympian deities. In their presence, Zeus could momentarily forget a prophecy that haunted him – that one day, one of his offspring would overthrow him, as he had with his father.

Every few years, the Muses celebrated a great festival, where mortals competed in poetry, dance, music and the other high arts. The Muses themselves were said to judge the contests, choosing the best in each field. Good sisters, the Muses did not argue about the victors, because each of them had a special talent and the other Muses would defer to her in that area. Urania was patron of astronomy, Melpomene of tragedy, Clio of history, Polymnia of sacred poetry and geometry. . . . Temples honoring the Muses were called Museia, and master artists, poets and sculptors left their works in them as offerings.

The Sequel (a modern addition)

As time went on, cities rose and fell, rivers changed their courses, and a strange thing happened. More and more men and women went to the sanctuaries of the Muses, seeking learning, beauty and knowledge, while fewer and fewer went to the temples of the Olympians. Desire for knowledge and grace now moved men and women, more than fear of the gods. Thus, the temples of the Muses prospered, giving rise to museums, universities, libraries and theaters. At the same time, the fortunes of the Olympians declined. Apollo's oracle at Delphi and Athena's shrine in Athens fell into disrepair. Without offerings or worship, the high gods slowly faded away, more forgotten than overthrown. Prayers and pleas to Zeus or Apollo soon seemed like old superstitions, quaint relics from an ignorant past. Thus, the ancient prophecy that Zeus would be overthrown by his offspring was fulfilled. Who would have guessed that the revolution would come from his daughters, the lovely Muses? Seeking knowledge and creativity rather than dominion and rule, the Muses inspired mortals to outgrow the Olympians, rather than overthrow them.

The Olympics of Arts

The Muses' competitions in the different cultural disciplines are not just myth. Historical records show that ancient Greek athletic contests, such as the Olympic, Nemean, and Isthmian games were accompanied by competitions in various arts such as music. The Pythian games even began as a musical competition, before adding on athletic contests.[3]

There are few mythological stories about how the Muses picked the winners in their contests.[4] However, by analogy with the Olympics, we can make a guess. In the classic Olympic games, contestants competed in specific sports, each with its own rules and traditions. Contestants in all sports promised to obey the regulations of their sport, and in addition, to follow basic rules of athletics, such as not bribing judges. This is an example of being true-to a promise but expanded to being true-to all the rules and traditions of a sport. The victor would be the one who was most **true-to** their sport, including its definition of winning. This is an example of **being true-to a discipline** or practice. For example, the winner in discus would be whoever threw a standard discus the farthest within the designated landing zone. The winner would be declared the champion in that sport in that Olympic contest. He would not be declared the best discus thrower for all time, because the next competition might have someone who performs even better.

We can imagine that competition in the Muses' arts would use the same concept of being true-to a discipline. For example, the winning contestant in astronomy, dedicated to the Muse Urania, would presumably have the most accurate observations or predictions of celestial events at that time, the traditional goals of astronomy. All contestants, of course, would also promise to follow basic rules, like not stealing someone else's observations. The winning contestant would be considered the one most **true-to** the discipline of astronomy at that time. Their work would also be considered the latest and best work **in** astronomy. That is, their work would be both **true-*to*** and **true-*in*** astronomy. Their narrative would not necessarily be the last word on the subject, just the latest one, because a later competition could reveal someone with even better observations and predictions.

We can apply the same concept of being true-to a discipline to the other contests in the Muses' arts. For example, in tragic drama, presided over by Melpomene, the winning play would have to be true-to the traditions of the field. In ancient Greece, this meant the play would have to be performed in public and evoke deep emotions in the audience. It must also articulate something of the tragic dimension of human life, such as the almost universal experience of suffering undeserved misfortune. As usual in a contest, cheating would be prohibited, such as plagiarizing. The winning contestant would be declared the champion of tragic drama in that competition. The play would be considered most true-to the discipline and true-in the discipline at that time although the next competition might feature an even better tragic play.

Being true-to a discipline is what we might call **disciplined truth**. It is often called **procedural truth**. An example from law helps explain the concept.

Disciplined truth is what juries aim at and must be distinguished from **actual** truth. The jury's job is to pick the winner between two narratives – one from the prosecutor and the other from the defense. The jurors must judge the evidence presented, and follow the rules and traditions established by their legal system. This is a judicial version of an Olympic match, dealing with competing lawyers rather than athletes. The winning side in the court case would then be considered to have the narrative that is most true-to the judicial discipline. And their verdict would be considered the best available judicial conclusion about whether the accused was guilty or not. The verdict would be an example of **disciplined** truth, but not necessarily **actual** truth, because new information might come out later about someone suppressing evidence, threatening a witness, and so on.

Nobel laureates also illustrate the difference between disciplined truth and actual truth. Winners must be true-to their specific discipline, for instance, physicists must make careful experimental observations or precise theoretical calculations. They must also follow the basic rules of the field, such as not making up data. Finally, the

Nobel winner must make what is considered a significant contribution to the discipline, e.g., with a new discovery, or a new way of making discoveries. The Nobel winner's contribution would be considered **true-*to*** and **true-*in*** their discipline. (This would be equivalent in the Olympics to an athlete making a record-breaking performance in a sport.) The judges for a particular Nobel prize could be wrong, of course, because new research might find a more accurate account – which is often the case in science. However, each year Nobel committees must pick a winner, just like each Olympic competition does.

Multiple Domains of Truth

The concept of disciplined truth gives us multiple domains of truth, depending on what discipline is involved – for example, we have what is true-to astronomy, what is true-to history, and so on. Multiple disciplines give us multiple types of disciplined truth. As mentioned before, a good example comes from Nobel prizes. But another instance can be found in tenure decisions from modern universities. They regularly hold competitions in each department, whether chemistry, psychology, literature or music. Contestants are judged on how true-to their specific discipline they are. This is exactly analogous to the Muses' cultural Olympics. Indeed, universities are descendants of the Musea, centers of learning and art dedicated to the Muses. The winners in university competitions do not receive a gold medal, but tenure. Their work is also considered to be most true-to their discipline at the time, the latest truth-in their field.

The different modes of disciplined truth constitute a pantheon of truth, like the pantheon of the Muses. Here an analogy comes in handy. In modern psychology, intelligence was initially thought to be a single ability. This monolithic concept of intelligence later split into two varieties – crystallized and fluid intelligence. The former reflects the ability to reason and solve problems based on a person's prior knowledge. The latter is the ability to solve novel problems without prior knowledge. More recently intelligence has been differentiated into multiple types, such as emotional, mechanical, musical, mathematical and kinesthetic intelligences. These distinct components of human intelligence were long ignored because abstract intelligence was considered uniquely human, and the others were essentially treated like minority ethnic groups – ignored or devalued. Not so anymore in psychology. The different types of intelligence are important in their own right just like the different modes of comprehension.

Disciplined truth is defined by a particular discipline and is thus relative to that discipline.[5] The arts that the Muses presided over in ancient Greece, for example, are not found in all cultures – virtually all societies have some kind of drama, but not the specific tragic genre of ancient Greece. More generally, what is true-to a discipline is relative to that discipline, which is usually a product of a particular culture. This means disciplined truth is relative to a specific group of people. That in turn entails that we can have multiple competing truths, depending on which group and which discipline are involved. Does this mean we return to the problem of postmodern relativism – we have multiple, competing truths and no way to decide between them? We avoid this problem if we have disciplines that are independent of culture.

Storytelling provides an example. All societies tell stories. **What** the stories are about – the content – varies greatly, but the fundamental storytelling **process** is similar across societies and time. Culture determines the **content** of the stories we prefer to tell, but **how** we tell and understand stories is shared across cultures. On an even more basic level, language usage is independent of culture. The specific language we use depends upon our culture, of course, and who raised us. However, all languages follow rules, which vary with the language. However, knowing that every language has some set of regular rules allows us to learn and understand foreign languages.

In a similar way, comprehension modes – objective, virtual, pragmatic and so on – represent even more fundamental culture-independent disciplines, reflecting core human "information processing" operations. Each mode follows specific rules. The mythic mode, for example, operates with the principle of transcendence, moving from a familiar world to unknown horizons. We can judge truth in the mythic mode by how true-to transcendence a narrative or experience is. (More on that in later chapters.) The faithfulness mode, in turn, uses convergence and integrates our actions around a goal to which we are committed. So, we can judge truth in the faithfulness mode, by how true an individual is to their oath, integrating their actions and experiences around their commitments.

In the next section of this book, Part IV, I retell stories that illustrate each comprehension mode and how we can judge truth in them. The tales give us examples which we can use as models for culture-independent judgments of truth. The stories' relevance to our contemporary difficulties will be readily apparent.

Notes

1 (Ehrenreich, 2007) I discuss the point with greater detail in *Beyond the Hero, Waking the World*.
2 (Graves, 1955)
3 (Rotstein, 2012), (Clarysse and Remijsen, 2012), (Allen, 2014), (BBy's Magazine, 2018)
4 (Carlier and Milanezi, 2005), (Rotstein, 2012)
5 Put in Wittgenstein's terms, different disciplines constitute different language games, which vary with culture. But all games, including language games, follow some set of rules, which we can usually figure out over time.

References

Allen, S. (February 6, 2014 (Updated: July 27, 2021)). "11 Notable Medalists in the Olympic Art Competitions." *Mental Floss*. Retrieved 8/24/21.

Bby's. (4 February 2018). "The Forgotten Medals of the Olympic Games." Retrieved 08/24/21.

Carlier, J. and S. Milanezi (2005). "Muses." *Encyclopedia of Religion*. L. Jones. Detroit, MI, Macmillan Reference USA. **9**: 6242–6243.

Clarysse, W. and S. Remijsen (2012). "Ancient Olympics: Music and Musical Competitions at the Games." Retrieved 8/24/21.

Ehrenreich, B. (2007). *Dancing in the Streets: A History of Collective Joy*. New York, Metropolitan Books.

Graves, R. (1955). *The Greek Myths*. Baltimore, Maryland, Penguin Books.

Rotstein, A. (2012). "Mousikoi Agones and the Conceptualization of Genre in Ancient Greece." *Classical Antiquity* **31**(1): 92–127.

Part IV

Judging Multiple Modes of Truth

Chapter 14

Judging Shoes and Facts

"The Elves and the Shoemaker"

Introduction

This German story is delightful, charming and satisfying – a classic fairytale. It also contains a profound insight – making shoes is analogous to making factual conclusions. The comparison may seem fanciful at first, like fairytales in general, but reading the story as a metaphor reveals many useful insights about the practice of fact-finding and the nature of factual truth. The story's insights are particularly relevant today, in a time of fake facts and fanatics.

The Story[1]

Once upon a time, a shoemaker and his wife fell upon hard times. No matter what they did, things went from bad to worse. One day, the cobbler found he had only a small piece of leather left in his shop. So, he sat down, cut the leather carefully and started to sew a pair of shoes. When evening fell, the shoemaker left his work unfinished and returned home to dinner with his wife.

The next day the cobbler found a beautiful pair of shoes in his shop! Someone had come in during the night and finished his work. The shoemaker sold the shoes and used the money to buy more leather. He spent the day cutting the new material, and when evening arrived, he put his work away and returned home to his wife.

The next morning, the cobbler found several more pairs of shoes in his shop! His mysterious helper had come again. And the new shoes were even prettier than the first ones. The shoemaker sold the shoes, bought more leather, cut the new hides carefully, and left the pieces in his workshop overnight. But he also studied the workmanship used in their shoes. The next day, the cobbler found boots, sandals, and shoes set neatly in a row on his table. This went on for some time. Each night, the cobbler left pieces of leather out in his workshop. And each morning, he found wonderfully made footwear in his shop. The shoemaker soon prospered and his reputation for marvelous shoes spread far and wide.

One day, around Christmas, the cobbler turned to his wife, and said, "We must find out who is helping us, so we can thank them!" His wife agreed. That evening they hid in the workshop, and waited anxiously. Right around midnight, the

DOI: 10.4324/9781003471028-18

shoemaker and his wife heard singing, and two elves leaped through the window. The elves were as naked as the dawn, barefoot and carefree. They danced, did somersaults, and sang. Then they sat down, started making shoes and boots, and in no time at all, they finished their work. They skipped around the room and vanished on a moonbeam.

The shoemaker and his wife could scarcely believe their eyes. "We must give the elves a gift to thank them for their help!" they both exclaimed. Since the elves were naked, and it was winter, the shoemaker and his wife decided to make them clothes. So, the shoemaker stitched two tiny pairs of boots, lined with fur, while his wife sewed two jackets and two pairs of pants, warm and fleecy.

On Christmas Eve, they set out their presents in the workshop. Then they hid and watched. At midnight, the two elves leaped through the window, and looked around in bewilderment. There was no leather for them to sew, and no tools to use! Then they saw the gifts.

"Ooh!" one elf exclaimed, as he picked up a tiny shoe and tried it on. "Ahh!" the other gasped, as he squirmed into a shirt and coat. The clothes fit perfectly, and the elves admired each other. They danced with glee and vanished in the moonlight. The shoemaker and his wife went to bed as happy as could be.

The next evening the elves did not return. Nor the night after, or ever again. "What have we done?" the shoemaker and his wife asked themselves. But they were practical people, so the cobbler started working once again. Having studied the elves' workmanship, he soon began making shoes just as beautiful. He and his wife prospered and lived happily for the rest of their days.

Shoes and Facts

Consider the cobbler's work: he collects materials, such as pieces of leather, cuts them into the right shapes and then sews them together correctly to make a decent shoe. In a similar way, a scientist considers the evidence available, judging what seems reliable, gathers new evidence, and then integrates the available information in a coherent narrative, i.e., a factual conclusion. The scientist is then true-**to** the discipline of fact-finding, as we discussed in the last chapter on the Muses.

What the shoemaker and a scientist work with differs, but **how** they operate follows the same deep logic – that of convergence, integrating the materials they deal with.

The parallel between making shoes and factual conclusions becomes clearer if we consider that the errors a cobbler and a scientist can make are similar. If the shoemaker uses inferior leather or if he works carelessly and misses stitches, he is false-**to** his discipline and his shoes are more likely to be defective. In the same way, if a scientist ignores evidence she does not like, works after drinking too much at lunch, or has a predetermined conclusion she wants to arrive at, then she is false-**to** the discipline of fact-finding and her factual conclusion is more likely to be proven wrong later.[2]

When the shoemaker falls on hard times, elves arrive and help him. They are quite skilled at shoemaking and the cobbler learns much by observing them. They illustrate an important part of shoemaking: it requires teachers and mentors. The shoemaker in the story presumably learned his craft from his father, or a working cobbler he apprenticed to. The elves play the role of master shoemakers who demonstrate the correct techniques and thus establish standards.

Much of shoemaking is determined by local traditions and tastes. However, the basic craft depends on physics, not culture: a shoemaker cannot use stone or bread to make shoes – the first is too difficult to work with and the second will not last in the rain.

The cobbler's practice involves making shoes – repeatedly. Practices in general, from teaching to plumbing, involve such repetition. Learning a new practice can be exciting, but after several years, most practitioners, whatever their discipline, begin to feel a little jaded or bored. (The same occurs with assembly-line workers, but much more quickly.) In the story, the cobbler suffers a slump, and this provides a good metaphor for a practitioner's ennui. He may have started his career with a bang, say, by winning a contest to prove his skill, perhaps making the shoes that the King chose for himself. But after that peak experience, come years of ordinary work for the shoemaker.

The same is true about fact-finding and this is especially clear in modern science: it is an ongoing activity, based on a community of scientists, and to survive, the practice must have teachers, mentors and referees to continue the discipline. Scientists have multiple projects, from geology to quantum physics, but they share the basic practice – the methodology of convergence, integrating experiences from many witnesses.

The elves specifically work only at night – secretly. This provides another metaphor about fact-finding, but now on a much more fundamental, unconscious level, concerning how we perceive objects in the world, from bread to birds to buildings.

Consider what is involved in an everyday example of perception – recognizing a friend named Bob walking on a street. We might start by seeing a person from behind, noting he wears the same kind of hat Bob always does. So, we draw closer, move to the side and see the person's profile, with the same strong nose and jaw exactly like Bob's. When we face the person, we see the slightly crooked smile that Bob always has. We integrate these multiple sensory experiences into a factual conclusion – "That is Bob!" Usually, we identify a friend effortlessly and immediately, but the conclusion results from rapid, unconscious cognitive processes – the work of skillful secret elves. Modern artists, I might add, such as Cézanne, Picasso and Bracque, were some of the first to notice how these secret elves create our visual experiences. For instance, Picasso in his painting "Head of a Woman" from 1960, painted the eyes and nose of a woman from both a profile and frontal view – in one image. He depicts simultaneously what we would normally experience sequentially as we move around a person. Picasso dissected the unconscious integrating process involved in recognizing people, painting the elves at work, so to speak.

Extraordinary Evidence

Elves are supernatural creatures and are analogous to extraordinary experiences, such as dreams, paranormal perceptions, mystical experiences and altered states of consciousness. Can we use these unusual experiences in making factual conclusions, the way the shoemaker uses the elves' handiwork? A classic answer comes from television, where stymied detectives turn to a psychic for help in finding a kidnapped person and the psychic's visions lead to rescuing the victim, thus corroborating the intuition. Science is also full of anecdotes describing how particular scientists made major discoveries after a dream or psychedelic vision. The often-cited case is that of the 18th-century German chemist August Kekule, who struggled to figure out the structure of benzene. Then one day, he reported, he had a reverie in which he saw a snake that was biting its own tail. This gave him the idea that benzene has the structure of a ring.[3] Similarly, Francis Crick, one of the co-discoverers of the structure of DNA is widely believed to have been on an LSD high when he had the image that gave him the double helix structure of DNA.[4]

Notwithstanding such dramatic anecdotes, a more judicious approach is that flashes of insight which seem real and true to the individual are important clues which a scientist must investigate further.[5] But this is the same approach we take with eyewitness reports (and memories in psychotherapy). We generally give credence to the testimony of eyewitnesses, but psychological experiments demonstrate that they are often mistaken. Any single bit of evidence by itself is not conclusive – it is the convergence of all available information that counts. This means that extraordinary experiences count as evidence – if corroborated.

The same principle applies to emotions. Emotions often contain important information about the world. If we meet a stranger, for example, we might feel very uneasy and anxious, although we cannot explain exactly why. But sometimes, such emotions are informative, because we pick up many clues unconsciously, such as subtle body language. Psychotherapists often use such emotional reactions with clients they meet for the first time, to quickly assess whether the person might be dangerous to them.[6]

Still, emotions are so idiosyncratic and changeable, it is easy to be suspicious of emotional experiences as evidence. However, the logic of factual comprehension specifies integrating evidence, not what kind of evidence, or who provides it. We might call this principle the **democracy of evidence**, as opposed to an **aristocracy** of evidence: in the "olden" days, the testimony of nobles (primarily men) was accepted in court, but not that of commoners (or women). Today, we reject such prejudices. Yet the aristocracy of evidence remains in subtler forms. Most of the time, for instance, we rely for evidence on what we see, hear and touch – our sensory experiences. We trust such aristocratic evidence, but remain dubious about emotions, even though they are a larger part of our experiences – just like commoners. Excluding whole categories of evidence is false-to the factual mode of comprehension and its deep logic of convergence.

If we accept emotions and any experience as evidence (if corroborated), we can classify facts into two categories. First, we have facts that can command wide agreement, such as, "It is sunny today," or "Dogs bark." These facts are based on shared experiences many people are familiar with. We might call these **wide facts** since they are widely accepted and based on widely experienced observations. The second group of facts includes emotional evidence. An everyday example would be job interview evaluations – interviewers usually draw on their emotional reactions to the candidate, and because emotions are often idiosyncratic, different interviewers may have completely different impressions. Factual conclusions based on emotional evidence thus do not command widespread agreement. So, such conclusions are not wide facts. However, we usually think of feelings as "deeper" than sensory perceptions, so we might call facts based on emotional evidence **deep facts**. This openness to evidence, no matter its content is true-to the fundamental logic of the factual mode.

Practicing the Factual Mode

A shoemaker's work brings up an aspect of factual assertions that we often overlook. Any self-respecting shoemaker would repair a defective shoe a customer brought back, like a boot that fell apart the very day the customer bought it from the cobbler. Most craftspeople and professionals take pride in their work and give an implicit warranty for their products or services. The same is true for making factual conclusions, which is, after all, also a discipline or craft. Consider an everyday example: if a tourist asks for directions to a nearby museum, and we know the answer because we live in the area, we normally will help the visitors by giving instructions on how to get there. If the tourists came back after a while, saying they could not find the museum, we would try to figure out what happened: were our directions incomplete or incorrect? Did they not understand? Did the museum move? We try to correct the problem because our directions came with an unspoken warranty.

Scientists, too, offer implicit warranties in their research conclusions. If someone challenges their findings with new, contradictory data, the original scientists will (or should) try to figure out why the new evidence differs. Of course, they could also ignore or reject the new evidence out of hand, in which case we might begin to suspect their work – are they engaged in fact-finding, or something else, like defending their reputation?

One last feature of the elves is noteworthy: they seem to treat shoemaking as a game or recreation and enjoy it. It is not tedious work for them, although they have made countless shoes before. The joy and magic they bring to the task is a good symbol of flow experiences, when we feel challenged by a task, but confident in our ability to complete it, and most important of all, feel carried effortlessly by our actions, like a surfer catching a wave. Flow experiences are the most dramatic examples of the intrinsic reward that activities can give us, irrespective of the final result. It is why tennis lovers keep playing tennis even after losing a series of games. Winning is wonderful, but the experience of playing is inexhaustible.

The process of integrating experiences is the core of the factual mode of comprehension. As we discussed previously, the practice of faithfulness, e.g., in religion, follows the same deep logic of convergence. With facts, we seek the convergence of evidence – we integrate our observations. With faithfulness, we integrate our actions around a promise or goal. As the next story illustrates, understanding the logic of faithfulness helps us identify common errors which are particularly important in religious and ideological disputes today.

Notes

1 (Grimm et al., 1975)
2 The parallels between fact-finding and shoemaking easily lead to the conclusion that we manufacture facts the way we make shoes and all other human artifacts. The story has an important caveat for us: the shoemaker does not create shoes out of nothing. He takes things already in the world, such as pieces of leather, and puts them together. Similarly, when we make factual conclusions, we do not create the world, but simply take our experiences of it and integrate them. We construct factual conclusions, but not the world they are about.
3 However, more recent historical research suggests that the story of the snake was based on a joke from Kekule, and that two other chemists published the structure of benzene before Kekule did (Browne, 1988)
4 However, more detailed research suggests this is not strictly true (Roberts, 2015)
5 (Charlton, 2007)
6 Prostitutes must also do the same.

References

Browne, M. W. (1988). "The Benzene Ring: Dream Analysis." *New York Times* Section C, 10.
Charlton, B. G. (2007). "Scientific Discovery, Peak Experiences and the Col-oh-nell Flastratus! Phenomenon." *Medical Hypotheses* **69**(3): 475–477.
Frood, A. (2008). "Albion Dreaming: A Popular History of LSD in Britain." *Springer Nature* **455**: 870–870.
Grimm, J., W. Grimm, A. W. Hunt, J. Stern and J. Scharl (1975). *The Complete Grimm's Fairy Tales*. London, Routledge and Kegan Paul.
Roberts, A. (2015). "Francis Crick, DNA & LSD: Psychedelic History in the Age of Science." *Psychedelic Press* **2**.

Chapter 15

Faith, Fact and Feat

"A Lost Shoe of Gold"

Introduction

Intractable disputes erupt today when our deepest commitments clash with those of other people. Our loyalty may be to a religion, ideology, political faction, culture, or tribe or combination thereof. **What** our commitments are about varies, but they all involve being true-to a promise or an oath. This is faithfulness, and the commitment mode of comprehension. The present Arabian story dramatizes the nature of faithfulness and highlights the errors we can make in it. Perhaps more important, it also points the way to how we can avoid those problems.

The Story[1]

Once upon a time there lived a Princess named Sit Lahab. Every day she joined other children at the house of their spiritual teacher for his lessons. One day, Sit Lahab went to school a little earlier than usual to bring her teacher a roasted goose. When she opened the door, she was horrified to see a dead horse hanging from the rafters, and her beloved spiritual teacher gnawing on it. Sit Lahab realized her teacher was really a ghoul and fled. In her haste, she left behind one of her shoes, which were woven of gold. That night, in her bedroom at the palace, the ghoul appeared and demanded, "Sit Lahab, Sit Lahab, tell me what you saw, please do, that made you flee without your shoe?"

The Princess replied, "I saw my teacher praying, reciting the Prophet's sayings." "If you don't tell me what you saw," the ghoul threatened her, "I will destroy all the wealth of your father, the Sultan." Sit Lahab simply repeated, "I saw my teacher praying, reciting the Prophet's sayings." So, the ghoul destroyed all the Sultan's property.

The next night, the same thing happened. The ghoul appeared in the Princess' bedroom, demanding to know what she saw. "Sit Lahab, Sit Lahab, tell me what you saw, please do, that made you flee without your shoe?" "I saw my teacher praying, reciting the Prophet's sayings," was all she replied. "I will take away your mother and father, and destroy their palace," the ghoul threatened. Sit Lahab

DOI: 10.4324/9781003471028-19

simply repeated her answer, and the next morning, she awoke to find her parents and the palace gone. She was now an orphan, and fled the city to escape the ghoul.

She walked all day, and finally came upon a group of potters, camping in the desert, on their way to the market. She fell asleep near them, but the ghoul awoke her in the middle of the night. "Sit Lahab, Sit Lahab, tell me what you saw, please do, that made you flee without your shoe?" And the monster threatened, "If you do not tell me, I will destroy all these people's pottery and kill their camels." Sit Lahab responded as she usually did, so the ghoul destroyed all the pots, and stole all the camels. The Princess realized she could no longer be near any people, and so fled deeper into the wilderness.

Sometime later, a Prince rode by and was astonished to see a beautiful young woman alone in the wilderness. Sit Lahab did not tell her story about the ghoul, but the Prince took her home, and his sister bathed and dressed her. Sit Lahab was then so beautiful, the Prince fell in love with her, and the two were soon married. Sit Lahab said nothing about the ghoul. In due time, she bore the Prince a beautiful baby boy.

That very night, the ghoul appeared. "Sit Lahab, Sit Lahab, tell me what you saw, please do, that made you flee without your shoe?" She replied, "I saw my teacher praying, reciting the Prophet's sayings." "I will take your baby away," the ghoul threatened, but Sit Lahab simply repeated her answer, and the ghoul seized the newborn boy. The next day, everybody was horrified at the baby's disappearance, and rumors spread that the Princess had killed her own child. The Prince loved her so much, he would hear none of this.

In due time, the Princess bore him a second baby boy. The Prince was overjoyed, but that very night the ghoul returned, threatening to take her second child, if she did not tell him what she saw. Sit Lahab refused to change her answer, so the ghoul seized the infant. The next day, when everyone heard about the baby vanishing, rumors swirled that the Princess was really a witch, and had eaten her own child. The Prince loved her dearly, and refused to believe the gossip.

Soon enough, Sit Lahab became pregnant again, and delivered a third baby boy. That night the ghoul appeared, and asked his questions. She gave her usual answers so the ghoul took her third child. The next day the rumors were too much for even the Prince to withstand, and he acquiesced to the crowd's demand that the Princess be burned alive as a witch.

As she was tied to a stake, surrounded by firewood, four horses came galloping, an old man in the lead. On each of the other horses sat one of the three boys. The old man came up to Sit Lahab, untied her from the stake, and said, "She is my pupil, and the best one I have ever had. Let no one harm her." Then he explained how Sit Lahab had seen him as a ghoul, but refused to be deceived by appearances. The old man turned to Sit Lahab, "These are your three boys," he declared. "And your mother and father are back at their palace, anxious to meet you and your new husband." The old man suddenly turned into a ghoul, and vanished. And so the Princess and her husband lived in happiness and contentment with their three children for the rest of their days.

Disruption

In her everyday routine, Princess Sit Lahab accidentally discovers her beloved spiritual teacher is a ghoul, and worse, eats dead horses. Overcome with horror she flees to the safety of her home, the royal palace. Later that night, the ghoul invades her bedroom, even though the Sultan's guards are presumably everywhere. Metaphorically speaking, the ghoul destroys the security of her home story: if the person she trusted and respected deeply, her beloved teacher, turns out to be a monster, can she trust anyone else, even her parents? She is thrown into an unfamiliar, frightening and bewildering situation. She has, in short, a mythic experience triggered by the horror of her discovery. (By appearing in her home the ghoul repeats Sit Lahab's initial terror of seeing him as a ghoul. His visitation is analogous to a post-traumatic nightmare or flashback.)

Sit Lahab's experience is no mere fairytale because we have many real-life analogues which do not require a supernatural being like the ghoul: we have clergy who abuse children, gurus exploiting their devotees, and many "family values" politicians caught in tawdry affairs. (To be fair, the ghoul is not actually doing anything criminal – eating an animal carcass is perhaps disgusting or barbaric, but not evil or illegal.)

That night, the ghoul specifically demands to know why Sit Lahab fled that morning, and she insists that she just saw her teacher praying. This is factually untrue, but she is clever enough to guess that the ghoul would want her to protect his horrible secret. This is certainly true of abusers in families, bullies in institutions, and harassers in corporations. They entangle their victims in webs of secrecy. Yet the ghoul persecutes Sit Lahab when she continues to deny seeing her teacher as a monster. If she is not protecting the ghoul's secret from the world, why does she persist in denial? She may be trying to protect **herself** from the ghoul's secret. Her teacher had become a central figure in her life, someone she respects, has affection for, and depends on psychologically. He is, in short, a keystone in her emotional life. His secret threatens to shatter her whole psyche. By repeating her story about seeing her teacher praying, she is in effect telling herself, "I know that my teacher is a good person, although he may look like a monster" – running away just in case she is wrong.

A small detail about Islamic culture is important here: when normally evil creatures like ghouls convert to Islam, they become genuinely good. Islam transforms them. So, when Sit Lahab insists that she saw her teacher praying as usual rather than being a monster eating a horse carcass, she really affirms that his appearance as a ghoul does not matter. She re-commits himself to her faith that Islam has transformed him. She must choose between her emotional reaction of horror, disgust and fear at seeing her teacher as a ghoul, and her faith that the ghoul has been transformed. In repeatedly insisting on her story that she saw her teacher simply praying, she consciously chooses to affirm her faith. This may be her first explicit, personal commitment to do so, because she was born into and raised in an Islamic culture – and in a presumably religiously observant household, since her father the

Sultan was both a spiritual and temporal leader. Belief in Islam would presumably be part of her home story which she simply took for granted.

The story emphasizes an important point about the faithfulness mode of comprehension in contrast to the home mode. The former requires conscious, voluntary commitment, rather than simply following habit or tradition. This is the difference between a faith community and a home community. The former is chosen, the latter is given. In this light, we can interpret the ghoul pursuing and persecuting her as a test of her faith. Despite progressively dire consequences of doing so, she remains steadfast in her faith. She is true to her covenant with Islam.

However, Sit Lahab also illustrates the errors we often make with the commitment mode of comprehension and faithfulness.

Errors of Faith

The prime error is imposing a covenant or oath on other people, without their consent, as the Princess quickly demonstrates. Although the ghoul threatens to attack her parents unless she reveals what she really saw, she insists that she just saw her teacher praying. So, the ghoul attacks her father the Sultan, destroys all his properties and apparently kills or disappears both mother and father. Her parents pay the price for Sit Lahab's religious faithfulness. She imposes her religious faith on them. To be sure, they probably were also Muslim believers, but it is unclear if they were willing to risk everything, including their lives, for their faith.

Now alone in the world, Sit Lahab takes refuge with a caravan of potters, but still gives the same answer to the ghoul when he threatens to attack the potters. In this case, she insists on her faith even knowing the likely result – the potters will be harmed or even killed by the ghoul. Here she is analogous to religious or ideological terrorists today who kill innocent people, even though those victims do not share the same commitments.

After the ghoul devastates the potters' caravan, Sit Lahab flees into the wilderness, so as not to endanger any other innocent bystanders. She recognizes that imposing her faith on unwilling individuals is an error in faithfulness. In the wilderness, she meets a Prince who naturally falls in love with her, since the story is a fairytale. However, when he asks why she is alone in the desolate landscape, she says nothing about the ghoul (also a typical theme in fairytales about young women).

Nevertheless, the Prince and Sit Lahab marry and in due time, Sit Lahab gives birth to an infant. It is then that the ghoul reappears and asks his usual question, but this time he threatens to kidnap her newborn infant. When she gives her usual answer, the ghoul executes his threat and abducts the child. This happens with two more of her babies after two more pregnancies. She keeps insisting on her story, and thus remains true-to her faith, apparently not worried about what happens to her newborn babies. Nor does she explain the situation to her husband, so evil gossip soon arises among the people, accusing her of being a witch who ate her babies. She is soon condemned to die at the stake.

In being willing to risk her babies, the Princess provides a metaphor today for parents who put their faith and commitments above their children's welfare. The most dramatic example comes from Islamic jihadists who send their children on suicide bombing missions – the parents sacrifice their children, although the latter may be too young to make such an ultimate commitment to a religion. In other religions, parents may risk the lives of their children by refusing medical treatment for them, following their religion's prohibitions. Secular courts regularly overrule the parents in these latter cases because the children could not give voluntary consent. Such informed commitment is the difference between a covenant and coercion, faith and forced labor.

Another error in faith involves a complementary problem – rather than forcing our faith on other people, we do not keep it ourselves, although we insist that others do. This is the problem of hypocrisy. Fortunately, Sit Lahab does not commit this error, but real examples abound – the political leader who rails against moral decay and marital infidelity and then is caught with a mistress; or the pastor who condemns homosexuality in public but practices it in secret. Such hypocrisy invalidates their exhortations to other people to follow their faith. If they are not true-to their faith, why should anybody else follow it?

To avoid these two errors in faithfulness, we can follow a simple motto: "Honor **all** your covenants and respect the stranger's." The former prevents "buffet" hypocrisy, where we pick a few rules in a covenant, ignore the ones we do not like, and insist everyone follow the rules we chose. Honoring the stranger's covenants is probably more difficult – we must treat their central commitments with the same respect we (ideally) approach our own.[2]

Faith versus Faithfulness

Clearly, practicing faithfulness is not only difficult at times but can also be confusing. This is where an education in faithfulness is essential. But here we must distinguish between training in **a** faith, as opposed to education in the practice of **faithfulness**. Religious education typically focuses on the former, instructing students in the doctrines and rules of their faith – like Sit Lahab learning from her teacher. The practice of faithfulness – the discipline of making and keeping commitments in general and not making errors – is much more difficult to teach. However, faithfulness is a skill just like reading or swimming, and both require instruction and practice.

Ironically, science education provides a good model for the difference between practicing **a** faith and practicing faith**fulness**. Traditionally, schools focus on **what** to teach in science classes, i.e., the specific content of instruction. Thus, we have arguments over whether creationism should be taught in schools. However, the content of science changes with new discoveries. Newton's physics gave way to Einstein's, and Darwin's theory of evolution may someday give way to something else. What does not change is **how** science operates, namely gathering evidence, making tentative conclusions, and testing them. And underlying science is practicing the factual mode of comprehension which involves commitment to revising our factual claims in light of new evidence and being open to new concepts.

Analogous considerations apply to religious and ideological faithfulness: instead of focusing on the content of a particular faith, e.g., the doctrines, we can focus on the fundamental process of faithfulness, namely commitment to a set of beliefs, and tolerance for those who do not make such an oath. While we might think that the commitment mode is straightforward – we make a vow and keep it – there are many issues we must confront.

Perhaps the most important question of all is how we resolve disputes, like who owns a particular land, with people who follow covenants incompatible with ours? Here we need to turn to another comprehension mode, besides that of faith and commitment, as the next story from China illustrates.

Notes

1 (Burton and Shumaker, 1977)
2 St. Paul gives analogous advice in First Corinthians, telling members of the church to judge fellow members for moral infractions, but not to judge those who do not belong to the church, because that is up to God.

Reference

Burton, R. F. and D. Shumaker (1977). *Tales from the Arabian Nights: Selected from the Book of the Thousand Nights and a Night.* New York, Gramercy Books.

Chapter 16

Virtual Understanding and Empathy

"The Rich Man's Dreams"

Introduction

The virtual mode of comprehension dominates contemporary culture. Some examples are evident, such as social media, video games, fantasy sports leagues, advertising and "fake news." They all construct a virtual world separate from the real one and draw us into the former. The process has lately become more subtle – and troublesome. Science becomes increasingly divorced from everyday reality in fields like quantum physics and molecular biology, which makes them seem more fantastical and therefore easier to dismiss as imaginary. Financial derivatives, like credit default swaps, future options and arbitrage positions, (also BitCoin) have evolved into powerful, abstract contracts, increasingly divorced from tangible assets or human consequences. For many, this virtual world becomes more important than experiences in the real one. This makes it easier for the haves to ignore the have-nots, as the present story from China dramatizes. The tale also illustrates the errors we commonly make in the virtual mode of comprehension. Fortunately, the story also illuminates a primordial example of the virtual mode – empathy – which helps resolve the problem and expand our concept of "rationality."

The Story[1]

Once upon a time there was a rich man who had a vast estate, with many workers and servants. He made them labor from dawn to dusk, so they all collapsed in exhaustion at night, while he lived in increasing wealth and luxury. Then he began to dream the same dream every night. In his dream, he was a servant of a cruel master, who forced him and all the other servants to work day and night, with little sleep or food. The rich man would awaken each morning feeling exhausted, his body sore, as if he had indeed labored the whole night. At first, he dismissed the dreams, but when they continued night after night, he consulted doctors and priests. None of their cures helped, and the dreams became a torment to him.

One day, he heard about an old servant in his palace. The servant had worked for the rich man for many years, but now with failing strength, the old man could barely complete his usual duties. But each night, when the old man collapsed into

DOI: 10.4324/9781003471028-20

an exhausted sleep, he dreamed that he was the King of a great kingdom, living in a palace of gold, with hundreds of servants, fulfilling his every whim. So, the old man did not complain about his hard lot. "At least, I am a King every night," he explained, "and that is a third of my life."

Puzzled by his dreams and the old man's, the rich man asked a wise friend about them. "It is the balance of nature," the friend replied. "If you live one extreme by day, you live the other by night." The rich man pondered this for several days, and then lightened the burden on all his workers and servants. They no longer collapsed with exhaustion at the end of each day – and he no longer dreamt of laboring all night.

Dreams and Virtual Worlds

The rich man pushes his servants and workers to the point of exhaustion. He "sees" their plight every day, but it does not register with him. As far as he is concerned, the exhausted workers all around him could be actors in a theatrical performance. The rich man treats the plight of his workers as a virtual reality, not a real one. Today, of course, we see the plight of people in Internet videos, and news broadcasts. And for the most part, we react to them as virtual realities because it would be too overwhelming to do otherwise.

What changes the rich man's perspective is a repeated – and disturbing – dream. Dreams are a paradigm of the virtual mode of comprehension – or more accurately, recalling a dream. When we dream, it is simply reality for us and only after we awaken, do we recognize we were dreaming. The recognition involves having two things in mind at once – recalling the dream and recognizing the real world around us. As we discussed In Chapter 2, attending to two things at once is characteristic of the virtual mode of comprehension.

Initially, the rich man dismisses his dream even though it was intense and vivid. In the dream, he felt physically exhausted from working so hard, and when he awakens in the morning, he was still exhausted. The dream thus spills over into waking life. This is unusual enough, but the dream recurs several times and understandably becomes disquieting to the rich man. So, he tries to get rid of the troublesome dream, consulting doctors and priests, trying medications and prayers to the gods. Then he hears about one of his servants having a recurrent dream of living in luxury – the complement of his own. Recurrent dreams are unusual in themselves, but two people in the same household having repetitive dreams is even less common, and more so when the dreams are about the same situation. The rich man is finally perplexed enough to consult a wise friend. This is another example of how a disturbing, baffling, situation – a mini-mythic experience – can break us out of our familiar home stories. (The equivalent in the last story about Sit Lahab is her seeing her spiritual teacher as a ghoul, eating a dead horse. In "A Christmas Carol," it was the specter of Marley screaming at Scrooge.)

The wise friend ventures an interpretation: the dreams are a revelation about the rich man's unbalanced life, overworking his servants, but not working himself. This is a classic Jungian interpretation, and the rich man recognizes its truth. Having experienced the physical plight of his overworked servants in his dream, the rich man finally can truly empathize with them. He could not do so previously, because he had no embodied experience of being exhausted from work – apparently being rich all his life. Now he has that experience even though it is virtual. What counts is not whether the experience is real, but how broad and deep it is, engaging mind, emotions and body. (Scrooge illustrated the point in his adventures with the three Christmas Spirits. Those experiences were transformative, even though they could have been dreams.)

The rich man reflects on what his friend said, and then responds to his uncanny dreams. He reduces his servants' workload and starts working himself. The rich man thus experiences a successful *katabasis*. He involuntarily descends into the unconscious and faces the parts of his life he ignored before, e.g., how his comfort depended on other people's unreasonable labors, and his own lack of experience with hard work.

In reflecting on his dreams and his real-life situation, and then changing the situation to the benefit of his servants, the rich man illustrates a core ideal of the Western Enlightenment – using reason to improve everyone's lives. We usually understand reason to be a matter of detachment, stepping back from our personal situation, and adapting an impartial, intellectual perspective. After all, if we remain in the grip of personal passions and convictions, we are much more likely to act selfishly and irrationally. Detachment seems to be the key to reason.

The story reverses this assumption. The transformation for the rich man does not come from detachment, but the opposite – having an intense emotional, embodied experience of **another** person's situation. We often need to detach from our own experiences to do this but detachment is only a first step. The more important task comes next – vicariously and vividly experiencing another person's situation, i.e., empathizing with them.

Degrees of Empathy

The story illustrates how our experiences of empathy fall upon a continuum. On one side is detachment from another person's experience, which the rich man illustrates at the beginning of the story, when he can see how overworked his servants are, without any noteworthy reaction. On the other side lies overinvolvement with a virtual experience, which the rich man illustrates when he is absorbed in his dream of being an overworked servant. In between, lies empathy, neither too detached, nor overinvolved, but just right, which is where the rich man ends up.

The extreme example of a detached approach, I might add, is a psychopath. They are good at intellectually understanding another person's experience, and especially their hopes, fears and desires – what psychologists call "cognitive empathy." But psychopaths **feel** little or no sympathy or compassion for other people and use their understanding to manipulate their "marks" more effectively.[2] A less extreme example of detachment would be the rich man's friend in our story reflecting on the dream and coming up with his interpretation. From his "outside" perspective, the friend could understand what the rich man could not. This positive form of detachment gives him a broader and deeper perspective.

The opposite of detachment is overinvolvement in someone else's experience. For example, when we see a person trip and fall flat, or cut their finger while chopping food, many of us instinctively wince, as if we ourselves were injured.[3] This instinctual empathy is visible very early in life: in a room with several infants, when one baby starts to cry in distress, soon a second child will join in, feeling distraught themselves, and then more follow.

A more common example of overinvolvement occurs when we identify with another person's experience so intensely, we forget it is their experience, and not our own. "I know exactly how you feel," we might exclaim excitedly, although we have not checked to see if that is true, for instance, by asking the other person. After all, when we conclude that we experience what the other person does, we make a factual conclusion, and we can be mistaken. Hence, accurate empathy requires reflection.

Reason and Entertainment

Our principal portals to virtual worlds are stories e.g., in novels, movies, gossip or video games. These familiar examples illustrate how we often treat virtual experiences today as **entertainment**, which we then do not take seriously. The word "entertain," however, originally meant something much more significant – to entertain was to provide for someone, for instance, provide for visitors (the familiar meaning), provide for family (an older meaning) or provide for workers (the oldest one).[4] In providing for someone, we create a place for them, where we consider their interests, independent from ours. This means we pay attention to two realms, theirs and ours – authentic empathy is hovering in this middle ground, neither disengaged nor overly engaged, but just right.

Like any other mode of comprehension, we can commit errors in the virtual mode – overinvolvement and detachment being just two basic ones. The next story illustrates other mistakes in the virtual mode and introduces us to an unexpected notion – we can judge truth or falsity in the virtual mode. More precisely, we can judge what is true-to the virtual mode, and what is not. This means we can identify what is true-in the virtual mode, and what is not. It may seem strange to talk about truth with respect to virtual reality, but the concept has important applications today, especially with free-speech controversies.

Notes

1 (Roberts and Zheng, 1979)
2 (van Dongen, 2020)
3 (Tully and Petrinovic, 2017) Such automatic empathy is probably hardwired in our brains, for example, because of "mirror neurons."
4 (Oxford, 2020)

References

Oxford (2020). Oxford English Dictionary Online. https://www-oed-com.ucsf.idm.oclc.org/.

Roberts, M. and S. Zheng (1979). *Chinese Fairy Tales and Fantasies*. New York, Pantheon Books.

Tully, J. and M. M. Petrinovic (2017). "Acetaminophen Study Yields new Insights into Neurobiological Underpinnings of Empathy." *Journal of Neurophysiology* **117**(5): 1844–1846.

van Dongen, J. D. M. (2020). "The Empathic Brain of Psychopaths: From Social Science to Neuroscience in Empathy." *Frontiers in Psychology* **11**: 695–695.

Chapter 17

Games and Free Speech

"The Princess Liar"

Introduction

Dreams are a paradigm of the virtual mode of comprehension, as we discussed in the last chapter. The story in this one illustrates two other familiar examples – first, telling stories that may or may not be true, such as fairytales and tall tales, and second, playing a game. We commonly make errors in the virtual mode with both, and these mistakes are particularly relevant to three major contemporary problems: addiction to Internet activity, such as social media; controversies in free speech, e.g., outrageous speech; and finally, misusing the game paradigm as a model for business and free enterprise.

The Story[1]

Once upon a time, there lived a Princess who constantly lied, so much so that her father the King worried she did not know the difference between truth and falsehood. So, he declared that anyone who could make her say, "You are a liar!" – which would mean she knew what truth was – would win half the kingdom, and her hand in marriage. Many men tried their best, but all failed. One day a young man decided to try his luck, even though his two older brothers had gone before him and failed. He set out for the palace, and came to the royal barn, where he met the Princess.

They greeted each other, and the Princess said, "I bet you have never seen a barn as large as this! It is so large, if the shepherd blows a horn on one end, another shepherd on the other end will not hear it."

The lad laughed, "That is nothing. In our barn, if a cow becomes pregnant on one side of the barn, and starts walking to the other, she will give birth before she reaches the other end."

"That may be," the Princess retorted. "But you do not have an ox as big as we do. If one man sat on one horn, and another man on the other horn, they could not reach each other, even if they use 10-foot poles."

"Such an ox is tiny," the lad exclaimed. "We have one which is so large, if you stood by one horn, and yelled, a man at the other horn would not hear it."

DOI: 10.4324/9781003471028-21

"Well, you do not have a cow as large as we do," the Princess boasted. *"The cow is so large, we have to collect her milk in a vat as large as a wagon, and we make cheese just as large."*

"Our cow puts yours to shame!" the young man insisted. *"She is so big and she gives so much milk, we need a vat as large as a house to contain it. And we have a gray mare that tramples the milk to make cheese. One day, the mare gave birth to a foal, but the colt fell into the cheese, and we did not discover it until seven years later, when we were cutting the cheese, and a full-grown horse stepped out. I took him to the mill to pick up a load of flour, but he broke his back on the way. So, I cut a spruce tree and replaced the broken backbone with a log which he uses to this day. But the tree kept growing into the sky so I climbed it to see if it reached heaven. At the top I saw a saint busy weaving a rope out of soup, but just as I greeted him, the spruce tree broke in half, so I could not climb down. The saint kindly gave me his rope and lowered me down to earth. The rope was too short, so I had to jump the last bit, and fell into a fox's den. And then I saw your father and my mother fixing old shoes. They got into an argument, and my mother slapped your father so hard, all the dandruff flew off his head!"*

"You're a liar!" the Princess cried out. *"My father has never had dandruff!"*

Virtual Worlds, Addictions and Anchors

Because his daughter the Princess constantly tells tall tales, the King becomes worried that she cannot tell reality from fantasy and sets up his tall tale contest as a test. The Princess may always tell tall tales because she is simply crazy i.e., she cannot distinguish virtual worlds from the real one. However, we have many people today who advocate all sorts of viewpoints on the Internet, many of which seem crazy. Like the King wondering if his daughter is psychotic, we wonder if many conspiracy theorists are too. But there is a more general problem, namely postmodernism, which often claims, "All is narrative." This is a modern version of the ancient Hindu tenet, "All is illusion." The modern Western version adds a slight egocentric focus, "All is narrative," and "My narrative is the best."

This brings us to a second reason the Princess might constantly tell tall tales: she simply likes doing so, and since she is royalty, she is accustomed to do what she wants – or so we presume. (Many people leaving comments on the Internet seem to have a similar, if unspoken, sense of entitlement.)

The Princess may even be addicted to tall tales and their virtual worlds, like some people today, endlessly playing Internet games, or commenting on social media. The technology is different today – the Princess only had oral storytelling – but the problem of conflating real and virtual worlds is the same.

One factor behind Internet addiction today is that websites are deliberately designed to be addictive, using psychological research to keep people glued to their screens. This contrasts with long-standing theater traditions, which have rituals to begin and end a theatrical production, such as lowering the lights, lifting the curtains and vice versa. Fairytales do something similar by starting with a ritualistic phrase, like "Once upon a time," to invite people to enter a virtual realm. And the stories end with other phrases, such as, "And they lived happily ever after." Analogous entry and exit procedures are used in traditional tribal initiation rites.

By contrast, little thought is given today to how individuals make the transition from computer-generated worlds **back** to reality. Web psychology is focused on luring people **into** virtual Web worlds. Websites have become like carnivorous plants – they attract attention, but then people, like insects, become trapped by the plant.

Attending to possible, virtual worlds is the defining aspect of the virtual mode of comprehension. Breaking or weakening the boundary between the two worlds is being false-to virtual comprehension. Conversely maintaining the boundary, keeping aware of both real and possible worlds, is **the** standard of truth and virtual comprehension. There must be some world considered to be real, anchoring all our experiences. Without such a reference, we float in an infinite variety of possible worlds. An extreme example of experience in such a floating reality is derealization, where everything seems unreal, as if we were watching a movie of ourselves.[2]

Virtual Errors

As a game, the tall tale contest creates a zone of "free speech," which suspends usual questions of truth and rules of propriety. This is not, however, a free-for-all territory, because virtual realms, such as sports, follow their own intrinsic rules. Presumably, for instance, the young man cannot physically force the Princess to say, "That is not true." The most basic rule for any free-speech situation, of course, are grammatical rules, because all storytelling and speech must follow proper grammar to be comprehensible to other people.

We usually understand free speech today as the right of every individual to express themselves in public without fear of retaliation or censorship. However, we have many older examples of protected speech, which reveal the basic rules they follow. Perhaps the best-known example of privileged speech in Western culture is the "seal of the confessional." What a person reveals in confession must be kept strictly confidential, to encourage people to speak freely and unburden themselves of their darkest secrets. A secular example of protected speech today is attorney-client privilege where the lawyer cannot reveal even a client's confession of guilt (unless they both conspired to commit the crime).

Doctor-patient confidentiality, for its part, keeps information confidential – unless a patient is an imminent threat to a specific person, or to themselves, in which case doctors must notify the authorities or the threatened victim. This exception should not be surprising because all speech situations separate the virtual realm of speech from the real world **for a specific purpose**. In medicine this is to foster the health and welfare of the individual patient.

The rules defining a free-speech situation are an example of what the philosopher Ludwig Wittgenstein called "language games." They range from cocktail party conversations to speeches in a Parliament. And language games, like games in general, maintain a boundary between the virtual playing field, and the larger world. Legislators may personally attack other parliamentarians in their speeches, but they are prohibited from physically attacking them. Breaching that boundary ends the free-speech situation, like soccer fans running onto the field, angry over a referee's call.

Something analogous happens when the Princess exclaims, "That is not true!" By taking the perspective of the real world, she steps out of the virtual realm of the game. She is now deadly serious, because the young man commits *lèse majesté,* when he claims that his mother slapped the King so hard that his dandruff flew everywhere. Outraging the Princess in this way was the young man's plan all along. He was not really competing to see who could be more creative with storytelling. He was simply trying to provoke her into saying that specific phrase.

Their contest provides a succinct metaphor for the problem with "outrageous speech" today. This is when someone says or does something, intending to provoke outrage or some specific action, while claiming the protection of free speech. A dramatic example is the 2015 cartoon of the Prophet Muhammad in the French satirical paper, *Charlie Hebdo.* The cartoon was intended to outrage Muslims, since images of the Prophet are blasphemous in Islam. And it succeeded. The cartoon sparked a deadly terrorist attack on the newspaper.[3] More common today are "dog whistles," which are specific phrases or images well known to a known set of people, and used to goad them into action.

In trying to provoke the Princess to act in a specific way, the young man uses the pragmatic mode of comprehension not the virtual one. We judge such pragmatic intentions by their real-world consequences – like any action. By contrast, we judge games by how engaging or entertaining is the virtual realm that they create, while protecting players and spectators.

Another example of breaking the boundary between virtual and real worlds is pornography. It uses the pragmatic mode and aims to draw people quickly into its sexual fantasy, and provoke viewers to specific actions, namely sexual gratification. The main concern with pornography is that the boundary between virtual and real worlds will break down, provoking viewers into repeating in real life what they saw in the pornographic film, e.g., raping and degrading women. The same applies to the pornography of violence, in films and computer games.

Fields of Play

Businesses and the free market are often conceptualized as games, especially sports. To take just a few examples, entrepreneurs are advised to "Keep your eye on the ball," or when problems arise, to "Adopt a new game plan." And a successful negotiation is hailed as a "big score."

Indeed, for the young man, the tall tale contest is an excellent business opportunity, a chance for enormous gain with minimal risk to himself, and he willingly enters the contest. This is not so with the Princess. If she loses the contest, she will be forced to marry the young man whether she wants to or not. Worse, following patriarchal tradition, her marriage means she gives up her independence and authority to her husband. In short, the Princess risks her life as she currently knows it, while the young man wagers nothing comparable. The Princess is not really playing a game because she is risking the only life she has known. (Other stories have a more equal playing field. In the opera, "Turandot," for example, men seeking the hand of Princess Turandot must solve three riddles from her, and if they fail, they are promptly beheaded.)

In taking advantage of the Princess' vulnerability, the young man is analogous to an ambitious hedge fund manager planning an uninvited takeover of a company. If the acquisition goes through, he can make enormous profits by "streamlining the company," i.e., dismissing much of the workforce, as well as looting the company's employee retirement fund. That is, the stereotypical takeover involves maximizing the acquirer's profit, without regard to the other participants, such as employees, the surrounding community, stockholders and bondholders. The takeover "game" is equivalent to a no-holds-barred mixed martial arts fight, where injuries to players and even spectators are ignored.

The fundamental problem in both scenarios – business takeover and free-form martial arts fight – is that there is no one minding the playing field. In any game, we have two basic roles – the players and what we might call the "game guard" by analogy with "lifeguard." Both lifeguard and game guard serve the same function – the former makes sure a beach is safe from real world dangers, like sharks, as does the latter, with metaphorical sharks.

Game guards include referees and regulators, but also basic rules which we often take for granted. This might be as simple as amusement park signs which say, "You must be this tall to ride" (so you will not fall out of the ride). Or it might be a basic understanding that Mafia-style murders are not allowed as a business strategy. Some games normally ended when one player died, like a Roman gladiator, or in Mayan ballgames where the leader of the winning (or losing) team was beheaded (or rewarded – which one is not clear). The logic of virtual comprehension prohibits such deadly games.

The tectonic logic of virtual comprehension illuminates fundamental rules involved in free speech and free enterprise. The next story shifts to pragmatic understanding and illustrates how it helps us approach several other vexing contemporary problems. As we shall see, the crucial point is differentiating objective and pragmatic comprehension – fact and faithfulness on one side, and practical problem-solving on the other.

Notes

1 (Yolen, 1986)
2 (Lucas Sedeño et al., 2014; Michal et al., 2016)
3 The newspaper had actually been attacked some years before, for a similar cartoon.

References

Lucas Sedeño, B. C., M. Melloni, A. Canales-Johnson, A. Yoris, S. Baez, S. Esteves, M. Velásquez, P. Barttfeld, M. Sigman, R. Kichic, D. Chialvo, F. Manes, T. A. Bekinschtein and A. Ibanez (2014). "How Do You Feel when You Can't Feel Your Body? Interoception, Functional Connectivity and Emotional Processing in Depersonalization-Derealization Disorder." *PLoS ONE* (June 26, 2014).

Michal, M., J. Adler, J. Wiltink, I. Reiner, R. Tschan, K. Wolfling, S. Weimert, I. Tuin, C. Subic-Wrana, M. E. Beuteland R. Zwerenz (2016). "A Case Series of 223 Patients with Depersonalization-derealization Syndrome." *BMC Psychiatry* **16**: 203. *https://doi.org/10.1186/s12888-016-0908-4*

Yolen, J. (1986). *Favorite Folktales from Around the World (1st ed.)*. Pantheon Books.

Chapter 18

Principles and Problem Solving
"Penguin Island"

Introduction

This story is originally from French author, Anatole France,[1] but over time, it has been passed from person to person, like Dickens' "A Christmas Carol." By now both stories qualify as folktales, and both contain invaluable insights for us today. The Penguin tale illustrates how the pragmatic mode of comprehension can resolve disputes over doctrines and ideology, which are commonly generated by the factual and faithfulness comprehension modes. These conflicts include contemporary battles over abortion, evolution or tax policy, among many others.

The Story

Once upon a time, a nearsighted saint went on a voyage, and came to an island where the natives gathered along the seashore. He could not see them clearly, except to note they were all unusually short. "But God loves all his creatures," the saint thought to himself. So, he went ahead, preached to them, baptized them and then sailed off

It turned out that the "natives" were penguins. In due time they died, and since they were baptized, they all went up to Heaven's gate and asked for entrance. This provoked an uproar among the Saints and Doctors of the Church. "Baptism guarantees them an immortal soul," said one Saint. "But animals do not have souls," countered a Doctor. After increasingly acrimonious debate, they turned to Saint Catherine, and asked what she thought they should do.

She pondered a moment, and then said, "Give the penguins souls, but little ones."

Objective versus. Pragmatic Comprehension

The nearsighted Saint launches the drama when he baptizes a group of Penguins by mistake. Baptism, as the story explains, guarantees entrance into heaven. Unfortunately, the Saint is shortsighted, and does not realize he deals with animals, who have no souls, and who are, by doctrine, not eligible for Heaven. When the baptized

DOI: 10.4324/9781003471028-22

Penguins die and arrive at Heaven's Gate, the Saints and Doctors of the Church start arguing over which principle to follow – that baptism guarantees entrance into Heaven, or that only humans have souls and can enter heaven.

Since God is apparently not present and does not settle the dispute, the Saints and Doctors are left disagreeing without end. This is, of course, our situation on earth – we have no universally accepted authority, whether God, King, science, etc. And so, we argue about everything under the sun – immigration, the meaning of life, banning books in school, the meaning of death, support for the poor. . .

The Saints and Doctors cannot come to a resolution because they use the objective mode of comprehension and its logic of convergence. For faithfulness, convergence involves commitment to fundamental oaths and the principles that derive from them. This means that the derivative doctrines and rules must be consistent with each other. The Penguins bring up a contradiction between rules, an inconsistency no one thought of before (until Anatole France).

Saint Catherine resolves the dispute by suggesting they give souls to the Penguins who were baptized – but only little souls. Her solution preserves the doctrine that baptism opens heaven to the baptized, but since the Penguins have only little souls, humans retain the unique status of being the only creatures with full-sized souls. Furthermore, only the mistakenly baptized Penguins souls, not all Penguins or all animals, can enter heaven. We have a compromise, but it is not a new universal doctrine – it is a local arrangement, applicable to a very particular group of Penguins.

Instead of sacrificing one doctrine or another, as dictated by the objective comprehension mode, Saint Catherine turns away from the entire objective comprehension mode itself, and opts for the pragmatic one. The primary focus of pragmatic comprehension is solving **this** problem in **this** situation now. By contrast, faithfulness and the objective mode focus on universal oaths and principles, which can therefore ignore many details. The latter are exactly what the pragmatic mode attends to. The difference between pragmatic and objective comprehension finds an analogy in the contrast between modern biology and physics. The former focuses on understanding these particular creatures and their kin. The latter seeks universal principles applicable everywhere.

The Saints and Doctors accept Catherine's pragmatic suggestion, apparently struck by her wisdom – they intuitively recognize it resolves the Penguin dilemma. The story does not explain exactly why they agree with Saint Catherine, but by introducing a new comprehension mode into the conflict, she switches to a broader, deeper, more comprehensive perspective than the objective mode can provide. Her suggestion is like a therapist's accurate and well-timed interpretation, which suddenly makes sense of all the issues the client is dealing with, while illuminating a new direction he or she can move in. Moreover, Saint Catherine's solution takes a compassionate view, empathizing with the plight of the individual Penguins waiting outside Heaven and genuine caring is essential for any effective therapeutic interpretation: insightful interpretations without empathy is like a fortune cookie's comment – they are impersonal and random and only coincidentally relevant.

Why Catherine?

How did Saint Catherine gain her unique wisdom? Traditional biographies, approved by the Church, give us clues. From childhood, Catherine had mystical visions of Jesus, which continued through her life. These inspired her enduring religious devotion and practice. At the same time, she rejected conventional roles and rules. She did not join a convent, which would be the traditional path for a religious woman in her time. She also refused to marry, despite intense parental pressure. Instead, she followed the biblical injunction to care for the poor and sick, giving away food and clothes, much to her parents' consternation. She thus had a deep religious life inspired by mystical visions and a strong independent character which eschewed conventional rules and roles. As her reputation for holiness and practical works grew, secular and ecclesiastical leaders consulted her, and she negotiated treaties for many leaders, including Pope Gregory XI.

With increasing personal prestige and influence, Saint Catherine undoubtedly faced the temptation to break rules for her own personal benefit. What counteracted such all-too-human impulses? I suggest that her ongoing mystical visions did. Such experiences involve transcendence, the encounter with something far greater than us which typically inspires a deep sense of humility. Only the intensity of mythic experience can counter the powerful temptations of egocentric goals.

Another factor in pragmatic wisdom comes from Carol Gilligan's research on gender roles.[2] She observed what happens when elementary school girls play together, and one accuses another of violating a rule. After a brief discussion, the girls typically change the rules of the game, so that everyone can keep playing. They focus on solving the immediate problem so they can continue the game. This is the essence of the pragmatic mode of comprehension.

By contrast, when boys play a game and someone is accused of breaking a rule, an extended argument typically ensues, involving questions like, "Was a rule really broken?" "What exactly do the rules say?" The argument – or looking up the rules – often terminates the game. Boys subordinate their specific game to the rules, because the rules must be universal and apply to everyone who plays the game, no matter who, where or when – no exceptions allowed. This perspective reflects the objective mode of comprehension: in playing a game, all participants agree to the same covenant, namely following the established rules,[3] and it is imperative that everyone follow them.

Compromising a principle is often experienced as a failure from the perspective of a hero, who is sworn to a quest. Such an oath is the fundamental logic of faithfulness. Any compromise is being-untrue to that vow – un-heroic, "giving in." This fosters being stuck-in the heroic archetype.

Practical Applications

Whether Penguins have souls or not is exactly analogous to the question of whether fetuses are human beings, one of the central issues in today's abortion controversy. Pro-life advocates say fetuses are fully human, so abortion is murder. Pro-choice proponents argue the contrary. Their dispute is interminable, just like the argument in heaven over the Penguins.

Claims about whether a fetus is or is not fully human occur in the objective mode. As we discussed previously, objective claims can be factual assertions or professions of faith. If factual, we would have to gather evidence, but it is not clear what counts as evidence for a fetus being human. On the other hand, if the claim is a matter of faith, it must be consistent with the fundamental commitments of that religion. But what constitutes those core vows? This is often not easy to decide, because most faiths include conflicting doctrines and rules. Moreover, if an individual concludes that abortion should be prohibited because that conclusion is part of the covenants they follow, the rule applies only to those who agree with those commitments. As the abortion controversy emphasizes, people of the same faith, e.g., Christianity, may disagree about what constitutes the basic vows and their application to abortion.

Saint Catherine's suggestion that they give the Penguins little souls is analogous to saying that someone is "a little pregnant." In objective comprehension, "a little pregnant" makes no sense at all. Someone is either pregnant or not pregnant. Like a jury verdict, objective comprehension seeks a yes or no answer, and if neither is available a new trial is required i.e., more argument.

If we approach the abortion issue in pragmatic understanding, everything shifts. We now focus on an immediate problem. The issue is no longer a sweeping generalization like, "Is abortion murder?" The question becomes, "What are the consequences if this specific woman in her particular circumstances does or does not have an abortion?" Focusing on concrete reality does not lead to moral relativism and situational ethics, I might add – it leads to **situated** morality, moral principles that are applied in specific real-life circumstances. And real-life problems are much more complicated than abstract or hypothetical scenarios. The latter are like experiments in a laboratory, which focus on a highly simplified phenomenon in a tightly controlled situation. Pragmatic comprehension is analogous to field work in the real world, where the phenomena are ill-defined and often unknown.

The next story from halfway around the world provides more details about how the pragmatic mode of comprehension helps resolve conflicting principles.

Notes

1 (France and France, 1909)
2 (Gilligan, 1993)
3 Of course, not all boys and men prefer the objective mode, nor do all girls and women opt for the pragmatic one. These are traditional gender stereotypes.

References

France, A. and A. France (1909). *Penguin Island*. New York, Blue Ribbon Books.
Gilligan, C. (1993). *In a Different Voice: Psychological Theory and Women's Development*. Cambridge, Mass, Harvard University Press.

Chapter 19

Creative Problem Solving

"Crossing the River"

Introduction

This story from Japan helps address an issue which underlies many of our contemporary dilemmas – insisting on a principle no matter the consequences. Single-issue politics is one example: "If you favor banning abortion, then we will campaign for you, no matter what else you believe – or do." A century earlier, the test was, "If you support prohibition of alcohol, we will do everything to help your election, no matter what else you have done." In this situation, disagreements easily become intractable conflicts. Our story shows us how we can resolve this situation by switching from principles to problem-solving, or more generally, from the objective mode of understanding to the pragmatic one.

The Story[1]

Once upon a time, a young and old monk traveled together. They came to a wide river and met a beautiful young woman sitting on a rock. When she saw them, she asked, "Kind sirs, I am afraid to cross the river, because I do not know how to swim. Would you help me?"

The young monk replied, "I want to help, but it is against the rules of our order to have physical contact with women. I'm sorry." He would have liked to pick up the beautiful young woman and carry her but did not dare. He then stepped into the river and crossed quickly by himself.

The older monk turned to the poor woman, and said, "Climb on my back. I will carry you across." He waded into the river with her and struggled a bit because the water went up over his knees. He finally arrived safely on the other side and gently put the woman down. She thanked him and the two monks continued their journey.

The young monk fumed as they walked, wondering how the elder could break the vows of their order so casually. Finally, the young man could bear it no more. "How could you!" the junior monk exploded. "You broke one of our most important vows! How am I supposed to learn from you and become enlightened?"

"Oh," the old monk said, "you are still carrying her. I put her down on the riverbank miles ago."

DOI: 10.4324/9781003471028-23

Principles and Problem Solving

There are various versions of this story from different cultures, I focus on this Zen version because it makes the least cultural assumptions. Its insights are consequently relevant to more situations, including our contemporary one.

The dilemma the two monks face is whether to help the woman cross the river when the only way to do so is to physically carry her. That would break their monastic vow to have no physical contact with women. On the other hand, the monks also have the basic moral precept of helping relieve other people's suffering, which is most dramatically expressed in the "Bodhisattva vow," to postpone their own enlightenment and liberation to help all suffering beings. Given these two conflicting rules from their faith commitment, which should they choose? Similar dilemmas occur in many other religious traditions. The Christian analog would be the parable of Jesus healing a sick person on the Sabbath – he must choose between showing compassion to a sick person, or breaking an oath, namely the Commandment to honor the Sabbath, and do no work. The general dilemma is commonly summed up as a choice between following the letter of the law, or its spirit.

The young monk insists on the former, obeying the letter of his monastic vows in contrast to the general bodhisattva vow. Thus, he does not help the woman across the river. Here, he also follows the objective mode of comprehension, focused on keeping faith with an oath or vow, ignoring any inconsistencies or inconvenient details. The young monk's objections and obsession with the senior monk touching the woman may seem strict, and harshly puritanical. A major reason for this doctrinaire approach is that with the faithfulness mode of comprehension, breaking any of the rules that follow from an oath is violating one's word. This is not simply a mistake, like miscalculating the square root of 4 and saying that it is 2.5 (rather than 2). Violating an oath is a moral failing, indicative of a character defect. It is not just a stain on one's social standing, but a pollution of one's soul or being. On the other hand, keeping all the rules – fulfilling one's promises – is being pure, without blemish or fault. This dichotomy of purity or contamination, virtue or sin, is an archetypal imperative for many individuals. This is especially true during youth, when it is easier to deal with stark dualities, rather than complicated shades of gray.

By contrast, the older monk illustrates the pragmatic mode of comprehension. He focuses on solving the practical problem at hand. He is less concerned with devotion to abstract oaths. From the viewpoint of faithfulness and the objective mode of comprehension, i.e., from the young monk's perspective, the senior seems to blithely abandon his oaths. Rather than being an idealist, devoted to core principles, the older monk seems more like a long-experienced politician, willing to compromise and make deals – including corrupt ones.

Here we come to the danger of a slippery slope. Make one small exception to a rule, and it is easier to make another exception, and then ever larger ones after that.

Carrying a beautiful woman across the river the first time might be titillating, so the next time a monk might carry another woman across and try groping her, going further with each new time. "Exception" is a gateway drug to "excuse" and then to "egregious error" and eventually – so the fear goes – having no principles or commitments at all. (Or as serial murderers explain on TV series, "The first murder is the most difficult. After that, it becomes easier.")

Our story dramatizes the slippery slope problem with its own metaphor, namely crossing a river on foot. Doing so risks slipping on a submerged rock, which can quickly lead to stumbling in the water, then falling completely into the river, and in the worst case, being swept away by the current and drowning. Carrying someone magnifies the risk.

The pragmatic mode of comprehension is a bottom-up viewpoint, starting with concrete details at hand, and looking for a solution to a specific problem. The faithfulness mode is a top-down perspective, starting with solemn oaths, meant to be applied in all situations and such vows are inevitably abstract. Pragmatic understanding is not concerned with purity of principle, but rather with solutions that work.

This is analogous to the difference between music and medicine. In the former, we either get a note right, or not. In medicine, if the patient improves, or does not get worse, that is a win! In music, perfection is a goal; in medicine, muddling through is acceptable. For many, the latter is unprofessional, unacceptable, immature: it is carrying someone across a river, both people falling in, but then getting across, wet and muddy – but alive.

Pragmatic understanding easily degenerates into trickery, where an individual finds the most expedient solution, advantageous to himself. Such trickery is often confused with the Trickster archetype in mythology, who is often misidentified with a con artist or deceiver.[2] Indeed, in Christian tradition, Satan is the chief Trickster. This understanding, however, ignores the larger context depicted in older mythology and indigenous tradition: the Trickster is typically sent by the Creator God to make the world safe for humanity. But the Trickster forgets his mission, and starts lying, cheating and stealing – until he remembers his mission and resumes it – only to repeat the cycle later. The pragmatic mode focuses on solving the problem at hand, but in a larger context, namely the fundamental charge to help humanity.

In keeping with the Trickster theme, a joke summarizes the difference between pragmatic understanding and expedient deception.

After weeks of intensive calculations, a supercomputer concluded: 1 + 1 = 2.0001. A mathematician immediately declared, "That is obviously wrong. 1 + 1 = 2."

A research scientist said, "That is obviously a random error in the computer, so we can ignore this result – the previous million calculations gave 2.0000 as the answer."

An engineer shrugged, "Well, the answer is close enough, and we can still rely on our calculations for how much weight the bridge can carry."

Finally, an accountant asked, "What answer do we want?"[3]

The mathematician and scientist operate in the objective mode, the engineer and accountant in the pragmatic one. However, the engineer and accountant use pragmatic understanding in different ways: the engineer focuses on *efficacy* – what will solve the problem they confront and make the project work. By contrast, the accountant focuses on *expediency*, i.e., what will produce a specific, desired result, whether it is accurate or morally acceptable.

Passion and Wisdom

So, how do we avoid becoming a selfish, tricky grifter?

Our story points the way in a small detail – it is the **younger** monk who follows the rule, "Do not touch women," treating it as a fundamental prohibition, while the **older** one breaks it, out of genuine compassion. The difference here is not just a matter of age, but rather of training and experience. This is one reason virtually all professions and practices require apprenticeships: law graduates clerk for respected judges, plumbers spend four years as apprentices, and electricians five, while physicians spend longer or shorter lengths in residency. Learning skills and knowledge is half the task, the other being absorbing the ethos of the profession, practicing under the watchful eye of senior practitioners who are dedicated to fostering the next generation of professionals.

Experienced individuals are then (hopefully) less tempted than the novice by egocentric rule breaking. The ideal result is twofold: first is learning practical wisdom, i.e., heuristics about solving common problems in their profession. The second result is more difficult and usually takes longer – learning the wisdom of practice, i.e., when to follow the rules, and when to follow the spirit of the rules, the deeper intention behind them.

Carrying, Putting Down and Practicing

At the end of the story, the wise monk notes that the younger one is still carrying the beautiful woman – psychologically. The old monk explains that he put her down physically **and** mentally after he carried her across the river, and he has not thought about her since. Instead, he continues paying attention to whatever situation he encounters, and any problems that he might need to solve. His attention is like the river itself, which continues to flow along, encountering new obstructions along the way, and going around them, i.e., resolving them.

The young monk by contrast is like a large obstruction which has fallen across the river and now dams it, forming a pond. Metaphorically, he has fallen from the riverbank and now blocks the stream himself, because he was not carefully watching how he was stepping along the riverbank.

Another way to put this is that the old monk keeps practicing the pragmatic mode in an ongoing effort. Meanwhile, the young monk focuses on one situation, namely what to do about the young woman, even though it is now in the past. He applies the pragmatic mode once, but then no longer uses it, instead obsessing about the past problem.

Diagrams are again useful.[4]

We might call the attention involved in practicing a craft or profession *inflective*, because the individual "bends in" her focus to a specific situation. ("Bending in" is the root meaning of "inflect.") A prime example of inflection is an athlete practicing her sport, say tennis. She focuses her attention on the present game, but if she loses it, it is not the end of the world, because she remains aware of future games she will play, as well as past ones. They are all part of her ongoing practice of tennis and her continual process of learning. However, the situation changes if she is playing in a championship tournament. She has trained for it – it has been her goal – for some time. Here she operates in the objective mode, focusing her efforts and time on the upcoming tournament. If she loses, it can be difficult to deal with, but awareness of her ongoing practice of tennis gives her a broader perspective, the basis of good sportsmanship.

Another example of inflective attention is an actor performing a script, bending their attention and emotions into the character they portray in that moment. But then they move on to the character in a different situation, attending to the new words and feelings required by the script, or perhaps a totally new character in another script. A more familiar example of inflection occurs in conversations – we normally inflect our emotions into our speech, raising our voices when angry, softening our tone when with intimates.

The next tale expands these considerations to religious practice and mythic experience in general.

Notes

1 (Forest, 1996)
2 I discuss this at greater length in *Beyond the Hero*.
3 Something like this occurred with one of Intel's early Pentium computer chips which made rare, tiny errors in complex mathematical calculations. Intel originally dismissed the errors as of no practical importance, since they were so small and uncommon, but was forced to redesign the chip after public backlash.
4 We can diagram the process of practicing as: ⟨diagram⟩ The rectangle represents the situation as we understand it; the curvy arrow represents the practice the individual is involved in, here the pragmatic mode of comprehension. The individual attends to the present problem, as indicated by the arrowhead pointing to the rectangle. In the story, this would be meeting the woman who cannot cross the river. But the practitioner also remains aware of the ongoing practice represented by the large, wave-like arrow. By contrast, the younger monk's attention is more like the diagram for convergence:

⟨diagram⟩ Square boxes represent the different thoughts the young monk has as he continues to walk, but all his attention converges on the dark circle, namely the situation with the young woman in the past. The young monk actually uses the objective mode of comprehension, where all his attention converges upon a single objective or object.

Reference

Forest, H. (1996). *Wisdom Tales from Around the World*. Little Rock, August House Publishers.

Chapter 20

Judging Mythic Experiences

"Krishna and Arjuna"

Introduction

This narrative about Krishna and Arjuna is a simplified recounting of the
Bhagavad-Gita, from the *Mahabharata,* a sacred story in Hindu tradition. Stories
like the *Bhagavad-Gita* were orally transmitted for many generations before being
written down. That is, they qualify as folk stories.

The episode with Krishna and Arjuna stands out from the rest of the *Mahabharata* because it focuses on their conversation. Their exchange is quite philosophical especially for a war epic. The abstract nature of Krishna's and Arjuna's
interaction has a major advantage for us: it makes their insights more easily applicable to other cultures, including our modern Western one, just like "The Turtle Tower," and "Ta'aroa" we discussed in Chapters 6 and 8. The *Bhagavad-Gita*
focuses on how we can judge the truth of different spiritual beliefs and practices.
This is particularly useful in today's religious and ideological disputes which can
be as intense and dismaying as any ancient war epic. Although the topics Krishna
and Arjuna discuss are metaphysical, Krishna uses striking, poetic metaphors
which make the stories more applicable to everyday situations.

The Story[1]

*Long ago a great kingdom was torn apart by civil war. On a fateful day, two great
armies faced each other across a field. Prince Arjuna, the leader of one side, asked
his charioteer to take him into empty space between the two armies. There Arjuna
cried out, "I see my uncles, cousins, friends, and teachers on both sides. How can
I kill people I have known and loved all my life? It would be better for me to lie
down and be slain, rather than slay others."*

*His charioteer was none other than the god Krishna in human form, who gently
chided the Prince, "You forget that when you slay your enemies, you only kill their
bodies, because all souls are immortal, parts of the Eternal Divine."*

*Arjuna fell silent a moment and then asked, "If no one truly perishes, why fight
this battle? Should I not just contemplate the Eternal Divine?"*

DOI: 10.4324/9781003471028-24

"Such contemplation would be an action," Krishna explained. *"No living crea-ture can avoid acting and if you do not act to defend what is good and right, evil people will create strife and suffering – just as they have in your kingdom. Even I, the incarnation of the Ultimate, take action in the world to prevent evil from triumphing – as I am now doing. You must do your duty as a warrior, and fight in this righteous war, lest people consider you a coward."*

"Yet if I kill my enemies," Arjuna responded, *"even though they are evil, they are still my kin or dear friends. I shall grieve deeply, and justice or victory will be bitter."*

Krishna replied, *"That is why the enlightened man detaches from sorrow or joy, pain or pleasure. Doing so is not easy, but there are many ways to succeed."* Krishna then proceeded to describe four fundamental spiritual practices Arjuna could use – the Way (yoga) of Action, Meditation, Knowledge and Devotion.

After a lengthy discussion, Arjuna inquired, *"Of those spiritual practices, which is the best?"*

"The endpoint of all spiritual paths is the same," Krishna revealed. *"Which practice is better depends on the person. For someone actively engaged in the world like yourself, the yoga of action is best – the yoga of meditation or the yoga of knowledge would be arduous. However, for someone who is reflective and intro-spective, the yoga of knowledge or meditation would be most effective."*

"Some paths also go farther than others," Krishna added. *"Those who devoutly worship the ancestors are reborn in their realm, while they who revere the gods go to them. Those who meditate directly upon the Ultimate will experience union with it and be freed from the cycle of rebirth. And those who mock spiritual paths and believe only in the material world are reborn in realms of darkness and illusion."*

"Best of all," Krishna confided, *"is devotion to me because I am the Ultimate Divine. And those who love me, however wretched or sinful, I will love in return, so they can be saved."*

"My mind understands," Arjuna exclaimed, *"but not my heart. Show me the Eternal Divine that you are, that I may understand fully."*

"Many yearn to see the Ultimate I am," Krishna answered, *"but few have attained this wisdom. I will reveal myself to you because you are dear to me. And I will protect you because no mortal can see the Infinite and survive."*

Krishna then revealed himself. Arjuna was awed and overwhelmed. Arjuna beheld the world arising from Eternity Itself – all the gods, demons, people, animals and things of the world, like the branches of a great tree rooted in the Divine. Arjuna fell to the ground, overwhelmed by the vision, and begged Krishna to return to his famil-iar human form. When Krishna reappeared as Arjuna's friend, the Prince exclaimed, *"Forgive me, great Krishna for treating you as an ordinary person, because when you are with me in your human form, I forget that you are the All, the Infinite."*

"Arise, Arjuna," Krishna said gently. *"You are born a warrior, and I myself established the castes of priests, warriors, farmers and servants, with all their duties. So, fulfill your duty as a warrior, and vanquish your opponents, the enemies of righteousness."*

So, Arjuna mounted his chariot. With renewed devotion to Krishna, and strengthened by insight, Arjuna went resolutely into battle and prevailed, but his true victory was his new understanding of the divine in the world and the world in the divine.

Dismay

The story begins with a terrible civil war which pits family members and friends against each other. Arjuna leads one army, assisted by the god Krishna himself. This means Heaven is on Arjuna's side, but we can assume that Arjuna's opponents also claim the same thing. This makes both sides unwilling to compromise. Their civil war dramatizes the dynamics behind most of our contemporary conflicts, from cultural wars within a single nation, to religious wars between countries – each side believes that they are right, and that God, destiny or truth favors them.

Recognizing that he must kill friends and relatives in the opposing army, Arjuna is horrified, confused and uncertain about what to do. He is thrown from his familiar, privileged, princely peacetime life into a world of suffering and tragedy. He moves from a known realm to one unfamiliar and bewildering. This is the process of transcendence, the core of mythic experience. Arjuna faces an incomprehensible situation which overwhelms him, and yet compels his participation. These are the three characteristic features of a numinous experience, namely the *mysterium*, *tremendum* and *fascinans* we discussed previously: the experience is mystifying, overwhelming, and yet one we cannot escape.

Most numinous experiences are attributed to supernatural causes – ghosts, gods and demons. However, there is nothing supernatural about Arjuna's dismay. It is a human reaction to an all too human situation – killing friends and family. Most people have a similar reaction when reading news such as the 2022 Russian invasion of Ukraine and their accompanying war atrocities, reliving the Twin Towers terrorist attacks, or visiting a Holocaust death camp like Auschwitz. The crimes are beyond our understanding, terrifying, and yet also fascinating in a horrifying way. The shadow – the impulses and temptations we would rather not face in ourselves or other people – can be as numinous as the divine.

Krishna tries to assuage Arjuna's revulsion and dismay by explaining that the Prince does not really kill anybody, since souls are immortal. Krishna offers Arjuna a Big Picture, in which any situation, including killing friends and family, is but a small part of reality. The Western Christian equivalent would be something like, "This earthly suffering is nothing compared to eternity in heaven." In both cases, a religious doctrine integrates multiple experiences, including a painful, overwhelming one of war into a coherent narrative. This is the integration process characteristic of factual conclusions and the objective mode of comprehension.

Notice how Krishna shifts Arjuna from an **experience** of numinous mystery, i.e., overwhelming horror over the impending battle, to an **explanation** of it, i.e., that Arjuna does not really destroy people because souls are immortal. Surprisingly, the Prince does not automatically accept Krishna's explanation – Arjuna raises a question: if souls are immortal, and part of the Divine, then should he not just contemplate the Divine, without bothering to act in the illusory material world? Arjuna looks beyond Krishna's traditional explanation, to wonder about the doctrine's implications and consequences. This experience of wondering – curiosity and questioning – may seem completely different from Arjuna's numinous horror over the coming battle. But the underlying process is the same – looking into the unknown. Questioning the doctrine of reincarnation involves moving from traditional religious teachings to unfamiliar alternatives and the discomforting experience of doubt. The difference between horror over killing friends and relatives, on one side, and questioning traditional religious doctrines, on the other hand, lies in the intensity and scope of transcendence. This is analogous to the difference between annoyance and road rage.

While dramatic examples of transcendence come from numinous experiences, the basic instance is illustrated by a young child asking questions like, "Why is the sky blue?" (Or Arjuna questioning Krishna's discussion of reincarnation.) The child's question, "What is God?" and the wise man's answer, "God is a question, not an answer" arise from the same tectonic logic of transcendence.[2]

Judging Spiritual Approaches

In response to Arjuna's questioning, Krishna turns to a practical answer, asserting that if Arjuna does not act in the world, evil will take over, just like his enemies are trying to do in the civil war. He even warns Arjuna that people might think their Prince is a coward if he does not fight. Krishna switches from objective understanding to pragmatic comprehension. He moves away from assertions about objective reality such as, "Everyone has an immortal soul," or "Reincarnation really does occur," which can – and often does – lead to interminable arguing. ("Penguin Island" and "Crossing the River" in the last two chapters were good examples.) Instead, Krishna now emphasizes specific actions and consequences, e.g., "If you do not fight now, evil will triumph." He shifts the focus from facts to acts.

Arjuna follows Krishna's lead and switches to the pragmatic mode. Arjuna notes that if he followed Krishna's advice and went to war, killing his friends and relatives, the practical consequence is that he would be overcome by grief and guilt for the rest of his life. Nothing supernatural is involved here – just ordinary human reactions to the death and killing of people close to us. In Arjuna's case, the intensity is great enough to call everything into question.

Krishna responds by continuing his practical advice. He describes different spiritual approaches by which Arjuna can detach from worldly life and free himself from emotional distress, like his horror over the impending battle. In the process, Krishna summarizes the traditional Hindu spiritual approaches. These are the way (or "yoga") of meditation, action, knowledge and devotion.

Arjuna then asks Krishna a crucial question: which spiritual approach is the best? It is the same question many ask today when religions and ideologies collide.

Krishna explains that all spiritual approaches have the same goal, which is directly experiencing the Divine in all its fullness. Exactly what that is, Krishna describes later, but at this point he emphasizes that not all spiritual approaches work for everyone. The yoga of meditation, for instance, would be difficult for people naturally inclined towards action, and conversely, the yoga of action would be hard for introverted, contemplative individuals. The optimal spiritual approach depends on the individuals and their situations.

Moreover, Krishna adds, some spiritual approaches have inherent limitations. Those who faithfully devote themselves to the ancestors, he explains, are reborn in the realm of the ancestors, while those who devoutly worship the gods, go to their domain. I interpret this to mean that an individual's spiritual practices, whether worship of ancestors or gods, define what they consider to be the ultimate state of existence. So, when a person experiences a radical transformation, where an old life structure collapses and a new one emerges, that new life is limited by their concept of the optimal one, the divine. Thus, someone who believes only in the material world is limited to experiences of just such a world. On the other hand, Krishna adds, devotion to him can lead a person directly to the goal of all spiritual practices, directly experiencing the Ultimate Divine. This is because he, Krishna, is the incarnation of the Ultimate Divine, and he will love and help anyone devoted to Him to experience the Divine.

In other words, spiritual practices are like modes of transportation such as walking, cars, airplanes or the space shuttle. Some are more difficult to use than others – virtually everyone can walk or ride a car, while astronauts must train strenuously, and not everyone can qualify. Each transportation also has its limits – cars can take us farther than walking, airplanes even farther and faster, and spaceships yet beyond that. Best of all would be a transporter, like in the *Star Trek* TV series and movies, which could send virtually anyone almost anywhere – the equivalent of devotion to Krishna.

Krishna gives us a way of judging any specific religious practice: the more fully it fosters the process of transcendence – the experience of wonder, openness and awe – the more true-to mythic understanding that practice is. The approach also applies to beliefs, such as religious doctrines. The latter are spiritual practices: according to Hindu tradition, learning and correctly understanding doctrines constitute the "Way of Knowledge," a means to experience the Divine. In Western tradition, by contrast, we evaluate religious beliefs by whether they are factually true or not, e.g., "Does God exist? Do souls exist?" The more important way of judging doctrines, Krishna suggests, is determining whether believing God exists fosters the experience of transcendence. (Or the converse, "Does believing that God does not exist hinder the experience of transcendence?")

Arjuna and Analytical Psychology

The conversation between Krishna and Arjuna is reminiscent of those between Philemon and Jung,[3] with Philemon playing the role of the teacher, analogous to

Krishna in the story. And just as Jung interpreted his conversations with Philemon in psychological terms, we can translate Krishna's metaphysical discussion
into phenomenology, i.e., as descriptions of fundamental human experiences. As
we saw before in Chapters 7 and 8, with "The Navajo Story of Emergence," and
"Ta'aroa," we can interpret creation stories as metaphors for the fundamental structures of human experience. This is also the logic behind Jung interpreting medieval
alchemy texts and astrology not as metaphysical treatises, but descriptions of the
human experience of deep transformations.

For Krishna, the focus of all spiritual quests is experiencing the Ultimate Divine,
which we can interpret more generally as numinous experiences. Jung was one
of the first modern Western psychologists to seriously look at such experiences,
rather than dismiss them as subjective fantasies – what Freud regarded as regressed
psychological states. As Jung knew from his own life and his work with patients,
numinous experiences can trigger profound changes in people's lives. His attention
to mythic experiences, of course, went against secular, scientific, Western tradition,
although there has been increasing interest lately in altered consciousness.

Like Krishna, Jung discussed several different ways of fostering numinous
experiences, such as active imagination i.e., guided visualization exercises, as well
as dream interpretation, and explorations of indigenous cultures (including medieval European alchemical tradition). Jung's answer to the question of what method
works best was like Krishna's – different methods work for different people. How
do we determine whether a method works or not? That is, how do we know when
a mythic experience is true or not?

An insight in psychotherapy, for example, may seem to be a numinous revelation to an individual, but the realization could also be mistaken, an example of a
"false memory."[4] Krishna provides a succinct way of judging mythic experiences:
they are true, if they foster further experiences of transcendence, i.e., opening the
individual up to new perspectives and discoveries. In psychotherapy, this usually
takes the form of greater openness to what an individual has ignored or repressed,
whether that involves intimacy, memories of traumas, or mystical experiences.
Simply put, true mythic experiences foster individuation and ongoing growth in
life. Mistaken insights usually do not because they are like fascinating roadways
that turn out to be cul-de-sacs. To put it another way, beliefs and practices are true
to the mythic mode of comprehension when they are emancipatory or liberating in
everyday life, helping individuals expand their experience of the world.[5]

By this point, my discussion has turned into a philosophical exposition and
risks becoming boring. Arjuna had a similar reaction and, in the story, wants something more than intellectual understanding. He therefore asks Krishna to reveal his
divine nature, and Krishna agrees. Arjuna then has a dramatic mystical experience:
he apprehends the Ultimate Divine and sees the whole world arising from that primordial unity – gods, goddesses, souls, people, animals, trees and everything else.
Each is a limited manifestation of the Divine and remains part of it. Arjuna feels
overwhelmed by Krishna's divine glory and begs Krishna to resume his mundane
human form as Arjuna's familiar friend.

Arjuna's revelation illustrates another important point. Although we usually think of Hinduism and other Eastern traditions as mystical and otherworldly, focused on transcendent experiences, Arjuna's conversation with Krishna emphasizes that the mundane world is equally important because it is part of the Divine – the everyday world arises from the Divine, and the latter permeates the former. This is a good description of experiencing mystery-in-the-mundane, the core of transcendence, moving from the familiar to the unknown, grappling with the tension between the two. Focusing only on numinous experience gives us mysticism, while focusing on mundane life gives us materialism, but neither by itself is transcendence. The latter involves the tension between both, moving from one to the other.

If a spiritual approach fosters authentic experiences of transcendence, including in mundane life, the practice is true-to mythic understanding. This gives us a pluralism of different religious beliefs and practices, but does not lead us to relativism, where any approach is true. We judge mythic beliefs and practices by a specific and culture-independent criterion – namely what is true-to the fundamental logic of transcendence.

Religious pluralism requires tolerance for multiple religious beliefs. The reason is that intolerance inhibits and even destroys the experience of exploration, wonder and awe. The tolerance required is more than letting others pursue their own religion without interference. The practice of transcendence requires skill and thus training – education **in** transcendence. Here we must distinguish instruction **in a** particular religion, from instruction **for any** religion. We usually think of religious education as indoctrination in a particular religion. Education for transcendence is much broader and more basic.

A surprisingly good analogy comes from teaching science. The usual focus is on the content of science, what science asserts to be objectively true. However, what is even more important is learning how scientists come to their conclusions. This requires instruction in the objective, factual mode of comprehension, e.g., how to collect, evaluate and integrate evidence into a conclusion – and then be willing to change the claim when new data appears. The content of science education changes, as scientists discover new evidence. However, the methodology – the objective mode of comprehension – remains the same. In a similar way, traditional religious education focuses on specific narratives and doctrines – the content of a religious tradition. More fundamental is training in the experience of transcendence, and especially how we can foster and recognize experiences of the numinous in everyday life.

Tolerance and freedom of religion are vital in today's multicultural world, but even more crucial is the freedom to **pursue** transcendence, and the education needed to succeed. This is freedom **for** religion, and not freedom **from** religion.

After their long discussion and Arjuna's vision of Krishna, Arjuna resumes his duty as a warrior, and leads his army into battle. So, his story ends with him following familiar, traditional roles and rules. We might ask why he does not question the caste system that tells him he must go to war and kill people. Arjuna seems to abandon the process of transcendence – looking beyond the familiar.

There are, however, very real practical factors compelling him to do so. If Arjuna constantly questioned everything, he would not be ready when the enemy attacked. Recall that his entire conversation with Krishna occurs when the two of them are in-between the two armies, on the verge of starting battle.

Returning to worldly conflict is perhaps the most difficult challenge of mythic understanding. We may be clear that the experience of transcendence demands religious and ideological tolerance, but not everyone supports the latter. Like Arjuna, we must sometimes return to deal with intransigent adversaries. The next story highlights the problem.

Notes

1 (Prabhavananda and Isherwood, 1975), (Arnold, 1970)
2 (Daoud, 2015)
3 (Jung et al., 1963)
4 (Scoboria et al., 2017)
5 (Apel, 1984)

References

Apel, K.-O. (1984). *Understanding and Explanation: A Transcendental-pragmatic Perspective*. Cambridge, Mass., MIT Press.

Arnold, E. (1970). *The Song Celestial, or, Bhagavad-Gita: (from the Mahabharata)*. Wheaton, Illinois, The Theological Publishing House.

Daoud, K. (2015). *The Meursault Investigation*. Place of publication not identified, BrightSummaries.com.

Jung, C. G., G. Adler and R. F. C. Hull (2014). *Collected Works of C.G. Jung. Volume 20; General Index*. Princeton, NJ, Princeton University Press.

Prabhavananda and C. Isherwood (1975). *The Song of God, Bhagavad-Gita*. London, Dent.

Scoboria, A., K. A. Wade, D. S. Lindsay, T. Azad, D. Strange, J. Ost and Ira E. Hyman (2017). "A Mega-analysis of Memory Reports from Eight Peer-reviewed False Memory Implantation Studies." *Memory (Hove)* **25**(2): 146–163.

Chapter 21

Transcendence and the Mythic Mode

"Moses Part II"

Introduction

We previously discussed *Exodus* in Chapter 12, where we focused on its two fundamental paradigms of truth – being true-to an oath, i.e., faithfulness; and second, being true-to the world, i.e., fact. I turn now to look at what *Exodus* reveals about mythic experiences. From the events at Mount Sinai onward, *Exodus* illustrates the evolution of mythic experiences and their connection to religious faith. *Exodus* also reveals common errors we make in mythic understanding and how these mistakes underlie many violent and intractable conflicts today.

The Story[1]

After leaving Egypt, Moses led his people to Mount Sinai, where God Himself descended upon the summit with smoke, lightning and earthquake. God declared, "I am the Lord God who has brought you out of Egypt" and then proclaimed the 10 Commandments. At the foot of the mountain, the people fled in terror and begged Moses to be their intermediary with God, so they did not have to deal directly with Him. Moses agreed and went up to the summit. There God told him more laws that His people were to follow – laws about property and theft, marriage and murder, servants and sabbaths. Moses wrote them down, returned to the people, and recounted God's laws to them, asking if the people agreed to follow them. When the people promised, Moses wrote God's laws down in the Book of the Covenant.

Moses returned to the summit of the mountain, and stayed with God for 40 days, in which time God told Moses further laws that the people were to follow. Moses wrote them down, and they were extensive and detailed: if a man stole an ox, he must return it with another, and if he could not, because he had disposed of the stolen ox, then he must give five oxen to the owner; the Ark of the Covenant was to be made of acacia, two-and-a-half-cubits long, and one-and-a-half cubits wide and high. . . . Finally, God gave Moses the stone tablets on which He Himself wrote the 10 Commandments.

Moses was gone so long, the people despaired that he would not return, and so at the urging of Aaron, Moses' brother, they molded a Golden Calf, which

DOI: 10.4324/9781003471028-25

they worshiped. When God saw what the people were doing, He flew into a rage and threatened to kill everyone, but Moses managed to mollify Him. Then Moses descended from the mountain and saw for himself his people dancing around the Golden Calf. He angrily destroyed the idol, and the Tablets upon which God himself had written the Commandments. Moses then summoned all the people who had remained loyal to God, rejecting the Golden Calf. When the faithful gathered around him, Aaron among them, Moses told the people that God commanded each man among them to draw his sword, and kill the unfaithful, whether brother, companion, or neighbor.

After thousands perished, Moses went back up to Mount Sinai to ask for God's forgiveness on behalf of his people. God forgave them but promised a later punishment to the people for breaking their Covenant with him. He also instructed Moses in further laws that the people were to follow. Finally, God wrote the Commandments on two more stone Tablets, and gave them to Moses.

When Moses returned to his people, he had them build the Ark of the Covenant, following God's instructions. Then Moses placed the Tablets in the Ark and wherever the people went, from then on, they carried the Ark with them. As they moved from place to place, Moses pitched his tent apart from all the people. Periodically God would visit Moses there, where the two would converse like friends. One day, Moses asked to see God in all His glory. God warned Moses that this would be fatal to any mortal, and to protect Moses, God put him in a cleft in a rock, and when He went past Moses God turned his Face away from Moses to spare him.

The people wandered in the wilderness for many years, which was God's punishment for disobeying Him and worshiping the Golden Calf. Along the way, they fought with numerous kingdoms, but with God's help, they prevailed. In some lands, they slew men, women and children, while in others, they enslaved survivors, or took virgin girls for brides. Finally arriving in the Promised Land, they defeated the Canaanites in a great battle, and claimed their homeland.

Mythic Understanding and Transcendence

When God reveals Himself in divine glory at the summit of Mount Sinai, the people are terrified and flee. Yet they are also filled with wonder and awe and so they constantly turn back to stare at the tumult atop Mount Sinai. The experience of overwhelming yet fascinating mystery is the hallmark of mythic experience as we discussed previously. It is the *mysterium, tremendum* and *fascinans* of numinous encounters.

God's initial numinous appearance atop Mount Sinai gives the people an **experience** of divine mystery. God then speaks and identifies Himself as the Lord God who brought the people out of Egypt. Here He **explains** who He is, shifting from the **experience** of mystery to an **explanation** of it. This is a move from mythic comprehension to factual understanding. God then begins reciting the 10 Commandments, further explaining what is involved in keeping the Covenant with Him. This is an exposition of the precepts and principles the people are to follow.

After proclaiming the 10 Commandments **orally**, God has Moses ascend alone to the summit of Mount Sinai and then **write** down the detailed rules God gives him. The shift from oral to written communication is epochal. Oral commandments must be short and general because we cannot accurately remember long lists of complicated rules. Switching to written rules, by contrast, makes possible an infinite number of detailed rules, which God promptly provides Moses, as extensively described in *Leviticus*, the next Book of the Bible. Moreover, with oral rules, there is always some doubt as to what God said, human memory being fallible. With written rules, there is much less leeway for doubt and discussion, and more temptation to dogma and orthodoxy.

Moses is gone so long at the summit with God, his people at the bottom begin to despair. Having one numinous encounter with God, they yearn for another experience of transcendence. So strong is this need for mystery and wonder, the people violate the Covenant they just made with God and build a Golden Calf to worship. This thirst for experiences of transcendence is a powerful human characteristic, clear throughout human history in art and architecture, from prehistoric cave art and megalithic monuments.

Secularists often dismiss mythic experiences as subjective, mistaken, primitive and superstitious. However, devaluing mythic experience in this manner has an instructive precedent in many religions: they condemned and suppressed sexual drives and experiences. Such an ascetic tendency is a traditional part of many religions, whereas dismissing or repressing mythic experiences is a relatively new cultural development. Psychoanalysts have long pointed out the psychological effects of repressing sexual desires, such as projecting them on other people or generating "neurotic" symptoms. Only now do we discover the many consequences of repressing **mythic** experience. With no conscious celebration of mythic experiences in shared quests, rituals and gatherings, the yearning for transcendence takes indirect forms, especially the conviction that God is on our side, and everybody else is wrong. Human hunger for transcendence easily inflames religious and partisan convictions and heightens conflicts. This is the "return of the repressed" except involving mythic yearnings, not just sexual ones and provoking societal conflicts, not just intrapsychic ones. As the next event in *Exodus* illustrates the consequences can be intensely destructive.

Exaltation

When God sees the people worshiping the Golden Calf, He flies into a rage and threatens to kill everyone, but Moses manages to placate Him. Then when Moses descends from the mountain and sees for himself his people dancing around the Golden Calf, he, too, becomes enraged – enough to destroy the Golden Calf and the Tablets on which God Himself had written the Commandants.

Moses next orders the people who remained faithful to God to kill all those who had worshiped the Golden Calf. Moses explains that God commanded the massacre of the apostates, although *Exodus* contains no explicit reference to God doing so. Quite the contrary, God earlier had spared the people for building the Golden Calf when Moses begged him to do so – something that subsequent religious or ideological zealots forget: God did not kill the apostates.

How are we to understand Moses' massacre? A short explanation is that it reflects the emotional power of mythic experience. When Moses descends from Mount Sinai, for instance, *Exodus* describes his face as "shining." Metaphorically speaking, Moses has become filled with God's glory. This is the original meaning of "enthusiasm," from the Greek root meaning, "to be filled with God." It is being "possessed" by divine energy, and not being in control of oneself, a kind of temporary insanity. It is **exaltation**, perhaps the fiercest form of passion and emotion. Exaltation inspires idealism and noble deeds but also atrocities. After all, if God is on our side, it is tempting to wreak havoc on our enemies – the stubborn or perverse unbelievers. Fear of exaltation and what it prompts people to do was one motivation for the Western Enlightenment in the 17th and 18th century, after the atrocities of European religious wars made all mythic experiences seem primitive, dangerous and contagious.

However, exaltation is the antithesis of transcendence and reverses the tectonic logic of mythic understanding. Instead of moving from the mundane to the numinous, looking up to mystery with wonder, we move from the numinous to the mundane, looking down in disdain. This is **condescendence**, not transcendence and when we devalue or dismiss our opponents, it is easier to dispose of them.

What makes condescendence even more tempting is the duality inherent in transcendence, the difference between the familiar and **not** familiar. This is the basic cognitive process of **negation**. And one of the most consequential examples of negation is *"us versus not-us,"* i.e., *"us versus them,"* which motivates suspicion of foreign immigrants and prejudice against unfamiliar ethnic groups.

The key role of negation in mythic experience helps explain a striking feature of the 10 Commandments – 8 out of the 10 rules are **prohibitions**, i.e., negations. These include, "Thou shalt have no other God before me," "Thou shalt not kill," and "Thou shalt not commit adultery." (Only two commandments are formulated in a positive way, "Honor thy mother and father," and "Honor the sabbath." The meaning of the last two injunctions, however, also involve prohibitions – on the sabbath, do not cook, do not conduct business, or do not ride animals. And honoring parents means not swearing at them, disobeying, or mocking them.) As we discussed in Chapters 7 and 8, with "The Navajo Story of Emergence," and "Ta'aroa Creates the World," transcendence and negation are two forms of the same process: transcendence is "Not-this, but everything out there."

The emphasis on negation and prohibition in many religions often extends into social policies, such as prohibiting dancing, music and festivities, prohibiting theft by amputating the hands of thieves, rather than discouraging theft in the first place with social justice and education.

Exaltation and negation in turn often lead to another error we commonly make with mythic understanding – universalization. When we are in a state of exaltation, it is easy to mistake our current beliefs and rules to be true for everyone – with no exceptions. We generalize our convictions. *Exodus* provides a good illustration when God pronounces the 10 Commandments from atop Mount Sinai. This makes it easy to mistake the 10 Commandments for universal laws applicable to everyone, everywhere for all time, rather than rules which apply only to those who adopt the Covenant with God. Such universalization is the converse of adopting an oath or covenant: it is imposing an oath on **other** people, rather than on everything **we** do.

Idol and Ark

Idols like the Golden Calf represent another form of mythic experience. Today, when we say someone uses idols, it is usually meant pejoratively. However, there are different ways we can approach idols. First, we can experience a numinous **presence** as we behold the idol, which is often explained by saying that the idol **is** the god, or a god is **in** the idol. (This is the usual meaning of "idolatry," worshiping a statue **as** a god.) We could also explain the numinous experience by saying that the idol is a **re-presentation** of a god rather than a presentation. As a representation, the idol is analogous to a portrait, a visual or verbal description which might be literal or metaphoric.

There is a third way we can approach the idol – not as the presentation or representation of a god but treating the object as a means of **transportation** to the divine, a **portal** to the numinous. Icons in Orthodox Christian tradition and mandalas in Tibetan Buddhism provide good examples. They include images of saints or Buddhas, which are not meant to be accurate representations of individuals. Nor are they considered sacred in themselves, like an idol or relics. While icons often illustrate precepts of their religions, that is not their principal function. They are rather used as foci for prayer or meditation – they function as tools for experiencing a connection with God or the Ultimate. They are not portraits but rather **practices** intended to foster our experience of transcendence. These icons are not experiences, explanations, or expositions of the numinous, but rather **exercises** to help us experience wonder and awe in everyday life. They are telescopes making the transcendent visible.

After destroying the Golden Calf and the Tablets, Moses has his people do penance and returns to the summit of Mount Sinai to ask for God's forgiveness. God does so and then writes the 10 Commandments on two more stone Tablets, instructing Moses on how to build the Ark which will contain them. The importance of the Ark is reflected in the length of instructions about building it. For the rest of their journeys, Moses and his people carry the Ark with them.

The Ark reflects another form of numinous experience, and it can be used as part of a practice that evokes mythic comprehension. The Ark does not contain God, like an idol might. Nor is it a representation of God, depicting or describing God. Neither is it an exposition of doctrines or rules – it contains the Tablets with the Commandments, but the Ark does not display them for all to see or expound on. Quite the opposite, the Tablets are kept hidden, in the Ark, which is concealed by a curtain in the Tabernacle of worship. The Ark conveys no information, but rather helps carry people into an experience of the numinous. This is, of course, the original meaning of the word "ark" – it is a mode of transportation, like Noah's Ark, or a chest used to carry belongings during transport. The Ark helps people move from the mundane to the numinous, and back again.

We can interpret many of the practices and rituals prescribed in *Exodus* (and *Leviticus*) in an analogous way – the practices are Arks that can carry us between the numinous and the mundane, or to put it another way, to bring the numinous into the mundane, and vice versa. The Sabbath evening meal, for instance, takes a mundane, everyday event, but ideally evokes a sense of divine presence, bringing down numinous mystery into a familiar routine. The Eucharist in Christian tradition similarly takes a mundane event, eating bread and drinking wine, then infuses it with a numinous mystery.

Overemphasizing the mundane or the numinous leads to common errors in mythic experience. Idolatry, for example, involves equating a material object like a statue with numinous mystery, and the mundane can then eclipse the divine. Dogmatism makes an analogous error: we take a narrative or doctrine, and make it fixed and holy, just like an idol. This is the process of fossilization, taking a living body of beliefs and turning it into something dead and fixed, but ancient and thus mysterious. The result is ideology, another form of an idol.

After the ancient Israelites resume their journey, Moses pitches his tent apart from everyone else, and periodically God visits Moses there in person. At one point, Moses asks to see God in all His glory, just like Arjuna did with Krishna, in the last chapter. God warns Moses that no human can survive such an experience and protects Moses by putting him in a cleft in a rock. And when God passes Moses, He turns His face away from Moses to shield him further. The theme is a common one in mythology around the world – direct encounters with divinities can be deadly to mere mortals. In psychological terms, numinous experiences can overwhelm us. A good example comes from the "Jerusalem syndrome." Here individuals visiting Jerusalem for the first time feel emotionally overwhelmed by a place holy to three world religions. Individuals often have no previous psychiatric history, and yet in extreme cases, individuals become psychotic, identifying with a biblical figure, and acting as if they were that person. Most individuals spontaneously recover. Similar experiences have been reported in Mecca. Less dramatic, secular forms of this phenomena occur with the "Stendhal syndrome" where an individual may be overcome by seeing art they find spectacularly beautiful: they suffer from palpitations, chest pains and fainting but spontaneously recover.[2]

The ancient Israelites carried the Ark with them as they travel, and this provides another good metaphor for how mythic narratives function. We carry them wherever we go. They are the stories that we initially apply to any situation we find ourselves – just like the 10 Commandments.

In *Exodus*, the ancient Israelites continue their journey, fighting hostile tribes and kingdoms along the way, until they arrive at the Promised Land. With careful planning and preparation, they invade and conquer the territory, establishing their own kingdom. After all, God promised His people this specific land as part of his

Covenant and if people were already there, they must leave. The killing during the invasion of Canaan also recalls the execution of those who worshipped the Golden Calf. Both are a consequence of the mythic mode: the conquered Canaanites are the Other, the outsiders – defined by their **not** being the people of God. That fundamental negation obliterates their humanity. The same applies to all the ancient Israelites who worshiped the Golden Calf. They were oath breakers, who betrayed their Covenant and the community of the Covenant.

However, there is one important difference between the two events: Moses' rage over the Golden Calf is directed at his own people who broke their Covenant, the same one everyone else took. The invasion of Canaan, by contrast, was directed at foreigners who may have never heard of the Covenant of Israel.

After their numinous interactions with God, the ancient Israelites return to all-too-human struggle and conflict in the everyday world. This is reminiscent of the ending to "Krishna and Arjuna," where Arjuna returns as a warrior to the civil war about to begin and proceeds to kill his enemies. The fundamental motivation in both narratives is the longing for home – a quest to find it in *Exodus*, and in Arjuna's case, to defend it.

The experience of home arises from the last fundamental comprehension mode to discuss. The home mode is paradoxically the most familiar and yet perhaps the hardest to understand – we are immersed in the home mode of comprehension most of the time, and so do not reflect on it. We take it for granted, just like home. So, attempting to understand it turns us into the proverbial centipede trying to figure out how it walks – we stumble on our hundred feet. An even greater problem is how home and the mythic intersect. God promised the people a specific homeland during a nearly overwhelming numinous experience atop Mount Sinai.

The next story is a heartwarming introduction to the complexities of the home mode of comprehension.

Notes

1   (Bible, 1979)
2   (Bar-El et al., 2000)

References

Bar-El, Y., R. Durst, G. Katz, J. Zislin, Z. Strauss and H. Y. Knobler (2000). "Jerusalem Syndrome." *British Journal of Psychiatry* **176**(1): 86–90.
Bible (1979). *The Holy Bible, New King James Version*, Thomas Nelson.

Chapter 22

The Place and Practice of Home
"Baucis and Philemon"

Introduction

Although charming and seemingly simple, this ancient Greek tale gives us a deep look into the experience of home and the home mode of understanding. Home is (ideally) where we can sleep without fear, break bread with those we love and converse with people we like or consider family. This is the type of understanding we need today: besieged by terrorists, rising sea levels and immigrants entering our neighborhoods, how can we experience home in a world like ours today?

The story points the way with a key insight: there is a difference between the *experience* of home and the *practice* of home. The latter is the process of creating the former, such as parents making a home for their children. But it is also the only way in which everyone can make the planet into a home.

The Story[1]

Long ago, there lived an old couple who had no children and were quite poor. The wife was named Baucis, and the husband Philemon, and they were content with their lot, because they had been married for many years, and loved each other very deeply. They lived in a small hut just outside a village of wealthy people. One day two strangers came by, but no one in the village would welcome them, because they were too busy.

When the two travelers arrived at the home of Baucis and Philemon, the old couple welcomed them with open arms. They brought out all the food they had – black bread, old cheese and new wine. As they shared their meager fare with the two strangers, the old couple was astonished to find that the bread, cheese and wine were the very finest they had ever tasted. Furthermore, no matter how much bread and cheese they ate, or wine they drank, the food never ran out. The old couple realized that the two strangers were no ordinary humans. At that moment, Zeus and Hermes revealed themselves.

"We thank you for your hospitality," Zeus said. "No one else in the village offered us kindness, and they will pay for their selfishness." As he spoke, water rose and flooded the village, forcing everyone to flee. Then the old couple's humble hut

DOI: 10.4324/9781003471028-26

was transformed into a temple, with tall, golden columns. "For your kindness,"
Zeus went on, "name anything you wish, and you will have it."

Baucis and Philemon turned to each other, and conversed quietly for a moment.
Then they told Zeus, "The one boon we ask is that when the time comes for us to
leave this life, we both die at the same time, so neither will have to bury the other
and grieve."

So it was that Baucis and Philemon continued to live in the temple for several
more years. Then one day, as they sat together just outside their home, they trans-
formed into two magnificent trees, whose branches intertwined over the temple,
their leaves murmuring of eternal love and devotion.

Hospitality

Like many protagonists in "elder tales," Baucis and Philemon are old and poor at
the beginning of their story.[2] They have few material possessions, and even less
chance of improving their situation in the future. Yet when two travelers come
calling, seeking shelter for the night, the old couple welcomes the strangers and
shares what simple food they have with their guests. By contrast, the neighbors of
Baucis and Philemon are rich, yet refuse any hospitality to the two travelers. The
pattern is all-too-familiar today, when it is easy for us to walk by a poor person sitting on a city street, just as intent on our business as the rich neighbors were in the
story. Our reaction to Baucis and Philemon today is likely to be perplexity at their
unusual generosity.

However, Baucis and Philemon follow the customs of most cultures for most of
human history, namely, offering hospitality to strangers. Nomadic hunter-gatherer
bands – the original human society – routinely shared their resources with other
groups they came across if they needed food, even though they were strangers to
each other. In following original human culture with their hospitality to strangers,
Baucis and Philemon are not just old individually, but culturally, too.

The question of why Baucis and Philemon are so generous is the opposite
of the real puzzle: why are their rich neighbors – and most of us today – so
inhospitable?

Baucis and Philemon's generosity to strangers highlights an important aspect
of the home mode of comprehension. To experience home, someone must provide
it. Although we often identify home with a particular place, like a house, and with
key people, like a family, the experience of home is a result of specific actions. We
can, for instance, make an impersonal office cubicle into a more home-like work-
place, by putting up favorite and often idiosyncratic knickknacks. These actions
are part of the **practice of home**. The practice is so basic even very young children use it: they often carry a special blanket or teddy bear with them, to comfort
them in new or strange situations. The special, almost-magical object creates home
around them.

Significantly, there is no single good term for the practice of home. "Hospitality" seems too superficial. "Sheltering" is incomplete. "Homemaking" has

unfortunately taken on pejorative connotations today, while "homesteading" implies a permanent settlement, which home does not. "Nesting," in turn, usually refers to animals more than people.

The reason I think we have no good term for the practice of home is that we take that practice for granted. Here the ancient Greeks provide an instructive metaphor. Hestia was the goddess of the hearth fire, the center of a home in ancient Greece. She was one of the original Olympians, like Zeus and Athena, but she voluntarily gave up her seat, so that Dionysus could join the pantheon of 12 divinities. Unlike the other Olympians, Hestia had no need for fame or worship. In fact, she had no temples, because every home contained a shrine to her – the simple hearth fire. We take home for granted as well as the practice of home – which Hestia personified.

The practice of home reflects a fundamental and unique human instinct. The primordial example of creating home is parenting – providing a home for off-spring – which many other animals do. But humans have extended such care to include distant kin, neighbors and other people's children. In the ultimate practice of home, many people have risked their lives rescuing strangers from peril.

Sufficience and Cherishing

When Baucis and Philemon share a meal with the two strangers, the old couple are astonished to find that their old bread, cheese and cheap wine are the best food they have ever tasted, and furthermore, their scant supplies never run out. This is a common event in folk stories – an act of kindness is magically rewarded. But it also reflects a familiar psychological event – eating with other people is more satisfying than doing so alone. Yet there is genuine magic involved, as the story quickly dramatizes.

Zeus and Hermes[3] reveal themselves to the old couple and offer to grant any wish that Baucis and Philemon may have, at the same time they transform Baucis and Philemon's humble abode into a magnificent temple. We have here a surprising juxtaposition of a humble home and a numinous reality – two gods and a numinous temple.

After husband and wife confer with each other (something that rarely occurs with midlife tales), they ask for a modest boon: they want to live together as they have done for years, until the day they die, and they will die at the same time, so neither will be left alone and bereaved.

The request is astonishing – it is the equivalent of winning a mega lottery and then turning the fortune down. Consciously choosing a familiar if simple situation as home in this manner is common in "elder tales," folktales about "old" people, but it rarely occurs in stories about youth, or the middle-aged where greed or fool-ish requests are more common.[4] Here Baucis and Philemon accurately reflect three crucial psychological developments in the elder years.

First, they reflect on their home life and home story and **consciously affirm** it. They could have any other life they wish, courtesy of Zeus and Hermes, but choose the one they already have with each other. In other words, they transform their **home story** into their **favorite story**. Second, Baucis and Philemon affirm that their life together gives them all they need – it is **sufficient** for them. They consciously turn down what many of us would consider an ideal situation – wishing for anything they might want. They change the tectonic logic of home from **presence** to **sufficience**. As we discussed previously, presence is the WYSIWYG principle – "What You See Is What You Get." We assume that what we see is all of reality. Sufficience is the principle of WISIWIN – "What I See Is What I Need" (or even more specifically, "What We See Is All We Need"). Third, Baucis and Philemon demonstrates what Erik Erickson called "ego-integrity."[5] It is consciously affirming a life just as we lived it, after coming to terms with its imperfections, disappointments and regrets. It is a central task for the last years of life, and it is fundamental to the wisdom we ideally develop in later life.

Ultimately, the practice which makes a home story a favorite one is **cherishing**. The beloved is usually another person, but it can also include a place. Cherishing another person contrasts sharply with infatuation, i.e., falling head over heels in love with another person. In the latter, we see an ideal in the beloved. The magic of falling in love inevitably involves illusion – which is why we use the metaphor of falling into love or floating on clouds for being in love. Cherishing comes later if it does at all and requires learning about and embracing the beloved's faults and quirks, too. Only if we can accept the beloved, just as they are, I might add, can we finally accept ourselves and our lives, just as we lived them. Cherishing is the candlelight which can make everything look magical,[6] in contrast to infatuation which is more like the magnificence of dawn that inevitably fades.

We usually attribute love and cherishing to what or whom we love: we cherish the beloved because they are kind, witty and beautiful. Would not anyone cherish our beloved? We rarely credit ourselves for cherishing something or someone, e.g., "I cherish him or her because I am a kind and loving person at heart (and so are they)." But cherishing is a practice and skill we can consciously apply to different people or things. This is a central insight behind the Christian motto, "Love thy neighbor as thyself," and similar injunctions from other religions. Loving self and others takes effort and repeated practice. Cherishing anyone, including ourselves, is a skill and accomplishment.

This is the importance of the practice of home with cherishing at its core. Both arise from deep emotional and instinctual roots: the practice of home is archetypal. At the same time, the practice of home is something we can learn, exercise and teach, like singing. Everyone can sing but becoming a successful opera singer requires training, talent and hard work. Similarly, everyone can speak, but we all can benefit from practicing public speaking and rhetoric. The difference with the practice of home is that we recognize the importance of training in singing and speaking, but not its equal importance in the practice of home. We take the latter for granted, often assuming that it is a personal trait, which does not have wider societal implications. However, the practice of home sustains tolerance in society. Ideally, we accept people who disagree with our basic moral or religious convictions, the way we (ideally) tolerate difficult family members and in-laws. Such tolerance takes effort and perseverance ("tolerance" comes from the root words which mean "to struggle").

The Trees of Life

At the end of the story. Baucis and Philemon turn into two trees, with entwining branches. Trees provide shelter to all who come to it, whether they are nesting birds, or humans seeking respite from the sun. Trees do not care what home stories the creatures have, simply providing a basic home story for all. It is the epitome of hospitality, the practice of home. And just as large trees often anchor the ecology of a whole forest, the practice of home anchors human society.

A campfire provides a perfect metaphor to summarize this discussion of the home mode of comprehension. At the dawn of human history, fire provided protection against wild beasts and gave people the ability to cook – which made food easier to eat, more nutritious and prevented diseases, compared to raw food.[7] Fire, in short, transformed any location into a temporary home. Providing food and shelter, of course, is the fundamental characteristic of any home and the same is true with home stories. They provide us psychological sanctuary and sustenance.

Fire-making is independent of any place or person. It is a practice, a skill that people can (and had to) learn. The same is true about the practice of home: the skill to create fire, and thus shelter and food. Indeed, fire-**making** is the only thing that distinguishes humans from other animals. As we now know, other animals use tools, solve abstract problems and use what seems close to language. Some animals even **use** fire deliberately, e.g., taking a burning brand and carrying it to a new location, spreading fire to make prey animals flee and thus become vulnerable.[8] But only humans can **make** fire at will, not depending upon lightning strikes or other spontaneous sources of flame.

Fire, of course, can be dangerous, especially when used carelessly. The same applies to the home mode of understanding: errors can be catastrophic. Another ancient Greek tale explains why.

Notes

1 (Bulfinch, 1913)
2 I discuss this further in *In the Ever After.*
3 Note the pairing of Zeus, the paramount Olympian God, and Hermes, the trickster. Occurring frequently in Greek mythology, they illustrate the connection between the Trickster and the primary deity, found in aboriginal cultures around the world, as we discussed in Chapter 10.
4 I discuss this at greater length with *In the Ever After* and *Once Upon a Midlife.*
5 (Erickson, 1980).
6 Other stories show that cherishing is also the key to understanding spiritual enlightenment in both Eastern and Western traditions.
7 Indeed, it is difficult to survive on a diet of only raw food, in contrast to animals. Humans evolved with fire and now we depend on it.
8 (Coghlan, 2018)

References

Bulfinch, T. (1913). *Bulfinch's Mythology: The Age of Fable; The Age of Chivalry; Legends of Charlemagne*. New York, Grosset & Dunlap.

Coghlan, A. (2018). "The Birds that Steal Fire." *New Scientist* **237**(3160): 4–4.

'Erickson, E. H. (1980). *Identity and the Life Cycle*. New York, Norton.

Chapter 23

Absolute Truth

"Procrustes"

Introduction

This horrifying story comes from ancient Greece and dramatizes fundamental errors we can make with the home mode of comprehension. Most people find the tale repellent precisely because these breaches in the home comprehension mode threaten our basic sense of human decency. To put it another way, our experience of home defines what we consider human or monstrous, normal or sick, right or wrong.

The Story[1]

Once upon a time, a man named Procrustes lived by a road that led to the famous pilgrimage site of Eleusis. Whenever Procrustes encountered a traveler, he invited the stranger to his home, offering him a meal and a night's lodging. He told his visitors that he had a magic bed which always fit the person who lay in it. But when the guest lay down to sleep, Procrustes would reveal the "magic." If his guest was shorter than the bed, Procrustes stretched the person until he fit. If taller, Procrustes would cut off the person's feet, so the hapless traveler matched the bed. To make sure his victim did not fit, Procrustes had two beds, one extremely short and one extremely long. In this way Procrustes killed all his guests. The hero Theseus finally ended Procrustes' crimes, by putting Procrustes on one of the villain's own beds, forcing Procrustes to fit and thus killing him.

Home and Strangers

Procrustes meets travelers outside his home and offers them dinner and a safe place to stay for the night. Both are core elements in the experience of home and Procrustes follows the traditions of his time in extending hospitality to travelers. He is just like Baucis and Philemon in the previous chapter except Procrustes does not have hospitality on his mind. He plans to murder his guests.

Why does he? Ancient Greek myths are full of horrifying events, somewhat like social media on the Internet today. If we take a psychological view, several

DOI: 10.4324/9781003471028-27

details of the story help explain Procrustes' behavior. First, he must work for a living, as a smith or innkeeper, depending upon the version of the story. At the same time, he sees many pilgrims going to Eleusis who were well off enough to stop working and go on a long journey. We can imagine that Procrustes felt jealous of the pilgrims. In one version of the story, Procrustes is even a son of Poseidon, the god of the sea, which would make the situation even more aggravating for Procrustes – how could mere mortals be better off than him, a demi-god? Today, similar feelings of envy – often with despair – fuel resentment toward immigrants and refugees: why do they get government support, when native citizens – really, neglected demi-gods – lose their jobs because of foreign factories?

Second, pilgrims from all over ancient Greece, and even outside, would travel to Eleusis, going past Procrustes' home, carrying many different customs and convictions with them. His is a situation familiar to most of us today, where religions, ideologies and even brand names compete for our loyalty. Which should we choose? The overwhelming number of choices can be threatening to our familiar home stories, raising doubt, and the impression that alien cultures invade our homeland. To allay such doubts, it is tempting to forcefully embrace our familiar home traditions, forcing visitors to follow them.

Significantly, Procrustes lives by himself. He has no one to provide the experience of home for him. He must do it by and for himself, which can be difficult for some people. Living alone also means there is no one to challenge Procrustes' assumptions – his home story. He can become progressively more absorbed in his own beliefs, ever more convinced they are true, just like solitary terrorists or serial killers and, more generally, people absorbed in "Internet bubbles." Indeed, given enough time and repetition, we can accept almost anything as normal, from historical American slavery to contemporary female genital mutilation. Only in retrospect, many years later do we react with horror. Habituation is the reason for many previously unrecognized crimes against humanity.

Home Rules

Procrustes specifically makes people fit in his bed, stretching short people on the rack, and amputating limbs for those who are too tall. And everyone succumbs because Procrustes has two beds and chooses the one which his guests will not fit. There is no better way of dramatizing the principle, "My way or no way." No one else counts in his home. This is a surprisingly common conviction in today's polarized politics and power disputes. The underlying belief is, "This is my homeland, so you must follow my home story, which means you must do what I say."

Underlying Procrustes' dichotomy, "My way or no way," is an axiom that most of us intuitively accept as self-evident – "**As long as you are in my house**, you have to follow my rules."

There are three errors in this assumption. First, it excludes an unspoken rule, namely, "You must follow the rules when you are in my house, **but you are free to leave at any time**." This is the difference between a home and a dungeon.

Second, it forgets the hospitality requirement: "You must follow the house rules, but they include providing you with hospitality." Difficult though honoring offering hospitality might be, it is much easier to do so than a challenge to follow the injunction "Love your neighbor", and certainly much more likely to happen than, "Love everyone." The hospitality rule is human kindness; loving your neighbor is a lifelong challenge; and loving everybody is surely enlightenment.

Finally, "My house, my rules" confuses "home" and "own." When we say something like, "This is my home," we mean it belongs to me, like property, and usually we can dispose of our property, whether house or car, as we wish. However, when we say something like, "This is my family," we do not mean (at least today) that I can do what I want with my family. In this case, other basic rules override an individual's preferences, such as, "Do not abuse or murder your children." Another way to put this is that deeper rules underlie, "My house, my rules," namely, "When in this home, follow the rules of **this** home and the **basic** rules of home." The latter are independent of any particular individual because they arise from the home mode of comprehension. And the fundamental process or logic of home comprehension is cherishing.

The confusion between home and own has surprisingly deep roots, as the etymology of "domestic" and "dominate" reveal. "Domestic" derives from the Latin "dom," meaning "home," while "dominate" comes from "dominare," meaning "to rule," which also derives from "dom."[2] This connection help explains why "My way or no way," has more to do with power, than home. We can paraphrase this perspective: "My house rule is that everybody does what I want." This then becomes, "Everybody must do what I want." But notice the presuppositions behind this last claim. First is, "Everybody must follow my rules because everyone is in my house," which is not true; and "Everybody **must** be in in my house," which is insane.

Often, we impose house rules on ourselves – we force our psyche to fit a Procrustean bed. We attack ourselves, in our own homes, like adolescent boys desperately lifting weights, and girls trying to lose it to fit social ideals. And those ideals seem self-evidently desirable – we do not question them. They are absolute rules. Sometimes parents play the role of Procrustes, pressuring one child to be an athlete, or to become a lawyer. Inner Procrustes are much more common than external ones and less obvious.

House Rules and Self-Evident Truths

Home stories contain many beliefs which seem to be "self-evident truths." Some are convictions we have never reflected on or challenged, such as, "No one should torture and kill babies." We have others we have reflected upon and accepted as true for long enough that their truth seems self-evident. The American Declaration of Independence provides good examples, e.g., "We hold these truths to be self-evident that all men are created equal, that they are endowed by their Creator with certain unalienable Rights, that among these are Life, Liberty and the pursuit of Happiness." At the time it was written, the rights the Declaration enumerated were **not** self-evident to most people, including the slave owners who signed the Declaration, and settlers seizing territory from Native Americans. By now, however, human rights seem self-evident to anyone raised in the Western liberal tradition. Another way to put this is that human rights are self-evidently true today because they are now part of the Western home story. Here we come to the tectonic logic involved in self-evident truths – it is that of a home story: "If you enter my home, as long as you stay, you must follow my rules and beliefs."

Some self-evident truths are also "necessary truths," statements which we **must** regard as true. The simplest examples are definitions, such as, "In English, 'bachelors' are unmarried men." We **must** hold this definition to be true, otherwise English speakers will not understand our speech. For instance, when we say "bachelors" and mean "the constellations of the zodiac," we get incomprehensible statements like, "The bachelors are unusually pretty tonight." When we enter the English language, we must follow its basic home rules, including its definitions.

Another example comes from geometry. In ancient Greece, Euclid described the basic rules of geometry, beginning with five assumptions, and then using pure logic to derive all the other conclusions of geometry. These explanations and deductions were so clear his conclusions about geometry were considered self-evidently true. However, in the last few centuries, various mathematicians eliminated some of his axioms and then derived different geometrical conclusions – the "non-Euclidean geometries." These alternative geometries were not self-evidently true at the time, but one of them was crucial to Einstein's theory of relativity. The assumptions that Euclid makes – his axioms – are equivalent to the basic rules of a home. Accepting Euclid's axioms is the same as entering his house and obeying his home rules – his axioms. However, we can enter the home of another mathematician, the way Einstein did, and follow those alternative house rules to discover a wholly unexpected new reality.

Our experience of certainty arises from the home type of understanding. More specifically, indubitable truths are simply the house rules in a home story we follow. This means certainty and truth are relative to whose home story we are in and what house rules we obey. What, then, do we do when we have conflicts with someone who follows a different home story? Whose house rules do we follow – ours, theirs, something else?

In this third section of the book, "Judging Multiple Modes of Truth," we focused on specific comprehension modes, and how we can judge truth in each of them. We analyze how we understand the world and judge truth, exploring distinct, unique modes of comprehension. We need now to put everything back together into a coherent process – judging truth and fostering deep transformation. Moreover, there is one last implicit question we have not yet addressed: why bother about truth? The topic is relevant today, because of postmodernist claims that there is no truth independent of a speaker. Does this mean that anything goes? Fortunately, we have two tales that provide an alternative. One is Native American, the other, Arthurian.

Notes

1 From (Graves, 1955)
2 (Oxford, 2020)

References

Graves, R. (1955). *The Greek Myths*. Baltimore, Maryland, Penguin Books.
Oxford (2020). Oxford English Dictionary Online. https://www-oed-com.ucsf.idm.oclc.org/.

Summary. Truth, Transformation and Re-Forging: "How Nanapush Brought the Peace Pipe to the People"

Introduction

We come now to a Native American story which summarizes all the themes we have been discussing about comprehension, transformation and truth. With so many folktales at this point, the book may seem like a jigsaw puzzle scattered on a table. The present tale provides a picture of the finished puzzle, like the cover on the puzzle box. The story summarizes the process of deep transformation with its descent into primordial modes of comprehension – and a return to everyday life. The narrative also illustrates two forms of this reforging process, one that is typical of youth, in the form of a heroic initiation, and another that occurs in maturity, with the elder initiation. Heroic initiations focus on an individual's quest and commonly leads to conflict between individuals pursuing different quests. The elder initiation focuses on reconciling such conflicting commitments with the deep camaraderie of shared practices. Without this second elder initiation, society remains stuck in conflict.

The Story[1]

Long, long ago, the Spirit of the West fell in love with a human maiden and married her. She bore him a beautiful boy whom they named Nanapush, and their joy could not be greater. But tragedy soon struck and illness took the life of the young mother. The Spirit of the West was overcome with grief and departed for his home in the far West, entrusting Nanapush to the care of the boy's grandmother.

As the years passed, Nanapush grew in strength and skill as a hunter. He often asked his grandmother what happened to his mother and father. Each time she promised to tell him when he was older. All the people in the village, however, whispered that the Spirit of the West had murdered his wife in a rage, and abandoned Nanapush. His grandmother told him not to believe false gossip, but over the years Nanapush heard the same story so often, he became convinced. He vowed when he grew up, he would avenge his mother's death by finding and killing his father.

Finally, Nanapush came of age and gathered his weapons and bid his grandmother farewell. She pleaded with him not to go, telling him that his father had not murdered his mother. Nanapush was so intent on his quest, he ignored her and departed. He searched far and wide, asking everyone he met on the way where he might find his father, the Spirit of the West. No one knew, but Nanapush persisted in his search.

One day as he rested in a forest, a woodpecker spoke to him. "Nanapush, be very careful. Your father is a powerful Spirit and from far away in the West, he already sees you looking for him, and knows you want to kill him. You cannot harm him with the weapons you have now. To find one that can, you must go to the Valley of Flint, and take a sharp stone from there." Nanapush thanked the woodpecker for its advice, found the Valley of Flint, picked out a sharp stone, and took it with him.

A short while later, a man came up to Nanapush and said, "I am your father and I know you have come to kill me. But you have listened to lies. I did not murder your mother. She died of a terrible illness, and I left because I could not bear the grief. And I knew that I could not raise you properly." Nanapush rejected everything his father had said. "I have come to avenge my mother's death," Nanapush insisted. The Spirit of the West knew he could not avoid a fight – if he fled, Nanapush would pursue him to the ends of the earth. That is what The Spirit of the West would have done himself, and Nanapush was his son, after all.

Reluctantly the Spirit of the West took up his weapons. They fired arrows at each other, and when they ran out of arrows, they grappled hand-to-hand. They fought so mightily the earth shook, and they breathed so furiously, they stirred up a storm in the heavens, with thunder and lightning. For days they battled, until Nanapush began to tire, so, he pulled out his magic flint, and wounded his father. The Spirit of the West stepped back and said, "We have fought enough. You cannot defeat me, and I cannot defeat you. Let us put aside our weapons."

The Spirit of the West then brought out his peace pipe, lit it, drew deeply on it, and then offered it to Nanapush, saying "Let us smoke this pipe in peace." Too exhausted to continue or say anything, Nanapush nodded. The two sat quietly side-by-side, sharing the pipe, and even though they spoke no words, an affection grew up between father and son.

Afterwards, Nanapush spent several days with his father, and they had much to talk about. Then the Spirit of the West told his son, "I must return to my place in the West, just as you must return to your people. But take this peace pipe as a token of our reconciliation and teach your people its use just as I have showed you." Nanapush accepted the gift, they embraced, and the two parted ways.

Nanapush returned home to find his people in a great dispute, arguing among themselves. Many had even come to blows. He gathered all the people before him, and showed them the peace pipe, instructing them in how to use it. With the pipe, they settled their dispute, and from then on, they used the peace pipe in the way that the Spirit of the West had taught his son, and Nanapush had taught the people.

Home Stories and Revenge

Nanapush's story is long and complex, but if we focus on the comprehension modes that the young man experiences, we can see the reforging sequence at work.

As a youth, Nanapush heard everyone in his tribe repeat the story that his father murdered his mother, and so came to believe the narrative. The tale of his mother's murder became part of his home story, just as it had become part of the tribe's. This is the domain of everyday life where we go about our lives, following familiar narratives which we do not reflect on or question. Nanapush's story is tragic – growing up without mother or father, and as far as anyone could tell, without any special talents.

Even as a child, Nanapush wanted to avenge his mother's murder, but he did not impulsively rush off to do so. He reflects enough to know that he cannot succeed on such a venture as a child. So, he waits until he comes of age, all the while learning how to be a hunter and warrior. Such reflection is characteristic of the virtual type of understanding, where we consider alternative scenarios, and not just the one in front of us.

When Nanapush comes of age, he embarks upon his quest to avenge his mother's death. That quest is now the paramount focus in his life, and he organizes his subsequent decisions and actions around it. Quests reflect the objective mode of comprehension in the form of faithfulness: we commit ourselves to an objective or goal and remain loyal to it.

The problem is that Nanapush's quest is based on a false belief – that his father murdered his mother. This is a central problem with quests and commitments – how do we judge our goals and objectives? How do we know which are true or mistaken? At this point, Nanapush does not reflect on his quest – he simply enacts it, organizing his life around one objective – avenging his mother's death. Curiously, Nanapush's grandmother does not correct the youth's mistaken belief that his father murdered his mother, although she knew what had really happened. This is psychologically perceptive: even if she told Nanapush the truth, he is not ready to hear it. At this point in his youth, he needs a heroic quest for his development.

The Confrontation

While searching for his father, Nanapush gets advice from a woodpecker, telling him that the only thing that can wound his father is a blade made from magic flint. The bird helpfully tells Nanapush where to find such a stone. This is a typical event in fairytales about young heroes – they receive aid from unexpected, magical sources. The bird personifies the virtual mode of understanding characteristic of fairytales and its advice brings up a viewpoint Nanapush had not considered until then. Nanapush needs help because his father is a powerful spirit who has already seen Nanapush from far off, coming for vengeance. Even though a skilled warrior, Nanapush is no match for his father. However, had the woodpecker told Nanapush to give up his quest, the young man probably would not have listened, unable to hear the advice.

When father and son finally meet, Nanapush rejects his father's explanation about what happened to his mother. Such an impasse is common when one or both disputants have devoted much time and effort to their positions, making any rational or productive discussion impossible. Although reluctant, the Spirit of the West resolves to fight his son. The Spirit does not try to avoid a difficult problem, the way he did when he fled from grief at the beginning of the story – he has matured. Nor does he fight as part of an instinctual reaction, the fight/flight reflex. He consciously decides to risk his life in a deadly duel, while ensuring his son is safe.

The Spirit of the West is engaged in two competing projects, namely challenging his son in a dangerous fight, yet protecting both from injury and death. Nanapush's father plays the role of an actor-director on a movie set. As an actor in a drama, the Spirit of the West must fight with enough ferocity to make his role believable, while as a director, he must make sure the whole production goes smoothly, keeping all the actors and staff safe in the process, in this case, his son Nanapush. This twofold task is characteristic of an elder rather than a young hero – attending to the overall situation, while intensely engaged in the specific one at hand. The young hero or heroine, by contrast, must focus on their objective, their quest, because everything else would be a distraction. Most of us do not play the role of professional actor or director, much less both at once, but it does come up in a common situation – parents struggling with adolescent offspring, like the Spirit of the West and Nanapush. Both sides become entangled in terrific arguments, but the parent does not try to kill the teenager or vice versa.

The battle between father and son is a kind of dialogue – the only one that Nanapush, at this point, can understand. He enacts two ancient archetypal dramas – the noble hero battling a villain and the son fighting the father for a place in the world. Mere words or reflection cannot interrupt or satisfy heroic energy in this phase of life – sometimes risky struggle is necessary.

When Nanapush begins to tire, he uses his magic flint and wounds his father. This is the only mention of an injury, suggesting that Nanapush was the first to inflict a wound. The Spirit of the West unexpectedly proposes a truce, almost as if he were waiting for his son to draw first blood. Even more surprisingly, Nanapush accepts the truce. His great thirst for vengeance has apparently been appeased, and I think this is specifically because the Spirit of the West shows his vulnerability to his son. Moreover, we glimpse a need that Nanapush has that is deeper than vengeance: on some level he wants to know that he could affect his father, even if he could not defeat him, and that Nanapush mattered to his father.

The Fellowship of Practice

Two enemies who battle furiously and then befriend each other like Nanapush and his father are a surprisingly ancient and important theme in mythology. An example comes from one of the oldest known written stories, the Sumerian tale of Gilgamesh. The King of Uruk, Gilgamesh encounters Enkidu, a wild man in the wilderness, and the two fight furiously, but neither can defeat the other. They finally call a truce, after which they become fast friends and comrades in arms.

What explains the surprising transformation from deadly combat to deep fellowship between Gilgamesh and Enkidu, as well as Nanapush and his father?

The key, I think, lies in the two practices that the combatants share with each other. First is the way of the warrior where each pursue their own goals – which conflict with their opponent's. And so, they fight to make sure their own goal prevails. The second practice is even more important – it is the practice of striving for **any** goal. This is the practice of faithfulness, commitment to a noble end, and heroic persistence in pursuing that quest. Warriors learn specific ways of fighting – spears, later arrows, swords, and now missiles and drones. So do business executives and politicians, although the tools and techniques of their professions vary – strategic plans for the former, appeals to voters, for the latter. But even more important, all the combatants must learn the importance of faithfulness to a goal or oath. Such perseverance and loyalty require extensive training and skill, quite apart from the specifics of the profession. The practice of faithfulness – the commitment mode of comprehension – provides a shared ground for the disputants, namely **how** they conduct themselves. And this is independent of their commitments and convictions, **what** they seek.

A modern example comes from lawyers. Attorneys for the plaintiff and defendant pursue conflicting objectives in court and may go at each other ruthlessly, pressing their cases. But outside of court, especially on weekends, they may amicably play tennis or golf. The lawyers are committed to incompatible projects at work, but in off hours, they share a delight in the same two practices: first, the sport they play, and second the profession they pursue as warriors-at-law.

An even more dramatic example today of the difference between project and practice is the international organization, Doctors without Borders – a group of physicians, nurses and other healthcare workers, who travel to places in dire need of medical aid, such as war zones or pandemic hotspots. The volunteers provide care regardless of which side the wounded fight on, or what tribe the sick belong to. The medical staff themselves may have conflicting ideologies or loyalties, but they can cooperate in their shared practice. One way to put this is that what the caregivers **do** is more important than what ideologies they **believe** – actions outweigh convictions. The camaraderie of deeds overrides differences in dogma. Their shared practice is more important than conflicting projects.

Neither Gilgamesh nor Enkidu could prevail in their initial fight. The same is true for Nanapush and his father. Because successful heroic quests end with victory, a stalemate, especially a permanent one, means that the hero's archetypal script ends in failure. Here is the crucial importance of a shared practice – it provides an alternative to the heroic focus on victory.

Quests may end in success, but consider what happens next – does the victorious hero bask on his laurels? A few do, but most do not – they embark upon new quests, repeating the drama of the young hero or heroine. Today they often become serial entrepreneurs. The same applies to military leaders from Alexander the Great, to Genghis Khan and Napoleon: after a successful invasion of a country, they proceed to invade others, until they die or are defeated. Today, a third alternative to death or defeat is even worse. Each new quest becomes a project, and after repeating enough projects, it becomes a job, then a boring job. The alternative to the latter is consciously embracing a practice or profession.

Nanapush's father, the Spirit of the West, quickly introduces the alternative. He proposes a truce to Nanapush, who immediately accepts. This is astonishing, since all his life he focused on avenging his mother's death.

Why this dramatic transformation? While a shared practice or profession may foster an experience of deep solidarity, three other archetypal factors play a role. First, as events soon show, Nanapush feels an archetypal connection to his father, something he undoubtedly felt before: beneath his quest to kill his father lies a deeper need to simply connect with his father for the first time. Second, Nanapush's father is teaching him the Way of Peace, which Native American tradition recognized to be as important as the Way of War. Just as warfare is a practice, so is peacemaking. Both require learning new skills, ancient rituals and traditions. These were probably known to other members of his tribe. (Many other hunter-gatherer tribes, such as Australian aborigines, also had peacemaking techniques and rituals.)

Altering Consciousness and Conflict

When father and son stop fighting, the former does something surprising – he brings out his peace pipe and proposes that he and Nanapush smoke it together. This is a third factor in reconciliation between father and son. Smoking tobacco was a sacred ritual for Native Americans, and a long-standing tradition (which according to the story, Nanapush and his father started). However, the historical Native American experience of smoking tobacco was quite different from that of modern smokers. Native tobacco was almost a completely different species compared to contemporary tobacco crops, which were bred for centuries to produce high nicotine content. Maximizing the (addictive) nicotine high was the goal of the cigarette industry. The many other compounds in the original tobacco plant – along with their subtler, psychological effects – were ignored.[2]

Smoking native tobacco generates a mildly euphoric experience, a sense of deepened meaning and well-being. That expansive mood is an example of transcendence, opening to unfamiliar possibilities. This is the fundamental process of mythic experience. As we discussed previously, such openness can apply to any content of experience from a sublime sunset to witnessing a child's first step. A modern, more intense parallel to the peace pipe experience is the drug "Ecstasy," which helps most users experience a sense of openness, empathy and a deep connection with other people – just like Nanapush and his father smoking the peace pipe.

Nanapush spontaneously recognizes that his experience of connection with his father is true on a deeper level than his vow to avenge his mother. The basic principle here is that when we come to a deeper, more encompassing understanding which includes our previous viewpoint as a special case, we recognize that the new perspective is truer than the old one: it is a more complete understanding.[3]

We have encountered the importance of mythic experience in resolving conflicts in previous stories. Nanapush' story introduces the conscious use of techniques, in this case the peace pipe ritual, to generate the mythic mode of comprehension. This approach is an ancient practice, reflecting shamanic tradition. Modern interest in shamans usually focuses on the individual shaman going into a trance to heal an individual with an illness. However, an even more important function of shamans is resolving conflicts within a group and there are many techniques to do so, frequently involving altered consciousness.[4]

In Western tradition, using altered consciousness to resolve conflicts seems irrational – and terrifying. Euripides sums up the attitude in his ancient Greek play, "The Bacchae," where the devotees of Bacchus, god of wine, fall into a frenzy, and tear apart their King. Most horrifying of all is the fact that one of the attackers is the King's mother, also in a frenzy. Avoiding such emotional frenzies was a major motivation for the Western Enlightenment in 17th- and 18th-century Europe, especially after the many religious wars that tore the region apart. Fierce devotion – an altered state of consciousness on its own – made any intense conviction or feeling suspect. So, detachment from emotions seemed the more rational approach. But detachment – which uses the virtual type of understanding – cannot reconcile deep conflicts. In contrast, experiencing all the comprehension modes in sequence can, descending from the home, virtual, objective and pragmatic levels to a shared mythic experience: descent and return can reforge seemingly permanent conflicts.

Nanapush returns home with the peace pipe and finds his people caught up in disputes and fights. Here he is like Moses descending from the summit of Mount Sinai, with the 10 Commandments written on stone tablets, only to find his people dancing and worshiping the Golden Calf. Moses flies into a rage because his people had broken their Covenant with God, not long after making it, and attacks the apostates.

In contrast, when Nanapush encounters his people caught up in disputes and fights, he teaches them how to use the peace pipe, and the altered consciousness it engenders, to reconcile conflicts. Nanapush thus brings back a **procedure** or **practice** for reconciling differences, rather than the **principles** and **oaths** that Moses carried with him. The peace pipe protocol is independent of the content of any dispute, and this contrasts with peace treaties, which focus on particular issues. Today, when many religions and ideologies fight – and even kill – each other, Nanapush's peace pipe procedure, and other similar indigenous traditions, are sorely needed. Those techniques constitute a technology of transformation and reconciliation.

As an indigenous tale from a tribal culture, the story of Nanapush may seem distant from contemporary problems, and any attempt to apply it to the latter, a stretch of imagination and abstraction. The next story comes from the heart of Western tradition and repeats central themes of Nanapush's drama, highlighting the practical application to current disputes. It is the tale of King Arthur and the Round Table.

Notes

1 (Hitakonanulaxk, 1994)
2 (Paper, 1988) (La Flesche, 1939)
3 This is the role of Jung's "transcendent function" following Hegel's principle of dialectic as we discussed in Chapter 6. One party asserts a thesis, and the other asserts the

antithesis, which generates a conflict. A synthesis on a deeper, more comprehensive level resolves the dispute. Mark Twain illustrates this principle: "When I was a boy of 14, my father was so ignorant I could hardly stand to have the old man around. But when I got to be 21, I was astonished at how much the old man learned in seven years." By 21, Mark Twain had gained a larger perspective from life experiences, and finally could recognize his father's wisdom.

4 I discuss this at greater length in *Beyond the Hero*.

References

Hitakonanulaxk (1994). *The Grandfathers Speak: Native American Folk Tales of the Lenapé People*. New York, Interlink Books.

La Flesche, F. (1939). *War Ceremony and Peace Ceremony of the Osage Indians*. Washington, U.S. Government Printing Office.

Paper, J. D. (1988). "The Sacred Pipe: The Historical Context of Contemporary Pan-Indian Religion." *Journal of the American Academy of Religion* **LVI**(4): 643–665.

Epilogue. The Practice of Chivalry and Comprehension Today: Kings Arthur's Roundtable

Introduction

One question remains unanswered in our discussion of conflict, truth, and transformation. Why bother with reconciling disputes? We could, after all, simply let power or force determine the outcome of our disagreements, which history suggests is the more commonplace approach. We have moral considerations, but these usually lack enough oomph to determine outcomes. So just what could motivate us to seek reconciliation? And specifically, what can counteract the temptation of settling disputes by declaring, "Because I said so" and "Or else!"

The stories of King Arthur and the Roundtable provide key insights for us. The tales reflect core elements of modern Western tradition, including American culture. Surprisingly, Arthurian stories have deep parallels with the tale of Nanapush in the last chapter. Both depict how the reforging process can resolve deadly conflicts. Arthurian tales focus on conflict in large groups of people, whereas "Nanapush" focuses on one-on-one interpersonal disputes. The content of the dispute varies, but the process of resolving them involves the same succession of progressively deeper comprehension modes. The parallels between the two stories are astonishing because "Nanapush" reflects nomadic hunter-gatherer culture, the original form of human society. By contrast, Arthurian tales arise from the most recent type of culture, that of organized states based on specific geographic areas. The fact that both the first and the latest cultures rely on the same reforging process emphasizes just how fundamental it is.

The Stories

Stories revolving around King Arthur are too numerous to recount, and too varied to identify any one as the most important. So, I will recount only the background the stories share, their common context.[1]

Arthur grew up in a time when all the land was divided into small territories, each ruled by a feudal lord. And the lords all quarreled and regularly invaded each other's territories, leaving their people miserable. The problems of his time mirror those of our own, except we call it a free market, and we do not contend with warring feudal aristocrats but something worse: we now have the democracy of truth and threat, where anyone can claim the truth and use frightening weapons to threaten opponents.

When Arthur pulled the enchanted sword from the stone, proving that he was the true King of Britain, he established a fragile, initial peace among the warring lords. It took a miraculous – mythic – event to stop the constant raids and wars. As we have seen in previous tales, mythic experiences are often required to resolve intense disputes. Arthurian tales go one step further: to solidify the new peace, Arthur and Merlin created the Roundtable. Its members were Knights victorious in combat over villains. Members also kept the code of chivalry, righting wrongs, helping the needy and punishing evildoers. Members of the Roundtable were deemed the worthiest and most honorable of Knights, so all the aristocracy wanted to join. (The analogs today would include conferences like the World Economic Forum at Davos, and TED talks among others.)

At the Roundtable, all members were considered equal, no matter what their birth, wealth, or power. That was the importance of the Table being round – no one sat at the head of the table, not even King Arthur himself. All hostility and disputes were suspended at the Roundtable, replaced by chivalry and tolerance. From the Roundtable, Knights would embark upon quests to battle villains and monsters of various sorts returning to recount their deeds.

To put it simply, King Arthur and Merlin invented a new profession – that of the chivalrous Knight. What united the fractious nobles was a shared practice, namely the way of the ethical warrior. We saw the same theme in the last chapter with the story about Nanapush. He reconciled with his father only after they engaged in hand-to-hand combat that went on for days and nights: Nanapush and his father shared the warriors' profession. Sharing other practices or professions can have the same effect. During the Cold War, scientists and physicians organized ongoing campaigns for nuclear disarmament and measures to prevent catastrophic climate change: the practice of science and the desire to help humanity bridged the gap between conflicting ideologies, nationalism, and economic interests.

The Roots of Practice

Sharing a practice, whether that be music, literature, is only the first step on a longer journey, which the Roundtable illustrates. Everyone who becomes a Knight learns from someone else. Arthur learned fighting from Sir Kay and wisdom from Merlin, while Parsifal benefited from Gournemond's mentorship. Today, medical students learn from practicing doctors, and beginning teachers, from experienced ones. On the most fundamental level, we all learn language from other people. Practices are gifts which a practitioner shares with a novice. And any practice must encourage such teaching and mentoring to survive.

The motivation for training other people is deeply and uniquely human. Many animals, of course, teach their offspring how to survive – what not to eat, and even what plants can be medicinal. But very few creatures will train **another** animal's offspring.[2] Humans have made training non-kin individuals the foundation of human culture – for instance, teaching others such crucial tasks as how to make stone tools or build fire at the dawn of humanity. That teaching impulse expanded vastly over time giving rise to apprenticeships and schools. This paved the way for the flowering of ever more complex cultures.

Professional warriors, however, are better known today not as noble knights, but as opportunistic mercenaries. And the word "mercenary" often applies to some practitioners of other professions, like law, medicine, finance or science. Doctors who find a cure for a terrible disease once took pride in simply helping humanity, but many now also set up corporations to patent and profit from their discovery. What makes for the difference between a mercenary and an altruistic professional?

The question is backwards: professions all have a prosocial origin, namely learning and teaching others an important practice, from building fire to writing code. The question is why people turn away from that original motivation to pursue personal wealth or glory. And what can prevent such a fall?

Arthurian stories provide a surprising answer to this question in the quest for the Holy Grail. Significantly the nature of the Grail is left undefined or somewhat vague. Individual tales vary dramatically in how they describe the Grail. In some versions, the Grail is a magical stone, like the alchemical philosopher's stone, that can change base metals into gold; in other tales the Grail takes the form of a magic platter, which produces whatever a person asks for; many stories explicitly link the Grail to the cup used by Jesus at the Last Supper. The only thing that all the stories have in common is that the Grail is a mystery – its nature and location are unknown.

Many stories emphasize this mysterious aspect with a small detail: a Knight who comes upon the Grail must ask specific questions of the people around the Grail. In one version, the question is "Whom does the Grail serve?" in contrast to a more common human reaction, "What can I get from this magic Grail?" In other stories, a wounded King presides at a feast in which the Grail is brought out. The question in this version is "What ails thee, Grail King?" All the questions asked are about the needs or concerns of someone besides the seeker. This altruistic perspective is not what we might expect from someone when embarked upon a long, dangerous quest for the Grail. The altruism lies beyond our natural, familiar egocentric concerns, reflecting the process of transcendence, characteristic of mythic comprehension. It is that experience of mystery and transcendence which separates the mercenary from the altruistic professional.

We saw the same theme with Nanapush in the last chapter when he smokes the peace pipe with his father. The two then have a shared mythic experience. In "A Christmas Carol," the mythic experience is Scrooge encountering his neglected gravestone in the future, which terrifies him so much, he changes his ways. And in "Why the Platypus Is Special," it is the Platypus reminding all the warring clans of their common origin in the Creator, interrupting their disputes with a mythic experience.

The link between mythic experience and a practice still occurs today in a **vocation** or calling to a particular profession. The individual feels a mysterious summons to a specific occupation. The paradigmatic example is someone feeling called to a religious ministry, e.g., becoming a priest, rabbi or minister. A more familiar version of a vocation today is someone called to be an artist or writer, not for fame or wealth, but because they are summoned to the way of creativity. The inspiration may be strong enough to sustain them through poverty and public indifference. Many individuals today begin their careers with a similar sense of calling. Law students are inspired to work for justice, medical students, to alleviate suffering, and journalists to reveal and reform hidden causes of social problems.

Because a mythic experience is not tied to any content or profession an individual may experience a vocation in what seems like an ordinary job, even a menial or tedious one. A janitor in a hospital, for instance, always seemed cheerful and delighted to help people, even when mistreated by patients or staff. When asked how he could be so kind and giving, he simply explained that he felt it was his calling to help people in his daily work through whatever way he could.[3] A mythic experience of a job transforms it into a calling.

The Roundtable and the Quest for the Holy Grail involve two different kinds of quests. The Roundtable is for successful knights, who have succeeded on their heroic quests, defeating villains and fighting for a noble cause. A seat at the Roundtable signifies completion of a heroic initiation. The Quest for the Holy Grail, on the other hand, has a much more nebulous objective, and no clearcut measure of success. This quest is a post-heroic one and can be summed up in the title of a Russian story, "Go I Know Not Whither, Bring Back I Know Not What."[4] It is a journey into mystery and the mythic realm. It is a developmental task of an elder, rather than a youth. Success in this second initiation results in wisdom – and in many stories, healing a kingdom that had become a wasteland.

Many tribal cultures follow the distinction between these two types of initiation – the first for young men or woman who have proven themselves, and the second, for older men and women, who learned wisdom over many years. And mastering how to resolve dangerous disputes between stubborn opponents is central to the elders' wisdom. Arthurian tales, I might add, are thought to have arisen from ancient Celtic stories reflecting tribal times and ways. Yet their wisdom is as relevant today as it was before. The tales are like strands of DNA, which originated millennia ago, and which all modern humans still have, because the DNA still plays essential roles in our biology – and health.

Modern culture encourages everyone to speak their truth and created the technology for anyone with it wreak havoc on opponents. At the same time, it has given us the means to resolve our disputes and battles through the camaraderie of practice, from farming to pottery and on through plumbing, medicine, and business. It is not the solidarity of the proletariat that brings equality and justice to society, but rather the communities of trained and skillful practitioners.

Other stories explore this theme further, but we come now to the end of this book. Here I shamelessly resort to Scheherazade's strategy in *1001 Arabian Nights:* after telling stories all night, she ended her last tale at dawn, just before the resolution of the drama, promising the conclusion later, with even more stories.

Notes

1 (Unknown, 1660), (Unknown, 1697), (Bulfinch, 1913), (Malory and Morris, 1904)
2 There are cases, of course, of an animal adopting an orphan from their group, but this principally occurs when all the individuals in the group are kin and thus closely related genetically.
3 (Wrzesniewski, 2015)
4 I discuss this and other post-heroic stories in *Beyond the Hero*.

References

Bulfinch, T. (1913). *Bulfinch's Mythology: The Age of Fable; The Age of Chivalry; Legends of Charlemagne*. New York, Grosset & Dunlap.

Malory, T. and C. Morris (1904). *King Arthur*. New York, R.H. Whitten.

Unknown (1660). The famous history of that most renowned Christian worthy Arthur King of the Britaines, and his famous Knights of the Round Table, London, printed for Francis Coles at the signe of the Lamb in the Old-Bailey.

Unknown (1697). *Great Britain's Glory: Being the History of King Arthur with the Adventures of the Knights of the Round Table*. London, printed by and for W.O. and sold by the booksellers.

Wrzesniewski, A. (2015). "Callings and the Meaning of Work" in Yaden, D. B. N., Andrew B. – Road to Damascus Moments: Calling Experiences as Prospective Epiphanies. *Being Called*: 27–46.

Index

For Product Safety Concerns and Information please contact our EU
representative GPSR@taylorandfrancis.com
Taylor & Francis Verlag GmbH, Kaufingerstraße 24, 80331 München, Germany